Lecture Notes in Economics and Mathematical Systems

479

Springer
Berlin
Heidelberg
New York
Barcelona
Hong Kong
London
Milan
Paris
Singapore
Tokyo

Leopold von Thadden

Money, Inflation, and Capital Formation

An Analysis of the Long Run
from the Perspective of Overlapping
Generations Models

 Springer

Author

Dr. Leopold von Thadden
Deutsche Bundesbank
Hauptabteilung Volkswirtschaft
Postfach 10 06 02
60006 Frankfurt/Main, Germany

332.4
T36m
C.2

Cataloging-in-Publication Data applied for

Die Deutsche Bibliothek - CIP-Einheitsaufnahme

Thadden, Leopold von:
**Money, inflation, and capital formation : an analysis of the long run
from the perspective of overlapping generations models / Leopold
von Thadden. - Berlin ; Heidelberg ; New York ; Barcelona ; Hong
Kong ; London ; Milan ; Paris ; Singapore ; Tokyo : Springer, 1999**
  (Lecture notes in economics and mathematical systems ; 479)
  ISBN 3-540-66456-4

ISSN 0075-8442
ISBN 3-540-66456-4 Springer-Verlag Berlin Heidelberg New York

Typesetting: Camera ready by author
Printed on acid-free paper   SPIN: 10725092   42/3143-543210

Preface

This book is a slightly revised version of my doctoral thesis which I wrote during my time as an assistant at the Faculty of Economics of the University of Magdeburg. I am grateful that I had the opportunity to write my thesis in the stimulating atmosphere of this young and lively faculty. I owe a great amount of gratitude to my supervisor Prof. G. Schwödiauer who constantly encouraged my work and helped to improve it in many discussions. I also would like to thank Prof. K.-H. Paqué and Prof. P. Flaschel who, as members of my doctoral committee, commented on various details of this study in a very constructive manner. At various stages of my work I received helpful comments from many colleagues of mine, in particular T. König and A. Wöhrmann. However, it goes without saying that I retain full responsibility for all remaining errors.

Contents

Introduction

"To alter the terms on which the community will accumulate real capital - that is what monetary policy is all about."[1]   *(James Tobin)*

"In an important sense, Tobin appears to have got his results backwards. When the economy is modelled 'properly' - and what this means is bound to be controversial - the Tobin effect is reversed."[2]   *(Douglas Gale)*

Should one expect that a shift to a fully anticipated, more inflationary policy can permanently improve the terms on which the community accumulates real capital ? Given the widespread belief that inflation is something which harms the economy, economic theory is surprisingly ambiguous in answering this question. In fact, a casual look at the by now classical contributions by Tobin (1965), Sidrauski (1967), and Stockman (1981) suffices to sketch this ambiguity.

In his classical contribution to the debate on long run real effects of sustained inflationary policies, Tobin (1965) established a positive correlation between the level of the inflation rate and the capital stock of an economy, and hence the overall level of economic activity. Responding to Tobin's results from a monetarist perspective, Sidrauski (1967) argued that the long run should rather be characterized by a clear dichotomy between real and monetary forces. Accordingly, Sidrauski (1967) proposed a specification in which all real variables of the economy are entirely invariant to changes in the economy's inflation rate. Finally, in another influential contribution which deviates from Tobin's and Sidrauski's analysis, Stockman (1981) presented a rigorous framework that allowed inflation to have a negative long run impact on the economy's level of economic activity.

Subsequent research has not been able to settle the issue. In contrast, different authors continue to stress different aspects of money, and a large body of hardly comparable modelling devices has emerged in the field of monetary

---

[1] Tobin/Brainard (1963), p. 387.

[2] Gale (1983), p. 85.

2

economics. Hence, the ambiguity of results with respect to the long run effects of inflation has not disappeared, reflecting the ongoing dispute among economists of how to deal with money at a fundamental level.

We think that the theoretical dispute is deep enough to be of considerable interest in its own right. Ultimately, however, robust empirical results have to bear upon the assessment of theoretical insights. Interestingly, more recent empirical findings indicate that Tobin's original conjecture is hardly supported by the data. Instead, the majority of the empirical studies concludes that a negative correlation between inflation and economic activity as suggested by Stockman (or, more prominently, the Anti-Tobin conjecture) is not to be rejected. Taking the empirical dimension of the dispute into account, our approach has, therefore, a pronounced bias towards finding theoretical support for the Anti-Tobin conjecture.

Our analysis concentrates exclusively on the *long run* interaction of inflation and economic activity. Following the standard treatment of this issue in the macroeconomic literature, we let the long run be defined as a situation in which the process of capital formation is endogenous. Moreover, the price level is assumed to be fully flexible. Accordingly, we deal with models which are often classified as models of 'money and growth'. Following tradition in monetary theory, *long run* models of money and growth are primarily concerned with the question of whether money is *superneutral*, i.e. models of this type investigate how permanent changes in the inflation rate and, therefore, ultimately in the *growth rate* of the money stock affect the real sector of the economy. Correspondingly, the question of whether money is *neutral* (and the associated question of how to assess the impact of potential nominal price rigidities) is not addressed in this book. In other words, we entirely ignore the traditional *short run* battlefield between Keynesian and monetarist economists of how to assess the effects caused by changes in the *level* of the money stock for a given level of the capital stock.[3]

Far from attempting to resolve the superneutrality issue at the fundamental level, we argue in this study that the version of the overlapping generations model with production due to Diamond (1965) is well suited to be used as a framework to discuss the ambivalence sketched above in a transparent way. In particular, we attempt to show that the Diamond model, when appropriately modified, offers a suitable framework to address far more aspects of money than the narrow store of value aspect implied by the overlapping generations friction in its pure form.

To structure the presentation of the material we have chosen a largely self-explanatory scheme consisting of two main parts. The first part addresses the issue of 'money, inflation, and capital formation in the long run' from a rather general perspective: chapter 1 gives an overview of the theoretical

---

[3]This debate is covered extensively in the literature. For a detailed summary, see, for example, Blanchard (1990).

literature, chapter 2 reproduces main results from the empirical literature, and chapter 3 presents general reflections on how to account for essential features of money in monetary theory. Also in chapter 3, we substantiate our claim that the Diamond version of the overlapping generations model with production is a suitable framework to discuss the superneutrality issue.

The second part addresses the issue more narrowly, but also more rigorously, from the perspective of the Diamond model. Chapter 4 presents a base version of this model with money acting as single outside asset. In this base version, the mechanics of the model strongly resemble those of Tobin's original analysis. More specifically, it can be shown that the Tobin effect prevails unambiguously under conditions which ensure the existence of a unique monetary steady state. Also, local equilibrium dynamics are shown to be uniquely determined along a stable saddlepath. Drawing on various ideas discussed in chapter 3, chapters 5-9 propose variations on the base model. As a common theme, all of these variations give rise to the possibility that the Anti-Tobin effect predominates. Similarly, local equilibrium dynamics may no longer be uniquely determined.

Chapters 5 and 6 present modified versions of the base model developed by Azariadis/Smith (1996) and Schreft/Smith (1997). In contrast, chapters 7-9 present our own research. Throughout the second part of this study we use the model structure and the notation as introduced in the presentation of the base model in chapter 4. However, to prevent the main text from becoming overly redundant, some recurring technical details have been delegated to two common appendices at the end of the book. Also at the end of the book, we give a short summary of the main results established in this study.

Part I

Money, inflation, and capital formation in the long run: general remarks

Chapter 1

Summary of the literature: theoretical aspects

Modern analysis of the long run interaction of inflation and capital formation begins with Tobin's seminal contribution in 1965. Presenting a monetary version of Solow's growth model, Tobin (1965) considers a closed economy in which 'outside money' competes with real capital in the portfolios of agents. As a matter of definition, outside money is the part of the money stock which is issued by the government. Correspondingly, it represents, according to Tobin (1965), "...neither a commodity produced by the economy nor the debts of private individuals or institutions."[1] Moreover, "...its own-yield (i.e. the amount of the asset that is earned by holding a unit of the asset a given period of time) is arbitrarily fixed by the government. This may, of course, be zero but it is not necessarily so."[2]

To assess the long run impact of inflation on the economy's capital stock, Tobin (1965) draws on the "analytical distinction between choices affecting

---

[1]Tobin (1965), p. 676. The stock of *outside money* represents liabilities of the central bank. In other words, it constitutes the monetary base of the overall money stock which can be directly controlled by the monetary authority through outright purchases of assets (such as open market purchases of government bonds or purchases of foreign reserves), reverse transactions with repurchase agreements (such as discount window lending) or, if the monetary authority lacks independence, through unbacked injections of money on behalf of the fiscal agent. In contrast, the stock of *inside money* consists of all private credit arrangements with varying degrees of liquidity and transferability. Using the standard classification of monetary aggregates, outside money is given by the aggregate M_0 which consists of currency holdings of the private sector and the net reserves position of financial intermediaries. Broader measures of the money stock such as M_1- M_3 are obtained by adding inside money components depending on their degree of liquidity. Note that in a closed economy, for the private sector as a whole, inside money does not represent net wealth.

[2]Tobin (1965), p. 676. In fact, well in accordance with everyday experience, we assume throughout our analysis that zero nominal interest is paid on outside money.

the disposition of income and choices affecting the disposition of wealth."[3] And it is the second kind of choice that lies at the heart of Tobin's analysis: "Most models of economic growth are non-monetary. They offer no place for significant choices of the second kind - portfolio choice. They admit only one type of asset that can serve wealth owners as a store of value, namely reproducible capital...Different questions arise when monetary assets are available to compete with ownership of real goods."[4] Rather than to derive the demand for money from first principles, Tobin (1965) makes the plausible, yet 'ad-hoc' assumption that one should think of outside money and capital (or claims against capital as far as the process of capital formation is intermediated) as substitutes in the portfolios of agents. Equally ad-hoc and in the tradition of Solow's analysis, savings are assumed to be a constant fraction of income, i.e. the analysis concentrates exclusively on the portfolio effect. Moreover, the government is assumed to redistribute any revenue resulting from seigniorage in a lump-sum fashion, and agents are assumed to have a fixed labour supply.

Under these specifications, Tobin (1965) establishes the well-known result - the so-called 'Tobin effect' - of a positive correlation between the inflation rate and the economy's capital stock across steady states: acting like a tax on money, higher inflation reduces the return on real balances, and, since assets are specified as substitutes, the portfolio effect ensures that in the new equilibrium a larger fraction of the portfolio will be invested in capital than before.

In general, however, the interaction of the portfolio and the income disposition effect will decide about the strength of the overall effect of inflation on capital formation. As we will argue below, for a deeper understanding of this interaction one needs to address the question to what extent outside money holdings qualify as net wealth. Tobin (1965) himself discusses this aspect in his contribution in a colourful way:

"The community's wealth...has two components: the real goods accumulated through past real investment and fiduciary or paper 'goods' manufactured by the government from thin air. Of course the non-human wealth of such a nation 'really' consists only of its tangible capital. But, as viewed by the inhabitants of the nation individually, wealth exceeds the tangible capital stock by the size of what we might term the fiduciary issue. This is an illusion, but only one of the many fallacies of composition which are basic to any economy or any society. The illusion can be maintained unimpaired so long as the society does not actually try to convert all of its paper wealth into goods."[5]

---

[3]Tobin (1965), p. 671.

[4]Tobin (1965), p. 672.

[5]Tobin (1965), p. 676.

As discussed, for example, by Orphanides/Solow (1990), Tobin's result is robust with respect to a variety of different modelling strategies. Importantly, it is not caused by surprise inflations. On the contrary, changes in the inflation rate which are taken to be permanent are at the heart of the Tobin effect. It is for this reason that it still serves, in contrast to many other results from a pre-rational expectation perspective, as a benchmark result in ongoing research.[6]

In summary, Tobin's analysis predicts that sustained inflationary policies have a positive impact on the long run level of the capital stock, and hence on the overall level of economic activity. According to the standard classification of macroeconomic reasoning Tobin's approach belongs, therefore, firmly to a school of thought that sees itself in the tradition of Keynes. Tobin (1965) himself acknowledges that he thinks that the major contribution of his analysis lies in the extension of Keynesian reasoning to a situation of the long run. Thus, he writes in concluding his classical article: "In classical theory, the interest rate and the capital intensity of the economy are determined by 'productivity and thrift', that is, by the interaction of technology and saving propensities...Keynes gave reasons why in the short run monetary factors and portfolio decisions modify, and in some circumstances dominate, the determination of the interest rate and the process of capital accumulation. I have tried to show here that a similar proposition is true for the long run."[7]

Following Tobin's analysis a vast amount of research has been undertaken that investigates the robustness of the Tobin effect, and there are various surveys that summarize the debate in a detailed manner.[8] Here, without going into too much detail, we keep the discussion of this debate at an informal level and rather confine ourselves to some loosely arranged remarks.

i) In an early benchmark contribution to the debate, Sidrauski (1967) challenged Tobin's non-superneutrality result from a 'monetarist' perspective. To this end, Sidrauski (1967) proposed a framework that explicitly allows for an endogenous treatment of the savings behaviour of agents.[9] In particular,

---

[6] An analysis similar to Tobin's is due to Mundell (1965). Hence, the literature uses the terms 'Tobin effect' and 'Mundell-Tobin effect' interchangeably. For a more detailed description of the workings of the Tobin effect, see also Tobin (1969) and Tobin (1982).

[7] Tobin (1965), p. 684.

[8] For early surveys, see Burmeister/Dobell (1970) and Dornbusch/Frenkel (1973). More recent summaries are given by Howitt (1993), Wang/Yip (1992), and, in particular, Orpanides/Solow (1990). Jones/Manuelli (1995) address most recent contributions from an endogenous growth perspective.

[9] In his own words, Sidrauski (1967) summarized his intention as following: "What differentiates this product is the fact that, in line with Patinkin's presentation of the neoclassical theory of money, and with the classical Fisherian theory of saving, it is based on an explicit analysis of individual's saving behaviour, viewed as a process of wealth accumulation aimed at maximizing some intertemporal utility function" (p. 534).

Sidrauski's framework combines Ramsey's optimizing set-up of an infinite horizon economy with Patinkin's idea of ensuring a well-defined demand for money by inserting real balances into the utility function of agents.[10] Under these specifications Sidrauski's model delivers surprisingly simple results: money is superneutral in steady state comparison, and changes in the inflation rate leave, therefore, all variables describing the real part of the economy unaffected.[11] Moreover, as in Ramsey's original non-monetary contribution, the steady state real interest rate is determined by the modified golden rule, i.e. exclusively by 'real' forces such as the time preference of agents, the growth rate of the population, and the rate of technical progress.

However, subsequent research has shown that Sidrauski's results hardly survive changes to the rather specific set-up of the model. As we will discuss in the following, both the adaptation of Patinkin's approach towards money and the choice of Ramsey's version of an infinite horizon economy are essential for money to be superneutral.

ii) With real balances being specified as an argument of the utility function of agents, Patinkin's approach towards money uses a powerful short cut to account for the exchange facilitating role of money in an otherwise entirely 'real' economy. However, this short cut is by no means innocuous: the non-superneutrality of money may well reappear in Ramsey-type economies if the transactions role of money is specified in a more transparent manner.

Models in the tradition of Dornbusch/Frenkel (1973), for example, assume explicitly that trading is a costly activity. Yet, agents have access to a 'pecuniary' transactions technology, and under this technology additional holdings of real balances help to reduce transaction costs. By and large, Sidrauski's results can be confirmed in such a framework if one considers the special situation that only the purchase of consumption goods involves transaction costs. However, superneutrality of money vanishes if it is assumed that the production process itself is subject to transaction costs. Essentially, such an assumption implies that output should be thought of as being produced according to a generalized production function that includes the provision of the required transaction services. Moreover, real balances act now simply as a productive input, and the exact nature of the non-superneutrality result depends on the signs of the cross-partial derivatives of the generalized production function with respect to the inputs. If it is assumed, for example, that capital and real balances interact in a complementary fashion the

---

[10]For details, see Patinkin (1965). For a summary treatment of the Ramsey model, see, for example, Blanchard/Fischer (1989), chapter 2.

[11]Superneutrality of money means that changes in the growth rate of money have no effects on the real equilibrium. Moreover, across steady states changes in the growth rate of money are typically associated with corresponding changes in the inflation rate. However, we will return to this point in more detail below.

Tobin effect will be entirely reversed: note that under the complementarity assumption the marginal product of capital depends positively on the input level of real balances. Thus, a lower demand for real balances in response to a higher inflation rate reduces the marginal product of capital, and this depresses the demand for capital itself.

Similarly, Sidrauski's superneutrality result is not robust with respect to modifications that incorporate leisure as an additional argument in the utility function of agents.[12] As summarized by Wang/Yip (1992), the direction of the non-superneutrality result now depends on the signs of the cross-partial derivatives of the utility function with respect to consumption, leisure, and real balances. Evidently, economic theory places a priori no restrictions on these signs, and by appropriate choice of these signs either effect, Tobin or Anti-Tobin, can prevail.

iii) Similarly, the superneutrality result disappears if the decision problem of agents is changed in a way that some 'disconnectedness with the future' is introduced.[13] In Sidrauski's set-up, because of the infinite decision horizon of agents and a fully operative bequest motive, changes in the inflation rate cannot shift wealth between present and future consumers. In fact, the steady state consumption profile of the representative agent is entirely flat, and there is no channel through which changes in the timing of consumption patterns could translate into changes in the interest rate. In contrast, in life-cycle models - such as overlapping generations models in the tradition of Samuelson (1958) and Diamond (1965) or models with an infinite decision horizon of agents and no operative bequest motive in the tradition of Yaari (1965) and Blanchard (1985) - this channel becomes effective and superneutrality in steady state comparison no longer holds: now, redistributions of wealth across generations by means of seigniorage affect the life-cycle consumption pattern of agents and thereby the aggregate capital stock.

In particular, using a version of the Blanchard/Yaari model, Weil (1991) shows that the question of superneutrality is ultimately linked to the familiar question of whether real balances are perceived as net wealth. Following Weil's argument, in the Sidrauski model "...money is not net wealth...because the real monetary wealth...of agents alive today is identically equal to the present discounted real value of the future opportunity costs which currently

---

[12] In particular, upon this modification the steady state capital intensity is no longer tied to the capital stock per capita on a one-to-one basis. With leisure being an argument of the utility function of agents, the modified golden rule optimality condition of the Ramsey model is still valid, ensuring that the real interest rate and, hence, the capital intensity are independent of the inflation rate. However, whenever the steady state labour supply responds to inflation, the capital stock per capita needs to react as well in order to rebalance the optimality condition.

[13] For a summary, see Orpanides/Solow (1990). For a detailed treatment, see, in particular, Weil (1991).

alive agents bear, when the nominal interest rate is positive, to hold their wealth in monetary form."[14] Consequently, in direct analogy to the Ricardian question of whether government bonds are net wealth, redistributions via seigniorage across time leave the real part of the economy unaffected. In contrast, "in the life-cycle framework without operative intergenerational transfers, government bonds are...net wealth, and so is money - in the nontrivial sense that the real value of current monetary wealth exceeds, at any date, the present discounted value of the future opportunity costs of holding money incurred by the currently alive consumers."[15] Thus, faster growth of money will have in general two opposing effects on the wealth of currently alive agents: it increases the present value of future nominal transfers and it raises, by increasing inflation and the nominal interest rate, the opportunity costs of holding real balances. In Sidrauski's set-up the two effects exactly offset each other, resulting in the superneutrality of money. However, in a life-cycle framework some of the future benefits need to be shared with yet unborn generations. As a consequence, the net effect on wealth is negative and consumption smoothing requires the interest rate to fall - in other words: the Tobin effect prevails.

In summary, Weil (1991) arrives at the thoughtful conclusion "...that the long-run nonsuperneutrality of money in life-cycle models is a modality of the violation of the Ricardian debt neutrality proposition: the very same intergenerational redistribution effects which, on the fiscal side, are the source of debt nonneutrality are at work, on the monetary side, to create monetary wealth effects and make money nonsuperneutral in the long run."[16] Undoubtedly, the implications of Weil's analysis are substantial: in particular, by comparing results from different dynamical frameworks one has to be aware that there is a dimension to the debate about the Tobin effect which is essentially non-monetary in nature.[17]

iv) Research in the tradition of Clower (1967) and, more recently, Lucas (1982) and Lucas/Stokey (1987) concentrates exclusively on the transactions role of money by subjecting purchases of goods to a so-called 'cash-in-advance constraint'. Fundamentally, models which introduce money via the cash-in-advance constraint follow Clower's early dictum: "Money buys

---

[14]Weil (1991), p. 37.

[15]Weil (1991), p. 38.

[16]Weil (1991), p. 37.

[17]Furthermore, as shown by Danthine/Donaldson/Smith (1987) the superneutraliy result vanishes in a stochastic version of Sidrauski's model. However, while the authors demonstrate that the stationary distribution of real variables is qualitatively affected by changes in the growth rate of the money stock, the resulting Tobin effect is shown to be quantitatively insignificant. For a further discussion of the robustness of Sidrauski's result, see Orphanides/Solow (1990).

goods and goods buy money, but goods do not buy goods."[18] Technically, this is achieved by the requirement that transactions can only be realized if the corresponding nominal value of the transactions has been held in cash for at least one period in advance. Using such a framework, Stockman (1981) shows in his influential contribution that in a Ramsey-type economy, when augmented by a cash-in-advance constraint that applies both to consumption and investment goods, the Tobin effect will be completely reversed. The intuitive explanation of Stockman's result is as following: since inflation acts like a tax on investment goods, a higher inflation rate simply raises the marginal cost of investment goods and thereby depresses the demand for capital. Hence, Stockman's contribution is a particularly transparent example of an economy in which the Tobin effect is reversed because capital and real balances act in the production process in a complementary fashion. However, similar to studies in the tradition of Dornbusch/Frenkel (1973), the prevalence of the Anti-Tobin effect depends in Stockman's analysis sensitively on the range of goods being subjected to the cash-in-advance constraint.

v) In traditional growth theory, the analysis of the interaction of inflation and real activity used to be concerned with level effects: with real per capita variables growing in the long run at some exogenously specified rate, changes in the inflation rate could affect at best the steady state *levels* of these variables. This has changed with the advent of the new, 'endogenous' growth theory. In fact, virtually all more recent contributions to the superneutrality debate analyze how permanent changes in the inflation rate impact on the long run *growth rate* of real variables and use therefore frameworks that exhibit endogenous growth.

The difference between level and growth effects is of considerable importance from an empirical perspective. Yet, from the perspective of monetary theory the scope for new insights is rather limited, since the mechanisms are similar through which inflation affects real activity in exogenous and endogenous growth models. To illustrate this point in somewhat more detail, remember from our discussion given above that in the traditional growth setting of the Ramsey model money ceases to be superneutral in terms of levels of real variables, roughly speaking, whenever changes in the inflation rate affect the marginal product of capital. However, it is a common feature of endogenous growth models in the spirit of Romer (1986), Lucas (1988), and Rebelo (1991) that ongoing growth obtains, because the production function exhibits non-diminishing returns to the reproducible factors of production such as physical or human capital.[19] This feature implies that in endogenous

---

[18]Clower (1967), p. 5.

[19]Rebelo (1991) uses a technology that is linear in a broad measure of the capital stock. Romer (1986) assumes that there are non-diminishing returns to capital at the aggregate level due to externalities in the production process. Finally, Lucas (1988) considers a

14

growth settings, deviating from traditional growth theory, any policy that
changes the marginal returns to reproducible factors, as perceived by agents
at the individual level, affects the long run growth rate of the system. Thus,
irrespective of the particular transmission mechanism of monetary policy, endogenous growth models transform, as a general feature, level into growth
effects because of a different specification of the real side of the economy.[20]
As long as one is aware of this general feature, there is, therefore, no need
to draw a sharp line between old and new growth theory in the context discussed here. Nevertheless, we turn now to a brief summary of more recent
contributions from an endogenous growth perspective.

Using a Rebelo-type set-up, Jones/Manuelli (1995) show that growth rates
of real variables and inflation will be negatively correlated, if there are any
nominal rigidities in place (such as imperfectly indexed tax brackets or depreciation allowances) that allow inflation to reduce the real after-tax return
on investment. Similarly, De Gregorio (1993) shows within a framework with
constant returns to physical capital at the aggregate level, a pecuniary transaction technology applying to purchases of consumption goods, and an elastic
labour supply that the Anti-Tobin effect will prevail.

In related work, Roubini/Sala-i-Martin (1992) offer an explanation of the
persistence of high inflation regimes in various less developed economies from
a public finance perspective. Broadly speaking, Roubini/Sala-i-Martin (1992)
argue that high inflation economies exhibit typically a large degree of financial
repression which precludes the efficient allocation of capital. Addressing this
issue within a Rebelo-type framework, the authors present a specification in
which the overall productivity of capital depends negatively on the level of
financial repression. Under this specification, Roubini/Sala-i-Martin (1992)
show that ongoing financial repression may well reduce the long run growth
rate of the economy.

Gomme (1993) adapts a version of a Lucas-type economy with human capital production to an environment in which all market-related activities are
subject to a cash-in-advance constraint. In particular, Gomme (1993) em-
phasizes the labour supply decision of agents. To this end, it is assumed that
households allocate the time they work between some market-related activity
and the acquisition of new human capital. As far as the effects of inflation
are concerned, the cash-in-advance constraint ensures that any increase in
the inflation rate reduces the real value of ordinary wage income resulting
from market-related labour effort. However, assuming uniform return rates

---

two-sectorial growth model with constant returns to physical and human capital.

[20]Similarly, it is for this reason that the formerly clear distinction between growth and
business cycle theory has become somewhat blurrred. As shown, for example, by Ben-
habib/Farmer (1994) and Farmer/Guo (1994), virtually identical frameworks which differ
only in the specification of the production function can result in both (endogenous) growth
and business cycle scenarios.

in both activities, Gomme (1993) shows that higher inflation also reduces the production of new human capital. According to the mechanics of a Lucas-type economy, this translates immediately into a lower overall growth rate of the economy, i.e. the Anti-Tobin effect obtains.

A similar treatment of the labour-leisure choice with human capital production is given in Jones/Manuelli (1995). However, due to a rich framework which differentiates between cash and credit goods, Jones/Manuelli (1995) link the effects of inflation to the question of whether cash and credit goods are complements or substitutes. In particular, in the spirit of some of our results given in chapter 8, it turns out that the Anti-Tobin effect prevails if the two types of goods are complements. In contrast, if goods are substitutes a positive link obtains.

Van der Ploeg/Alogoskoufis (1994) extend Weil's discussion of the controversial net wealth dimension of money in a straightforward manner to an endogenous growth framework. Essentially, their life-cycle economy is specified as in Weil's original contribution, but it is assumed that returns to capital are linear at the aggregate level due to a Romer-type externality. Thus, Van der Ploeg/Alogoskoufis (1994) confirm, well in accordance with Weil's analysis, that the Anti-Tobin effect prevails, although now in terms of growth rates.[21]

vi) So far our discussion has been concerned with the long run interaction of inflation and real activity in terms of comparative statics analysis. However, this type of analysis leads only to meaningful results if one can show that equilibrium dynamics are stable. Moreover, we have silently assumed that there exists in steady state comparison a uniquely defined relation between the rate of monetary expansion and the inflation rate. Yet, this does not need to be the case and, therefore, we turn now briefly to the large literature on the issues of uniqueness and stability of equilibrium.

To clarify the terminology with respect to these issues, we find it useful to present a classification due to Howitt (1993) that addresses the steady state relation between the rate of monetary expansion and the inflation rate in exogenous and endogenous growth settings. According to Howitt (1993), the difference between the two settings can be simply summarized as following: while the relation is uniquely defined in exogenous growth models, this may well be different under conditions of endogenous growth. To illustrate this point, let π, μ, and g denote, respectively, the steady state inflation rate, the growth rate of the money stock, and the growth rate of output. Assuming that the velocity of money stays constant over time, the quantity theory of money implies that in steady state equilibrium the inflation rate is given by the excess of the rate of monetary expansion over the growth rate of output: $\pi = \mu - g$. As graphed in figure 1.1a, with g being fixed independently of

---

[21] A similar derivation of this result is given by Mino/Shibata (1995).

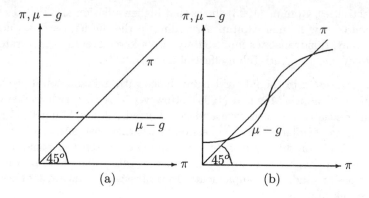

Figure 1.1: *Steady state equilibria: exogenous vs. endogenous growth*

π in exogenous growth settings, there is no scope for multiple steady state inflation rates for a given value of μ.

The situation is different in endogenous growth settings when it is assumed that output growth depends negatively on the inflation rate through one of the channels discussed above: now, as graphed in figure 1.1b, multiple inflation rates and growth rates of output may well coexist in steady state for some exogenously fixed value of μ. Thus, endogenous growth models are sufficiently rich to accommodate the fact that a growing money stock may equally feed the transactions demand of a growing economy at rather stable prices or fuel the inflation process of an economy with a poor growth record in real terms. And, indeed, there is no reason why growth frameworks which deal explicitly with monetary matters should exhibit a uniquely defined relation between the growth rate of the money stock and the inflation rate.

Returning to the exogenous growth literature, it turns out that all the classical contributions mentioned above exhibit in steady state a uniquely defined level of real balances, capital formation, and overall economic activity. However, there remains the important question of whether the steady state is stable. This question has been extensively analyzed in the literature, and in summarizing the results one needs to bear in mind that the underlying notion of stability itself has dramatically changed with the rational expectations revolution.

In particular, as shown by Nagatani (1970), Tobin's model is subject to 'saddlepath stability' under the assumption of perfect foresight. Thus, from the pre-rational expectations perspective of 'backwardlooking stability' this result implies that the steady state is unstable.[22] In contrast, this assessment changes once the rational expectations perspective of 'forwardlooking stability' is employed: from this perspective, Tobin's model exhibits a uniquely defined path - the so-called saddlepath - that converges asymptotically towards the steady state.[23] However, as demonstrated, for example, by Brock (1974) and Calvo (1979), this uniqueness result in the forward looking sense is not a general feature of monetary growth models, and adjustment behaviour towards steady state may well be 'indeterminate'.

Note that in the literature this type of indeterminacy in terms of adjustment behaviour towards a steady state is sometimes referred to as 'multiplicity of equilibria'. However, to avoid misunderstandings, in this book the term 'multiple equilibria' is reserved for a constellation with multiple steady states, while the term 'indeterminacy' refers to the stability type of a steady state with multiple stable adjustment paths.

vii) Generally speaking, it is a well-known result of intertemporal macroeconomics that in full employment models of the long run the maximum attainable level of output may well exceed the welfare maximizing level of output.[24] Clearly, under such circumstances the Tobin effect is of purely theoretical interest. Importantly, Tobin (1968) himself shows in his 'notes on optimal monetary growth' that he is well aware of this dimension to his analysis.[25]

---

[22]Responding to this undesirable feature, various authors have addressed the question of how to restore stability of Tobin's model under backwardlooking behaviour. In particular, Sidrauski (1967a) ensures stability in this sense by introducing adaptive expectations. Similarly, this is achieved by Olivera (1971) by assuming a policy of 'passive' money.

[23]In particular, once real balances are allowed to act as a 'jumping' variable with a free initial condition in the context of Tobin's model, the economy can always respond to a shock in a discontinuous way such that stability is restored.

With all variables being considered as predetermined, backward loooking stability implies that all roots of the Jacobian matrix evaluated at the steady state are non-explosive. In contrast, for the steady state to be forward stable the numbers of explosive roots must not exceed the number of 'jumping' variables. In particular, saddlepath stability requires that both numbers are identical, while adjustment behaviour towards the steady state will be stable, but indeterminate, if there are more jumping variables than explosive roots. For details, see Blanchard/Kahn (1980). For textbook summaries, see Farmer (1993) or Turnovsky (1995).

[24]In chapter 4, we discuss the associated problem of 'dynamically inefficient' equilibria in more detail.

[25]Although not addressed in this book in any detail, there is a large literature on the welfare costs associated with inflation. Broadly speaking, the majority of studies concludes that welfare costs of moderate inflation rates tend to be 'small', not exceeding 0.5% of GNP per annum for a 10% inflation rate. However, more recent contributions from an endogenous growth perspective show that costs may be 'substantially large' due to the growth effect of inflation. For a detailed summary of more recent estimates, see, for example, Wu/Zhang (1998).

However, more 'realistic' settings of long run economic developments (which might be hard to come by in a rigorous way) should incorporate various imperfections, at least some of them non-monetary in nature. From this perspective, first-best arguments seem no longer appropriate, and then it should be of considerable interest whether the Tobin effect is firmly supported by macroeconomic reasoning.

Despite the narrow perspective that we have taken so far, we think that our review of the theoretical literature has clearly demonstrated that the Tobin effect is not a general feature of monetary growth models. In particular, various more recent contributions have shown that one easily designs plausible frameworks in which the Tobin effect will be completely reversed. Thus, to put it mildly, more than 30 years after the publication of Tobin's analysis monetary growth theory is no longer in a position to recommend a policy that seeks to exploit a long run trade-off between inflation and economic activity.

Finally, it is an entirely different question whether the results which Tobin obtains by extending 'Keynesian' reasoning to the long run are still in the spirit of Keynes himself. Most textbook treatments suggest that Keynes' loose stance on monetary policy in the situation of a deep recession, as expressed in his General Theory, reflects his position on the proper conduct of monetary policy in general. Yet, Keynes was in his earlier writings clearly worried about detrimental effects of ongoing inflation. Interestingly, Keynes' concerns primarily reflect the 'distributional aspects of inflation' as the following passage from his early 'Tract on Monetary Reform' indicates:

"...Inflation is unjust and deflation is inexpedient. Of the two perhaps deflation is, if we rule out exaggerated inflations such as that of Germany, the worse; because it is worse, in an impoverished world, to provoke unemployment than to disappoint the rentier. But it is not necessary that we should weigh one evil against the other. It is easier to agree that both are evils to be shunned. The individualistic capitalism of today, precisely because it entrusts saving to the individual investor and production to the individual employer, presumes a stable measuring-rod of value, and cannot be efficient - perhaps cannot survive - without one."[26]

Up to this point, our summary of the theoretical debate on the long run effects of inflation has concentrated, quite in accordance with Tobin's original contribution, on the narrow 'money-taxing aspects' of inflation. Evidently, further aspects need to be considered, and we return to the issue from a broader perspective in chapter 3.

---

[26]Keynes, A Tract on Monetary Reform (1923), in: Keynes (1972), p. 36.

Chapter 2

Summary of the literature: empirical aspects

As a result of the renewed interest in growth theory in the 1980's due to the work by Romer (1986) and Lucas (1988), a vast amount of empirical literature has emerged which seeks to account for the remarkable variability of growth rates across countries. In this literature, numerous specifications of cross-country growth regressions have been tested to establish significant linkages between long run average growth rates and various indicators of economic policy. Together with other indicators of macroeconomic policy, the rate of inflation is widely used in these regressions as an explanatory variable, and there is a broad consensus that inflation is an important determinant of the rate of per capita growth. Drawing on this literature, we establish in this chapter a set of 'stylized facts', with the aim to summarize the available evidence with respect to the long run interaction between inflation and per capita growth.

In general, recent cross-country studies are surprisingly unanimous in assessing the long run interaction of inflation and per capita growth rates for the time period since the second world war.[1]

1) The overwhelming majority of recent post-war cross-section studies supports the Anti-Tobin conjecture, i.e. there is strong evidence that inflation

---

[1]There is a broad literature which confirms this result. For details, see: Kormendi/ Meguire (1985), Grier/Tullock (1989), Fischer (1991, 1993), De Gregorio (1992, 1993), Roubini/Sala-i-Martin (1992), Gomme (1993), Herbertsson/Gylfason (1996), Sarel (1996), Andrés/Hernando (1997), Barro (1997), Bruno/Easterly (1998), Ghosh/Phillips (1998). Deviating results are given in McCandless/Weber (1995) and Bullard/Keating (1995). Both studies argue that money is superneutral. For summaries of the literature, see Chari/ Jones/Manuelli (1995), McCandless/Weber (1995), and Herbertsson/Gylfason (1996).

Variable	Fast-growers	Slow-growers	t-statistic
Share of investment in GDP	0.23	0.17	5.18
Secondary-school enrollment rate in 1960	0.30	0.10	5.46
Primary-school enrollment rate in 1960	0.90	0.54	6.10
Government consumption/GDP	0.16	0.12	3.26
Inflation rate	12.34	31.13	-1.74
Black-market exchange-rate premium	13.57	57.15	-3.79
Share of exports to GDP	0.32	0.23	2.31

Source: Levine/Renelt (1992, p. 948). The sample includes 109 countries. Mean growth rate =1.92. Fast-growers (slow-growers) are countries with a growth rate exceeding (falling short of) the mean growth rate.

Table 2.1: Cross-country averages, 1960-1989

and per capita output growth are negatively correlated.

Inevitably, it is difficult to compare these studies directly due to differences in estimating procedures and characteristics of variables such as the countries and the length of the time period considered in the sample, the specification of sub-periods in panel studies, and the explanatory variables included in the regression in addition to inflation.[2] However, to give a rough illustration of the evidence we reproduce in table 2.1 a summary of fairly representative results as reported in the detailed study of cross-country regressions by Levine/Renelt (1992).

Not surprisingly, the precise estimates of the Anti-Tobin effect vary from one study to another. Yet, to give an idea of the magnitudes involved, Chari/Jones/Manuelli (1995) compare the results established in various studies and conclude that the standard linear regression model suggests that a 10 percentage point increase in the inflation rate is roughly associated with a decrease in the average growth rate between 0.3 and 0.7 percentage points.

Addressing the differences in estimating procedures across the empirical literature, results can be more accurately interpreted if the frequency of data is

---

[2]As a common feature, all the cited studies measure inflation, whenever the data situation allows this, in terms of changes in the CPI. Calculations of the CPI index do not depend on output figures. Thus, measurement errors will not induce any systematic correlation between inflation and output growth. Clearly, this is a problem if one uses instead the implicit GDP deflator. Then, any (systematic) overstatement of output growth due to measurement errors leads automatically to an understatement of the change in the implicit GDP deflator.

properly taken into account: while pure cross-section regressions use for each country only the long run average of each variable over the whole period, panel regressions, which combine cross-section and time-series data, capture also some of the information being available in the time series of each country. In the light of this distinction, the broad result given in *1)* can be restated with more precision:

2) Results on inflation and growth are weaker in pure cross-section regressions than in panel regressions, i.e. the negative effect of inflation tends to rise in the frequency of the data as one moves from the pure cross-section to ten or five year averages to annual data.

Further investigating this result, Bruno/Easterly (1998) show that it is primarily driven by a strong negative link between per capita growth and inflation during discrete episodes of unusually high inflation rates, i.e. per capita growth falls off during inflation crises and growth rates are quickly restored to pre-crisis levels once inflation is again under control.[3] Evidently, this type of pronounced short-run interaction of inflation and growth will not be detected by pure cross-country studies which operate with long run average values over periods of $20 - 40$ years.

Given the well-known differences to establish conclusive bivariate relationships between macroeconomic variables, the 'robustness' of the results summarized in 1) and 2) has been tested along several dimensions.[4]

In particular, in order to establish the robustness of inflation as an explanatory variable within a broad set of regressors, the majority of the studies cited above follows the strategy pursued by Levine/Renelt (1992) and specifies first variables with a widely accepted, strong explanatory power for per capita growth which are included in all regressions, such as the initial position of GDP, the investment share of GDP, and the initial secondary-school enrollment rate. Next, a conditioning set of variables is constructed which includes macroeconomic variables related to inflation. According to this strategy, inflation will only be considered as a robust explanatory variable, if the significance of the inflation coefficient survives alterations in the set of conditioning variables.[5] Typical examples for additional, conditioning variables

---

[3]Note that this finding is a challenge for the standard view that inflation is procyclical, i.e. that - as summarized by Mankiw (1989) - "in the absence of identifiable real shocks such as the OPEC oil price changes inflation tends to rise in booms and fall in recessions" (p. 88). We will return to this issue below when we discuss the possibility of systematic differences between low and high inflation observations.

[4]For a very informative survey of aspects related to the robustness of inflation effects, see, in particular, Ghosh/Phillips (1998).

[5]Ironically, according to Levine/Renelt (1992) inflation is not robust in this sense. However, this result is not confirmed by more recent studies, in particular, if non-linear

(which are deliberately chosen to impact sensitively on the effects attributed to inflation) are the share of government consumption expenditures, the public deficit, the premium on the black market exchange, the average growth rate of domestic credit, or the variability of the inflation rate itself.[6]

Moreover, since panel results combine both cross-country and time series information, the literature knows various techniques to control along both dimensions for potential effects resulting from omitted variables, i.e. from forces which are jointly correlated with inflation and growth and which are not, or only imperfectly measured, by other regressors.

To establish robustness of the findings in the cross-country dimension, most studies run additional regressions with country or continent dummies included (i.e. fixed effects regressions), and there is strong evidence that the common effect of inflation remains significant upon this modification.[7] Both Roubini/Sala-i-Martin (1992) and Fischer (1993), for example, report that the inclusion of continent-specific dummies for African and Latin American countries decreases the coefficient on inflation slightly, but does not affect its significance. Ghosh/Phillips (1998) include country dummies and show, somewhat surprisingly, that this even increases the common effect of the inflation coefficient.[8] Evidently, to control for cross-country variation by including country dummies is highly costly in terms of lost degrees of freedom. On these grounds, Barro (1997) prefers to include broad indices for the rule of law and the degree of democracy as additional regressors, thereby ensuring that fundamental cross-country differences are not picked up by the coefficient pertaining to inflation. Yet, it turns out that in qualitative accordance with the other studies the inclusion of such variables in Barro's regressions does not render the effect of inflation insignificant. Thus, in the light of this evidence we summarize:

---

effects of inflation are taken into account.

[6]The literature disagrees whether the inclusion of the variability of inflation brings additional, significant information. Barro (1997), for example, shows that the inflation coefficient remains virtually unchanged, while the coefficient associated with the variability of inflation is small and insignificant. In contrast, Kormendi/Meguire (1985), Grier/Tullock (1989), and Fischer (1993) find significant evidence that output growth depends negatively not only on the level of the rate of inflation, but also on its variability. However, these latter findings need to be interpreted with some caution because of the multicollinearity problem of including both inflation and the variability of inflation as regressors.

[7]As summarized by Barro (1997), fundamental characteristics of economies such as the enforcement of properts rights should be of prime importance in explaining differences in growth performances. Moreover, the ability of a central bank to achieve a stable and low inflation rate will be highly correlated with such fundamentals. Thus, in regressions, in which no attempt is being made to control for such fundamental, country-specific characteristics, the measured effect of inflation may well be misleading.

[8]In similar spirit, Herbertsson/Gylfason (1996) control for the cross-country dimension by running a random effects regression and establish significant effects of inflation.

3) There is strong evidence that the results summarized in 1) and 2) remain significant if one controls in the cross-country dimension for unmeasured country-specific factors associated with inflation and growth.

As far as the time-series dimension of the findings is concerned, the second stylized fact with its strong emphasis on the more pronounced short run interaction of inflation and growth hints naturally at the possibility of a strong spurious relationship, i.e. it may well be possible that the relationship reflects predominantly common responses of inflation and growth to policy changes and external shocks. In fact, assuming that velocity is not strongly volatile in the short-run, any policy of strict monetary targeting will translate shocks systematically into a negative relationship between inflation and growth.

However, controlling for the impact of external shocks by including the change in the terms of trade as an additional regressor, Fischer (1993) shows that this modification does not affect the significance of the inflation coefficient.[9] In similar spirit, Fischer (1993) runs distinct regressions for the subperiods 1961 − 72 and 1973 − 88, having in mind that the latter period was arguably more strongly affected by external supply shocks. Yet, he finds no evidence for a more pronounced relationship between inflation and growth in the second subperiod. Also with the intention to control for spurious effects, Ghosh/Phillips (1998) report that the inclusion of both contemporaneous and lagged changes in the inflation rate lead to largely unchanged results.

Closely related to this issue, proponents of the so-called 'reverse causation hypothesis' would argue that the evidence produced so far does not prove that causation runs indeed from inflation to growth.[10]

In order to disentangle effects resulting from reverse causation and components of inflation which are 'truly' exogenous to growth, various modifications which rely on instrumental variable specifications have been tested in the literature. Cukierman et al. (1993), for example, develop in their widely cited study for a sample of 55 countries an index of political vulnerability of central banks which measures the fraction of times that a political transition is followed within 6 months by a replacement of the central bank governor. Accordingly, a high index value stand for a comparatively high degree of exogenously caused changes in observed inflation.[11] Using this index as an instrument for inflation, Cukierman et al. (1993) show that the impact on growth is still significantly negative, though less pronounced than in their base regression.

---

[9]In fact, following Fischers's approach the majority of subsequent studies includes the change in the terms of trade in the list of controlling regressors.

[10]For an outline of the reverse causation hypothesis, see, for example, the study by King/Plosser (1984).

[11]As one would expect, Cukierman et al. (1993) report that the index is typically lower in developed than in less developed economies.

24

Commenting on this result, Barro (1997) doubts whether the actual turnover of central bank governors should be treated as being exogenous to growth. Moreover, he shows that indicators which measure the underlying legal independence of central banks, although more likely to be exogenous to growth, cease to be systematically correlated with inflation. Thus, Barro (1997) resorts to different instruments for inflation. First, he shows that the use of lagged rather than contemporaneous inflation leads only to slightly reduced coefficient estimates. Alternatively, he argues that the prior colonial status of countries, in particular in distinguishing between former Spanish and Portuguese colonies on the one hand and all remaining countries on the other hand, may well be used as an instrument for inflation. And it turns out that instrumenting inflation in this way leads, again, to largely unchanged results compared to his base regression. Thus, although using different techniques than Cukierman et al. (1993), Barro (1997) also arrives at the conclusion that causation runs largely from inflation to growth.

Further evidence of this view, though from a slightly different angle, is given in McCandless/Weber (1995). In their cross-section study, McCandless/Weber (1995) establish for the long run a high (almost unity) correlation between the growth rate of the money supply and the inflation rate. This correlation holds for various definitions of the money stock, including the narrow definition M_0 which is directly controlled by the central bank. Thus, the findings of McCandless/Weber (1995) suggest, contrary to the reverse causation hypothesis, that it is legitimate to assume that inflation is to a large extent exogenously caused.

In summary, we conclude in the light of this evidence:

4) There is strong evidence that the results summarized in 1) and 2) remain significant if one controls in the time series dimension for unmeasured effects associated with inflation and growth. Similarly, the empirical evidence suggests that the causation runs predominantly, though not exclusively, from inflation to growth.

The results presented so far do not attempt to distinguish systematically between episodes of high and low inflation. Yet, to account appropriately for the effect of inflation along this dimension is certainly the most controversial issue in the empirical studies cited above.

Studies along the lines of Barro (1997) and Bruno/Easterly (1998) which use linear regression set-ups reach the conclusion that the significance of the stylized facts 1) and 2) depends strongly on the inclusion of high inflation observations.

Most drastically, Bruno/Easterly (1998) report that the inclusion of observations beyond a threshold inflation rate of 40% is crucial for all their findings: "We find that there is no robust evidence of a growth-inflation relationship at any frequency excluding these discrete high inflation crises."[12] In similar spirit, though less drastically, Barro (1997) re-estimates his system with separate coefficients for inflation in three ranges (up to 15%, between 15% and 40%, and over 40%) and reports that the coefficient for low inflation observations, although still negative, is no longer significant.[13] Thus, less drastically than in Bruno/Easterly (1998), the negative effect of inflation on growth in Barro's findings is driven both by middle and high inflation observations. But, importantly, Barro (1997) also reports that the differences are not pronounced enough to reject the hypothesis of a common linear effect of inflation on growth across inflation ranges.

These findings are challenged by studies along the lines of Sarel (1996) and Ghosh/Phillips (1998) who point out that non-linearities are important and that estimates from standard regression set-ups which fail to account for non-linearities tend to be strongly biased. In fact, both Sarel (1996) and Ghosh/Phillips (1998) produce evidence that the relationship between inflation and growth is subject to two types of non-linearities: First, a positive relationship between inflation and growth for very low (i.e. single digit) inflation rates, with the structural break occurring somewhere in the middle of the single digit range, and, second, a negative and convex relationship for all other inflation rates.[14] Taking this second finding for granted, a move in the annual inflation rate from, let's say, 10% to 20% is far more detrimental in terms of foregone output than a move from 40% to 50%. Accordingly, both studies conclude that misspecified, linear estimates induce a severe downward bias to the estimated inflation coefficient over the range of greatest policy interest. Moreover, as summarized by Ghosh/Phillips (1998), the negative relationship between inflation and growth in this range does no longer depend on the inclusion of high inflation observations: "Taking both ...non-linearities into account, we find that the negative inflation-growth relationship is...evident in both the time and cross-section dimensions of the data, and that it is quite robust. Excluding high inflation observations, time averaging the data, or using various subsamples (defined according to time period or the degree of inflation) does not alter the basic findings."[15]

Interestingly, the first non-linearity in the transition from very low to moderate inflation rates in the single digit range detected by Sarel (1996) and

---

[12]Bruno/Easterly (1998), p. 4.

[13]The estimated coefficients are -0.023 in the low range, -0.055 in the middle range, and -0.029 in the upper range, i.e. an increase in average annual inflation by 10 % in low inflation regimes reduces annual per capita growth on average by 0.23 percentage points etc.

[14]Concerning the first non-linearity, Sarel (1996) estimates that the structural break occurs when annual inflation reaches 8%. In contrast, Ghosh/Phillips (1998) report a threshold level of 2.5%.

[15]Ghosh/Phillips (1998), p. 674.

Ghosh/Phillips (1998) is not unanimously confirmed by small sample studies which concentrate only on OECD observations, which are typically associated with low inflation outcomes. While McCandless/Weber (1995) establish indeed a positive relationship between inflation and growth in OECD countries, Grier/Tullock (1989) find that on average inflation has no effect on growth in these countries. In contrast, Andrés/Hernando (1997) find a significant negative relationship for these countries.

Thus, in the light of this mixed evidence we summarize:

5) The literature disagrees whether the effect of inflation differs systematically between low and high inflation regimes. However, non-linearities may play a role, and there is considerable evidence that the negative effect of inflation on growth is, at best, rather fragile for very low inflation rates.

The evidence established so far is more or less silent on the question why inflation affects growth. Broadly speaking, the literature agrees that sound monetary policies create in general a climate conducive to growth. Moreover, it is argued that the rate of inflation should be interpreted as an overall indicator of the government's ability to pursue such policies. Clearly, this vague assessment of the role of inflation is hardly satisfactory, but more detailed evidence that would help to identify distinct channels through which inflation affects growth is scarcely available. However, we conclude this chapter with a brief summary of this scattered evidence and leave some general reflections on the structural relationship between inflation and growth for the next chapter.

In his informative analysis, Fischer (1993) uses a regression analog of growth accounting which makes it possible to attribute the effects of inflation separately to changes in factor supplies and to changes in a Solow-type residual measure of productivity that approximates the efficiency with which inputs are used. Decomposing thereby the growth effects of inflation in 'extensive' and 'intensive' components, Fischer (1993) arrives at the conclusion:

6) Inflation is negatively associated with both capital accumulation and productivity growth.

Broadly speaking, Fischer's findings indicate that one needs to distinguish at least between two different mechanisms through which inflation affects the growth performance of economies. First, from a macroeconomic perspective, the negative effect on the level of investment suggests that high inflation rates are typically associated with policies that are perceived by investors as being uncertain, thereby making it less attractive for investors to commit themselves to new projects. Additional evidence supporting this assessment is given by Bruno/Easterly (1998) who report that the quick rebound in output growth after episodes of high inflation is typically not accompanied by a corresponding recovery in both capital growth and the investment/GDP-ratio, i.e. both measures remain according to these findings for a sometimes prolonged time period below the pre-crisis level. In other words, while the output recovery is mainly realized through improved rates of capacity utilization, investors respond to the reputation loss of the monetary authority by adapting a wait and see attitude with respect to new investment projects.

Second, from a microeconomic perspective, both the fact that the inflation effect remains significant after the inclusion of investment-related regressors and the negative correlation of inflation with overall productivity seem to indicate that high inflation rates interfere with an efficient allocation of inputs. Additional evidence supporting this microeconomic view is given in Roubini/Sala-i-Martin (1992) and King/Levine (1993). Roughly speaking, the evidence presented in these studies can be summarized as:

7) Ongoing rates of high inflation are typically found in financially repressed economies. Moreover, there is strong evidence that the growth rate of output and the level of financial repression are negatively correlated.

In their broad cross-country study, Roubini/Sala-i-Martin (1992) test for the effects of financial repression on growth, with financial repression being measured through various indicators such as a composite index of distortions in financial markets, the level of the real interest rate, and the level of reserve requirements of intermediaries. The results presented in the study strongly indicate that financial repression has a significant negative effect on growth, and, more importantly, inflation is shown to be closely correlated with all measures of financial repression. Interpreting this evidence, Roubini/Sala-i-Martin (1992) concede that short-sighted governments may well have a dominant revenue motive to engage in financial repression if they find it sufficiently costly to switch from an inflation tax regime to a more broadly based income tax regime. However, as a result of such a policy, long run gains from a more efficient allocation of capital in a liberalized financial system will remain unexploited and a comparatively low growth rate will be perpetuated over time.

Complementing this view, King/Levine (1993) address in detail the productivity enhancing aspects of well managed financial systems. Drawing on early insights by Schumpeter, King/Levine (1993) argue that the link between finance and innovation is central to the process of growth. In particular, the authors stress the active role played by financial institutions in evaluating, managing, and funding the entrepreneurial activity that leads to productivity growth. Given the risks associated with innovative activities, the authors conjecture that developed financial systems are better at monitoring these activities successfully, thereby improving the probability of successful innovation. In order to test this hypothesis empirically, King/Levine (1993) construct in their cross-country study various measures that are designed to approximate the level of financial development. Measures used by the authors include, among others, the size of the formal financial intermediary sector, the distribution of assets within the banking system between the central bank and non-central bank intermediaries, and the allocative structure of intermediated funds with respect to government and private uses. Using these measures, King/Levine (1993) also reach the conclusion that there is a significant relation between output growth and the level of financial development.

Chapter 3

Further reflections on money

In reviewing the literature on the superneutrality issue in chapter 1, we have exclusively focused on the *'money-taxing aspects of inflation'*. However, in the light of the empirical evidence given in the previous chapter this has been an unduly narrow perspective and, therefore, we turn now to a broader discussion of the issue. First, we discuss additional channels through which sustained inflation impacts on the economy. Second, we argue that despite the striking variety of results in monetary growth theory there has emerged a solid consensus among economists, as far as 'essential' features of money are concerned that need to be addressed in a rigorous way. Referring to these 'essentials', we discuss some consequences for monetary theory in general and present a broad classification of ongoing research. Third, drawing on this classification, we introduce the second part of the book. In particular, we argue that Diamond's version of an overlapping generation's economy with production may well serve as a benchmark model to discuss a broad range of aspects related to the question whether one should expect money to be superneutral.

Responding to the unsatisfactory variety of results in monetary growth theory, theoretical work in the aftermath of Tobin's contribution has attempted to clarify the situation, from a methodological perspective, by adopting certain 'standards' in terms of commonly accepted modelling techniques. In particular, the following two standards are by now widely regarded as indispensable: first, the issue should be addressed from 'first principles' within a fully specified intertemporal framework that allows for a proper understanding of the dynamics involved. Second, the role attributed to money should be 'well-defined', and the demand for money should be derived from some kind of explicit optimizing behaviour of agents.

But while there is by now widespread agreement on these technical aspects, things are more complicated as far as the content of the models is concerned. Generally speaking, issues that go beyond the narrow 'money-taxing aspects of inflation' are scarcely addressed in the literature in a rigorous way, although there can be no doubt that they belong intimately to the subject matter. A thoughtful classification of these issues in broad terms is given by Howitt (1993). In particular, Howitt (1993) distinguishes between two aspects. First, there are *'transaction-impeding aspects of inflation'* which make it, in summary, more costly for the economy as a whole to trade at any given level of real balances. Second, there are *'uncertainty aspects of inflation'*, accounting for the fact that high inflation rates are typically associated with uncertainty about the future course of macroeconomic policies in general.

As far as the 'transaction impeding aspects of inflation' are concerned, associated costs arise, broadly speaking, "...from society's inability to keep business and government accounts in real terms."[1] In particular, since goods and services are commonly traded at nominal prices, prices need to be adjusted more frequently under high inflation rates, and these adjustments by themselves create additional 'menu' costs. Similarly, higher inflation tends to increase the overall dispersion of prices, thereby leading to a rise in overall search costs. Also, prices that are specified in contracts for a fixed period of time are rarely indexed to the inflation rate. Thus, higher inflation forces agents to renegotiate contracts more frequently, thereby creating additional costs for the parties involved in the negotiation process. Finally, since tax brackets are stated in nominal terms, inflation distorts the efficiency of the tax system and raises the costs of collecting taxes in real terms.[2]

As far as the 'uncertainty aspects of inflation' are concerned, the literature suggests that various effects are at work. As indicated by Lucas (1973), one would expect that an overall increase in uncertainty about future policies (i.e. an increase in the noise in the system) tends to reduce the allocative efficiency of the price mechanism. Moreover, higher uncertainty tends to induce a shortening of contract terms, thereby raising the costs associated with a more pronounced 'short-termism' of contracted projects. Also, with financial markets being incomplete, inflation induced uncertainty impacts negatively on collective risk sharing arrangements. Finally, along the lines of the work by Dixit/Pindyck (1994), one would expect that higher uncertainty reduces the overall level of economic activity, in particular with respect to investment, since more agents will find it now profitable to postpone decisions until the additional uncertainty has been resolved rather than to commit themselves to new projects.

---

[1] Howitt (1993), p. 267.

[2] For a careful analysis of the interaction of inflation and the tax system, in particular with respect to capital income taxation, see Feldstein (1996). In this study, Feldstein reaches the conclusion that even for very low inflation rates welfare costs resulting from distortions in the tax system are substantial.

Disagreeing with the dismal picture of inflation presented so far, various authors point out that there are also beneficial, *structural change facilitating aspects of inflation*, to the extent that nominal prices exhibit a certain degree of downward rigidity. Leaving measurement problems of inflation aside, a 'low' rate of inflation seems from this perspective desirable since it helps to facilitate the readjustment of relative prices in a smooth way.[3] In particular, taking it for granted that the downward rigidity of nominal wages is a well entrenched characteristic of modern labour markets, Akerlof/Dickens/ Perry (1996) present in a widely cited study a model with heterogenous wage setting by firms, in which a policy aiming strictly at a zero inflation rate will even raise the long run level of unemployment.[4]

In summary, it seems fair to conclude that monetary theory is still far from having a framework that would permit a satisfactory treatment of all, or only the majority, of the above mentioned aspects of inflation in a rigorous way. Reflecting upon this unsatisfactory situation, Hahn (1969) arrives in his early work on 'money and growth' at the conclusion:

"Economic theory still lacks a 'monetary Debreu'. The study of some simple problems raised by considering the growth of a monetary economy which follows must therefore be regarded as tentative. At some future date the issues here raised may be found to be peripheral to a proper understanding of money...To say that money is 'neutral' if the steady state values of the 'real' variables are what they would have been had we never introduced a monetary asset is, therefore, misleading. In order to compare the two economies we should have to provide a theory of transactions for the non-monetary economy, and no one has yet done so. Money can be found to be 'neutral' in the above sense only if it is given no function to perform."[5]

Arguably, Hahn's gloomy assessment is at a fundamental level today as true as nearly 30 years ago. Yet, despite the widely acknowledged lack of a single, all-embracing paradigm in monetary theory, substantial progress has been made with respect to the identification of indispensable features of money that need to be analyzed in a rigorous way. Since any assessment of the role of inflation will ultimately reflect how these 'essentials' are addressed, we turn now to a more thorough review of central aspects of current research in the field of monetary theory.

The history of monetary economics knows various attempts to establish essential characteristics of money. However, with the collapse of the gold standard

[3] For a trenchant summary of arguments against a policy aiming at perfect price stability, see Krugman (1996).

[4] For a critical assessment of this study see, for example, Groshen/Schweitzer (1996) who argue that more dispersion of relative prices is not per se desirable, in particular if induced by larger forecasting errors of agents due to higher and more volatile inflation rates.

[5] Hahn (1969), p. 196.

and the emergence of modern fiat money regimes there is little disagreement
on these 'essentials' as discussed, for example, by Hahn (1965, 1982), Wallace (1980), or Fama (1983). Drawing on the distinction between inside and
outside money, this consensus can be roughly summarized as following:

Essential features of money:

i) *Outside money is 'inconvertible' and 'intrinsically useless'.*

ii) *Outside money is return-dominated by other assets. In particular, outside money coexists with interest-bearing outside assets (such as government
bonds) which have a perfectly safe return rate.*

iii) *Outside money coexists with interest-bearing inside money. In particular, payment by outside money is not the only way to carry out transactions.*[6]

The implications of these essential features of money for monetary theory are
substantial and constitute, by and large, the agenda of ongoing research. In
the following, we address these essentials in turn. Clearly, a detailed review
of the relevant literature is beyond the scope of this book and, therefore, we
confine ourselves to some broad remarks.

ad i) Invoking the well-known definitions of these two terms advanced by
Wallace (1980), "...*inconvertibility* means that the issuer, if there is one, does
not promise to convert the money into anything else - gold or wheat, for example. *Intrinsic uselessness* means that fiat money is never wanted for its own
sake."[7] Correspondingly, 'inconvertibility' and 'intrinsic uselessness' raise the
problem that "...the devices usually invoked to prove that an object has value
in equilibrium - basically, that supply is limited and that utility is increasing
in the amount consumed - cannot be used for fiat money."[8] Responding to
this problem, Wallace (1980) argues that monetary theory should "...attempt
to model explicitly the notion that fiat money facilitates exchange...In order
to pursue the notion that fiat money facilitates exchange, one must abandon the costless multilateral market clearing implicit in the Walrasian (or
Arrow-Debreu) general equilibrium model. Since exchange works perfectly
in that model, there can be no role for a device that is supposed to facilitate
exchange."[9]

---

[6]In the literature, and also in this book, the pairs 'outside' vs. 'inside' money and '(fiat)
money' vs. 'credit' are used more or less interchangeably. However, at this point we prefer
the former specification since it hints at the fact that both outside and inside money share
the main feature commonly attributed to money, namely to be accepted as a medium of
exchange.

[7]Wallace (1980), p. 49.

[8]Wallace (1980), p. 50.

[9]Wallace (1980), p. 50.

While Wallace's diagnosis of the problems caused by the special nature of outside money is widely accepted, there is less agreement on how to incorporate the exchange facilitating role of money in a framework that goes beyond the standard Walrasian setting.

Reflecting on desirable ingredients of such a setting, Hellwig (1993), for example, points out that the Walrasian formalism of how to deal with stocks and flows is at stake once the exchange facilitating role of money gets seriously addressed. In particular, Hellwig (1993) argues that it is not appropriate for the purposes of monetary theory to subject the demand for money to a logic which specifies that assets are to be held 'at the end of the period': "...The use of money as a medium of exchange is related to the process of transactions in goods and services. In this process of transactions, money is traded back and forth during the period rather than demanded to be held at the end of the period. The formalism that we use to deal with stocks and flows, asset markets and goods markets, fails to take account of this special role of money, which is an asset, but one that is used in goods market transactions."[10] In summary, Hellwig (1993) comes to the far reaching conclusion that for the purposes of monetary theory the Walrasian framework should be entirely abandoned.

In contrast, Wallace himself argues that some features of a setting in Walrasian spirit (such as the conventional treatment of money as a stock variable) can be retained as long as one specifies an explicit trading friction that inhibits the full operation of markets. In particular, Wallace (1980) arrives at the conclusion that the overlapping generations friction as developed by Samuelson (1958) gives rise to the best available model of fiat money. Broadly speaking, this friction exploits the idea that the population of an economy can be imagined to consist of different generations, with money playing the role of an intergenerational trading device that facilitates the trade between members of different generations. Yet, there is no need to interpret the term 'generation' in a literal sense: alternatively, agents can be imagined to live in distinct groups, and while members of the same group can engage in private credit arrangements, members of different groups lack this ability (for reasons of distance or absence of trust, for example). However, when engaging in trade, members of different groups can overcome this friction by using outside money as a medium of exchange. Moreover, while Wallace (1980) considers a version of a pure exchange economy in the spirit of Samuelson (1958), Diamond (1965) has shown in early work that the same friction may also play a role in models with production.

Similar to the diagnosis given by Wallace (1980), Mitsui/Watanabe (1989) acknowledge that "...the growth theory of a monetary economy should not ignore the imperfections of credit markets..., since the phenomenon of fiat

---

[10]Hellwig (1993), p. 224.

money itself is a logical contradiction without such imperfections."[11] Consequently, Mitsui/Watanabe (1989) claim that it is the main function of money
"to complement the function of the credit market whenever the latter fails."[12]
In other words, the authors argue that various credit market imperfections
cause money and credit to act not like substitutes as proposed by Tobin, but
rather like complements. Addressing the 'complementarity hypothesis' in a
rigorous way, Mitsui/Watanabe (1989) construct a version of an 'island economy' where agents move between islands according to a random scheme and
where the spatial arrangement constitutes the friction which generates the
demand for money: while spatially close agents (i.e. inhabitants of the same
island) are linked by credit markets, spatially separated agents rely on money
as a medium of exchange. In summary, the complementarity hypothesis helps
not only to deal with the issues of 'inconvertibility' and 'intrinsic uselessness'
in a serious manner, but it also defines at the same time a departing point
from standard monetary growth theory.[13]

ad ii) For entirely safe assets with different return streams to coexist, the
assets need to differ in some other respect such as the denominations in
which the assets are issued or the ease with which they can be transferred.
As summarized by Wallace (1983), such distinguishing features do exist as
far as government bonds and outside money are concerned, since bonds are
commonly issued in large denominations. Similarly, bonds cannot be used
as hand-to-hand media of exchange to the extent that they are not readily transferable bearer certificates. Yet, to account for the observed return
differential between government bonds and outside money additional 'legal
restrictions' need to be invoked. In particular, regulations against private
issues of bank notes and legislation on reserve requirements rule out that intermediaries undo differences between bonds and money by engaging in the
entirely safe business of emitting bearer notes in small denominations against
a portfolio of government bonds. Clearly, these institutional arrangements
strengthen the demand for outside money.

But why are there legal restrictions in place which allow money to compete
with other outside assets despite being dominated in return? Broadly speaking, there are two ways of how to rationalize the existence of legal restrictions.

First, without legal restrictions it would be far more difficult for the government to control the price level: essentially, as suggested by Patinkin (1961)
in his classical contribution, for the price level to be determinate the govern-

---

[11]Mitsui/Watanabe (1989), p. 124.

[12]Mitsui/Watanabe (1989), p. 124.

[13]As acknowledged by the authors, the complementarity hypothesis has been pioneered
long ago in the field of developing economics by Shaw (1973) and McKinnon (1973). Interestingly, these studies have received little attention in monetary theory. For a general
discussion of monetary models with spatially separated agents, see Townsend (1980).

ment needs to control the nominal quantity and the return rate of an asset which is sufficiently distinguished such that there exists no perfect substitute among alternative assets.[14] From this perspective, legal restrictions (such as regulations against privately issued bank notes) may simple serve the role to create an exclusive and stable demand for outside money.[15] Similarly, restrictions on reserve requirements make it easier for governments to secure funds by subjecting outside money holdings to inflation taxation.

Second, efficiency considerations may call for the imposition of legal restrictions. Addressing the spread between government bonds and outside money from this perspective, Bryant/Wallace (1984) present a framework in which the government simply behaves like a perfectly price discriminating monopolist who offers outside assets in different denominations at different prices.[16] In similar spirit, Bryant/Wallace (1980) argue that the legislation on reserve requirements can help to limit a misallocation of resources, resulting from adverse incentive effects under deposit schemes which are perceived as being fully insured by the government's lender of last resort function.

In the light of these arguments, there is no obvious way of how to approximate the existence of legal restrictions in the context of a rigorously specified model. Reflecting this dilemma, a large body of the literature includes rather ad-hoc an additional trading friction in an otherwise Walrasian setting which ensures that bonds cannot be used as media of exchange.

Alternatively, Wallace (1980) presents a set-up in which the composition of government liabilities is shown to be entirely irrelevant: in particular, Wallace (1980) argues that such an irrelevance proposition can be obtained if it is assumed that the costs accruing to the private sector from absorbing less marketable bonds are matched by government resource savings from issuing bonds instead of outside money. Consequently, Wallace (1980) uses a framework in which money is the only outside asset, and within this context he arrives at his famous dictum describing the effects of monetary policy: "The main result comes from nothing more than a careful consolidation of the balance sheets of the monetary authority and the public: without additional frictions, the portfolio of the monetary authority does not matter even for the value of fiat money. What counts is asset creation and destruction, not

---

[14]Strictly speaking, this is a necessary, but not a sufficient condition. In fact, in the second part of the book we produce various examples in which the price level turns out to be indeterminate in the neighbourhood of certain steady states despite an exogenously fixed growth rate of the nominal stock of non-interest-bearing outside money. For further details, see Calvo (1979) or Woodford (1994).

[15]However, as argued by Wallace (1983), potential benefits from the government's ability to control the price level need to be weighed against potential costs from subjecting private credit markets to binding constraints. For similar considerations, see Fama (1983).

[16]More specifically, Bryant/Wallace (1984) argue in close analogy to standard monopoly theory that the use of a non-linear pricing schedule in the sale of outside assets may well lead to an improvement in welfare.

asset exchanges, or in other words, outside money, not inside money, or in still other words, fiscal policy, not monetary policy."[17]

Yet, there are broader aspects related to the issue of return-dominance which cannot be reconciled with a Walrasian approach. In particular, from a Keynesian perspective money may simply be held because of its unique feature to be a fully liquid store of value. Thus, in a framework that allows for some form of genuine uncertainty there should be a premium attached to the liquidity services offered by money balances, since they enable agents to respond in a flexible manner to the arrival of new information. Addressing the liquidity aspects of money, Hahn (1980), for example, comes to the far-reaching conclusion: "One of the things about flexibility and money is that you may face trading uncertainties (not price uncertainties) which a Walrasian model completely rules out. By trading uncertainty I mean whether or not you will be able to trade what you want to trade at the going price. Now it is clear that trading uncertainties exist and that you may want to insure yourself against some of them. Indeed, trading uncertainties may give you a ranking of assets by liquidity. In any case, a formal theory of liquidity is still lacking, and yet it seems quite important for monetary theory."[18]

However, it is still a largely unresolved question in monetary theory of how to deal with the issue of return-dominance within the context of a fully specified theory of liquidity.

ad iii) Casual observation confirms that outright payment by cash is by no means the only way how market-based transactions are settled. Exploring this issue in considerable detail, Fama (1983) offers a useful classification that distinguishes broadly between two different modes of non-barter exchange. On the one hand, agents can use non-interest-bearing currency as a direct hand-to-hand medium of exchange. On the other hand, however, agents commonly own interest-bearing deposits which provide access to an accounting system of exchange offered by banks. In this system of exchange, transactions take the form of exchanges of claims against wealth among depositors. In particular, transactions are executed with bookkeeping entries rather than with a physical medium of exchange.

According to Fama (1983), both modes of exchange can coexist because they have different 'survival values': in particular, a currency with survival value is denominated in fixed quantities of a unit of account and trades at face value, i.e. no interest is paid on such a currency. By virtue of this feature, a currency has a clearly defined fixed value in terms of the unit of account used to state prices. Hence, information and calculation costs are minimized to calculate exchange rates between goods and the currency. In fact, the

---

[17]Wallace (1980), p. 51.

[18]Hahn (1980), p. 165. For a more detailed analysis, see Hahn (1990).

legal restriction not to pay interest on notes may not necessarily be a dis-
advantage, since it makes it more attractive to use them as a hand-to-hand
media of exchange. Yet, at the same time there are also advantages from
settling transactions in a cashless fashion by a transfer of wealth through the
banking system: "...Interest-bearing deposits have survival value because a
transaction executed in the accounting system of exchange accessed through
deposits only requires that transactors agree on the amount of wealth to be
exchanged. Broker-bankers, who specialize in pricing securities and trading
them at low cost on behalf of depositors, carry out the purchases and sales
of securities that are necessary to complete a transaction."[19]

The coexistence of multiple modes of exchange raises once more the question
of how to proceed in monetary theory as long as there is no generally accepted
alternative to the Walrasian framework. Again, the literature knows, by and
large, two complementary approaches of how to deal with the issue. First,
various authors introduce an appropriate, though ad-hoc friction into an
otherwise Walrasian framework of centralized exchange. Second, there is a
growing literature that addresses the issue in non-Walrasian settings.

Concerning the first approach, research in the spirit of Lucas (1982) and Lu-
cas/Stokey (1987) assumes, as already mentioned in chapter 1, that money
is used as a means of payment because for exogenous reasons certain goods
need to be bought by cash, i.e. these goods are subject to a cash-in-advance
constraint. In order to reconcile this trading friction with an otherwise Walrasian setting, events in asset and goods markets follow a special sequential
structure. Concentrating on the special situation in which all goods need to
be bought with cash, Lucas (1982) illustrates the assumed timing of the trading process as following: "At the beginning of a period, traders...meet in a
centralized marketplace, bringing securities and currency holdings previously
accumulated, and engage in perfectly competitive securities trading...At the
conclusion of securities trading, agents disperse to trade in goods and cur-
rencies. I find it helpful to think of each trader as a two-person household, in
which one partner harvests the endowment and sells it for currency to various
strangers while the other uses the household's currency holdings to purchase
goods from other strangers, with no possibility of intra-day communication
between them...At the end of a period, agents consume their goods and add
cash receipts from endowment sales to their securities holdings."[20]

Clearly, these special trading conventions help to ensure that money will be

---

[19]Fama (1983), p. 15. In practice, intermediaries are commonly subject to reserve requirements, and the settlement of transactions through the accounting system of exchange
is, therefore, closely related to the stock of outside money. However, as stressed by Fama
(1983), this institutional arrangement is not essential for the operation of such a system.
In fact, Fama (1983) holds the view that reserve requirements interfere with the smooth
operation of private credit markets and supports a pure currency approach with respect
to the control of the price level.

[20]Lucas (1982), p. 342.

held despite being dominated in return by other assets. Furthermore, with the money demand of agents being exclusively defined by the transactions motive, this timing of events leads to the sharp result that the demand for money holdings at the beginning of a period is simply given by the expected nominal value of the demand for 'cash goods'.[21]

More recent research has attempted to overcome some of the shortcomings of the cash-in-advance friction resulting from its strong ad-hoc nature. Questioning the plausibility of dividing goods rigidly into cash and credit goods, Schreft (1992) and Ireland (1994), for example, present closely related frameworks in which the choice between payment by cash or credit becomes fully endogenous due to a modified spatial arrangement of the economy. Importantly, in these studies the distinction between cash and credit goods is no longer invariant to changes in monetary policy: thus, rather ironically, these extensions of the standard cash-in-advance framework live up to the compelling standards of Lucas' own critique, as outlined in Lucas (1976).[22]

Nevertheless, there are other unsatisfactory features of the cash-in-advance approach (like the exogenously imposed timing of transactions across markets) which invariably reflect the limitations of a Walrasian approach in the context of monetary theory. Addressing these limitations, Hellwig (1993), for example, doubts whether the complementarity hypothesis as discussed above can be adequately addressed within the cash-in-advance framework: "Within the formalism of Walrasian market models, the cash-in-advance constraint gives the impression that the use of money as a medium of exchange impedes trade. This is rather at odds with the naive notion that the use of money as a medium of exchange facilitates trade and enables the economy to exploit opportunities that would be not available under barter."[23]

As far as the second approach is concerned, work along the lines of Kiyotaki/Wright (1989) abandons the Walrasian framework and designs explicitly decentralized trading schemes in which multiple modes of exchange

---

[21]Presenting a more general version, Lucas/Stokey (1987) assume that the cash-in-advance constraint applies only to a subset of consumption goods, so-called 'cash goods', while 'credit goods' can be purchased in exchange for interest-bearing assets.

Closely related to the analysis given by Lucas (1982), Svensson (1985) breaks the narrow cash-in-advance constraint by virtue of a timing of events that admits also a precautionary motive for money holdings. In particular, Lucas (1982) assumes that agents learn the realizations of stochastic state variables (such as productivity shocks and shocks in the money supply) before the trading in the asset markets begins. As a result, the demand for money balances becomes perfectly predictable in this set-up. In contrast, in Svensson (1985) agents need to decide upon their money holdings before the current state of the economy is revealed. As a result, the cash-in-advance constraint turns out to be non-binding in some states, i.e. in some states not all money balances are spent on cash goods. Instead, some money balances are simply carried over into the next period.

[22]A more detailed discussion of regimes with an endogenous cash-in-advance constraint is given in chapter 8 in the context of our own research.

[23]Hellwig (1993), p. 221.

can naturally coexist.[24] Basically, Kiyotaki/Wright (1989) develop a scenario in which competing media of exchange differ in terms of intrinsic properties (like their durability and their return rates) and extrinsic beliefs with respect to their general degree of acceptability. Agents are 'specialized' in production and consumption in the sense that they never consume the type of good which they themselves are capable of producing. Moreover, it is assumed that agents meet bilaterally over time according to a random scheme and follow strategic trading rules. These rules specify whether agents should immediately execute a trade or wait for a better match on some future occasion. In particular, Kiyotaki/Wright (1989) demonstrate that the use of money involves strategic elements: for fiat money to be valued in a non-cooperative Nash equilibrium, comparatively poor intrinsic properties of money need to be compensated by a sufficient degree of trust in its general acceptability. Importantly, the degree of acceptability is endogenously determined and results from a 'Diamond-type' trading externality: essentially, an increase in the acceptability of money by the trading partners of an agent makes the money holdings of this agent more valuable and increases in turn his own willingness to accept money. As a result, there is scope for multiple equilibria, and the exact degree of money-based transactions in equilibrium depends on the initial conjecture of agents about the willingness of their trading partners to accept money.[25] In a sense, Kiyotaki/Wright (1989) present a rigorous analysis of Fama's idea of distinct survival values of coexisting media of exchange. In particular, the authors show that the high survival value of money may result to a large extent from a self-enforcing social custom.[26]

Of course, current research in monetary theory is more diverse than suggested by this loosely arranged review of the literature. Nevertheless, we think that it is legitimate to conclude that research in this field knows, roughly speaking, three distinct approaches of how to deal with essential features of money as listed above:

First, there is a growing body of literature which uses decentralized trading frameworks in non-Walrasian spirit to capture essential properties of money from first principles. However, models of this type are still too 'primitive' to

---

[24]For further details, see also Kiyotaki/Wright (1993).

[25]For details of how the 'thinness' of markets, as determined by strategic considerations of agents, constitutes an externality in the trading process, see Diamond (1982).

[26]In related work, Aiyagari/Wallace/Wright (1996) return to the question of how to rationalize the coexistence of money and interest-bearing government securities. Extending the set-up introduced by Kiyotaki/Wright (1989), Aiyagari/Wallace/Wright (1996) assume the existence of special government agents who face the same trading friction as private agents, but also issue and redeem government securities. Moreover, government agents are assumed to refuse with positive probability not-yet-matured securities. Essentially, the authors argue that this or some other form of discriminatory treatment by government agents needs to be assumed in order to establish that not-yet matured securities will have a return advantage over money.

deal with questions traditionally raised in the macroeconomic literature, and with respect to these questions there is not yet agreement on some tractable alternative to the Walrasian framework.

Second, various authors use the overlapping generations friction as a device to create a genuine role for outside money. However, the overlapping generations literature is entirely Walrasian in being silent on how markets operate and how transactions are settled. In a sense, the overlapping generations literature puts too much emphasis on the store of value function of money.

Third, the cash-in-advance friction is widely used as a device to mimic the transactions role of money. However, although extensions are available which help to endogenize the use of multiple means of payment, the cash-in-advance literature also suffers from the shortcomings of an otherwise Walrasian setting.

In the light of this classification, the main argument to be presented in the second part of the book can now be summarized as following: essentially, we argue that critical aspects of the superneutrality debate can be addressed within the standard Diamond version of the overlapping generations model with production, when appropriately modified. Generally speaking, we show that the unequivocal predominance of the Tobin effect in the standard framework vanishes if mechanisms are incorporated that support the complementarity hypothesis with respect to money and credit. In particular, we demonstrate that such mechanisms can easily be established if informational imperfections in the credit market, liquidity aspects of money, and the notion of multiple means of payment are adequately included. To a certain extent, our decision in favour of the overlapping generations framework simply reflects the fact that a non-Walrasian setting is not yet available which would make it possible to analyze these issues comprehensively from a fully specified intertemporal perspective. However, less on the defensive side, we claim that Diamond's version of the overlapping generations model is sufficiently flexible to address far more questions in monetary theory than this has been traditionally done. More specifically, on various occasions we will exploit the fact that the overlapping generations model provides a transparent framework to study intertemporal equilibria of economies with heterogenous agents.

In chapter 4, we present a monetary version of the standard Diamond model with production. In particular, the proposed version resolves the return-dominance issue in the spirit of Wallace (1980) by assuming that money acts as the single outside asset. Moreover, the intragenerational capital market works entirely frictionless, and details of how transactions are settled remain unaddressed. In short, money operates in this economy only through the overlapping generations friction, i.e. money acts purely as a store of value. Restating a well-known result of the literature, we show that under conditions which ensure the existence of a unique monetary steady state the Tobin effect prevails in an uncontested manner. Also, we show that the dynamics around the monetary steady state are uniquely determined.

Chapters 5-9 propose variations on the base model as discussed in chapter 4, and in all cases we introduce modifications which give money a more interesting role to play. In particular, chapter 5 discusses a version of the base model due to Azariadis/Smith (1996) in which imperfections in the credit market ensure, well in accordance with the 'complementarity hypothesis', that money and capital cease to be close substitutes. In chapter 6, we offer a version of the base model with multiple outside assets developed by Schreft/Smith (1997) that stresses genuine liquidity aspects of money. Finally, in chapters 7-9 we present own research and develop versions of the base model which can be used to deal with the transactions role of money in a context with multiple means of payment.

As a common theme, all of the variations presented in chapters 5-9 give rise to the possibility that the Anti-Tobin effect prevails. Moreover, dynamics may well be indeterminate and multiple monetary steady states may well occur. In short, drawing on a common framework, chapters 5-9 attempt to show that the mechanics of the Tobin effect as established for the base model are seriously at risk if one accounts for aspects of money that go beyond the rather narrow overlapping generations friction.

Part II

Money, inflation, and capital formation: the perspective of overlapping generations models

Chapter 4

The Diamond model with money as single outside asset

This chapter serves the purpose to establish a version of Diamond's overlapping generations economy with production as a benchmark model for a detailed discussion of the superneutrality issue of money. Basic elements of the model and, in particular, the notation introduced in this chapter will be shared by all modified versions of the benchmark model presented in the following chapters.

In his original contribution, Diamond (1965) used the overlapping generations structure as pioneered by Samuelson (1958) to question the long run dynamical efficiency of competitive production economies in the absence of standard static sources of inefficiency. However, apart from efficiency concerns Diamond's model has become a standard tool in macroeconomics to study aspects of dynamical equilibria in general. In the monetary version of the Diamond model presented in this chapter, we assume, as a convenient point of departure, that money acts as the only outside asset. Importantly, agents have perfect foresight with respect to all future events. Moreover, we assume that capital markets operate frictionless, and details of how transactions are carried out remain unaddressed: in short, money acts in this model as a pure store of value.

Following the instructive terminology introduced by Tirole (1985), the overlapping generations friction gives rise to a 'bubbly' view on money: according to this view, the demand for money relies exclusively on the speculative conjecture that the future exchange value of money in terms of goods will be positive, because future generations will also express a positive demand for money. In the absence of uncertainty and with money not being explicitly required for transaction purposes, the bubbly view implies that in a monetary equilibrium the return on money needs to be identical to the return on competing assets such as claims on productive investment projects. As a consequence, the overlapping generations friction provides an extreme specification of Tobin's substitutability hypothesis with respect to (outside) money and capital. It is for this reason that we introduce a monetary version of the Diamond model as a benchmark structure to analyze the mechanics of the Tobin effect.

More specifically, restating a well-known result of the literature, we show that there exists at most one outside money steady state. At this steady state, the Tobin effect prevails in an uncontested manner. Also, we show that local dynamics around the steady state are uniquely determined along a stable saddlepath and display monotone adjustment. Thus, the long run effects of monetary policy are rather favourable: a shift to a more inflationary policy not only stimulates economic activity, but it also leads to adjustments which occur in a smooth and uniquely defined way.

The Diamond model is well documented in the literature. However, the here presented version with money acting as single outside asset draws particularly on the versions developed by Azariadis (1993) and Tirole (1985). Our brief discussion of non-monetary equilibria follows closely the detailed analysis given by Galor/Ryder (1989).

4.1 The model

The economy is assumed to be inhabited by an infinite sequence of overlapping generations. Each generation consists of an infinite amount of agents with unit mass.[1] Members of each generation are identical and live for two periods: when being in the first period of their life, agents are 'young' and have a fixed labour endowment. Young agents derive no disutility from work and have no wealth apart from the value of their labour endowment. When being 'old', i.e. in the second period of their life, agents have no labour endowment. Old agents die at the end of the period and leave no bequests. Thus, as graphed in figure 4.1, in any representative period t the economy is populated by young and old agents who are members of two distinct generations.

Agents have access to a productive technology that uses two inputs, labour and capital, and produces a single output good. The output good and capital are perfectly homogenous, i.e. there exists only one good that can be equally consumed or invested. To realize consumption in their old age, agents need

---

[1]This assumption is not important for the purposes of this chapter. However, in some of the following chapters it is a convenient way to account for heterogeneity among agents.

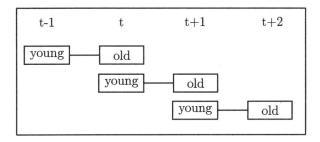

Figure 4.1: *Time structure of the overlapping generations model*

to save a part of their wage income when being young. Savings can take the form of deposits or holdings of real balances.

More specifically, savings can be deposited with intermediaries who have access to the investment opportunities of the economy. Intermediaries do not belong to the overlapping generations population, but to an exogenously imposed scheme, ensuring over time that savings and investment projects are matched in a competitive manner. When deposited with intermediaries, savings simply take the form of shares that represent a claim to the return stream earned by capital in the production process. Thus, reflecting the pattern of labour endowments over the life cycle of agents, in any period t output is jointly produced by young and old agents: while young agents offer the labour input, old agents own the capital stock as a result of investment decisions taken in period $t - 1$.

Alternatively, savings of young agents can be sold to old agents against un-backed outside money. Money is the only outside asset of the economy and acts as a device to facilitate intergenerational exchange. We also assume that the government increases the money stock over time in order to finance some government activities by subjecting agents to inflation taxation. The scheme according to which the money stock evolves over time is deterministic and known to all agents.

Agents do perfectly understand how the economy operates and hold ratio-nal expectations. Because of the entirely deterministic specification of the economy the rational expectations assumption implies that agents make all decisions under perfect foresight. In other words, expectations about future events are not governed by proper probability distributions, but by degener-ate point expectations which always turn out to be correct. Thus, with ex-pectations of all variables always being validated by subsequent realizations, the entire analysis can rely on a forwardlooking, deterministic framework.[2]

In more detail, the essential features of the economy can be summarized as following:

Production: In period t, let L_t and K_t denote the labour endowment and the capital stock per member of the young generation, respectively. Output per young agent is produced according to a time-invariant, neoclassical production function $Y_t = F(K_t, L_t)$ with constant returns to scale and diminishing marginal products. Let $f(k_t) \equiv F(K_t, 1)$, where k_t is the capital-labour ratio per young agent. Furthermore, we normalize: $L_t = 1$. Then, $f(k_t)$ and k_t denote output and capital stock per young agent, respectively. At this stage, the function f is assumed to have the following standard properties:

(A 1) The function $f(k)$ is twice continuously differentiable, positive, increasing, and strictly concave:

$$\text{(i)} \ f(k) > 0, \quad \text{(ii)} \ f'(k) > 0 \quad \text{(iii)} \ f''(k) < 0 \ \text{ for } k > 0.$$

(A 2) The function $f(k)$ satisfies the set of Inada-conditions:

$$\text{(i)} \ f(0) = 0 \quad \text{(ii)} \ \lim_{k \to 0} f'(k) = \infty \quad \text{(iii)} \ \lim_{k \to \infty} f'(k) = 0$$

It is assumed that all markets operate under conditions of perfect competition. Thus, constant returns give rise to the familiar result that profit maximizing behaviour will lead to a constellation in which inputs get paid their marginal products and factor payments exhaust output. Let δ stand for the rate at which capital depreciates within the production process. Then, with w_t and ρ_t denoting the wage income of young agents and the gross rate of return on capital received by old agents, respectively, we have for all periods:

$$\rho_t = f'(k_t) + 1 - \delta \tag{4.1}$$
$$w_t = f(k_t) - f'(k_t) \cdot k_t = w(k_t) \tag{4.2}$$

Government: In period t, let M_t denote the nominal stock of outside money per young agent. With μ being the constant net growth rate of the money stock, M_t evolves over time according to the law of motion:

$$M_t = (1 + \mu) \cdot M_{t-1} \quad \text{with: } \mu > 0 \tag{4.3}$$

---

[2]The rational expectations assumption on the side of agents, though standard in the literature, is a far-reaching one. It precludes any autonomous expectation-formation mechanism. Instead, expectations are deliberately assumed to be such that perpetual market clearing becomes possible. For a critical assessment from a Keynesian perspective, see, for example, Hahn/Solow (1995), p. 28.

In period t, the government is assumed to consume g_t units of the output good per young agent. Moreover, we assume that the government levies no taxes. Let p_t represent the period t price of the output good in terms of money. Thus, with outside money acting as the only outside asset, the budget constraint of the government takes the primitive form:

$$g_t = \frac{M_t - M_{t-1}}{p_t} = \frac{\mu}{1+\mu} \cdot \frac{M_t}{p_t} \qquad (4.4)$$

Equation (4.4) simply states that at the beginning of period t the government brings $M_t - M_{t-1}$ additional units of money per young agent into circulation in order to finance all government expenditures via seigniorage.[3]

Problem of the representative agent: In period t, young agents face the decision to allocate wage income $w(k_t)$ between expenditures on current consumption c_t^y and savings s_t in order to finance consumption c_{t+1}^o one period ahead when being old. Preferences of agents are represented by the intertemporal utility function $U(c_t^y, c_{t+1}^o)$.[4]

(A 3) The function $U(c_t^y, c_{t+1}^o)$ has the standard properties:

(i) The function $U(c_t^y, c_{t+1}^o)$ is twice continuously differentiable, strictly quasiconcave, and increasing in both arguments on the interior of the consumption set R_+^2.

(ii) 'Starvation' is avoided in both periods:[5]

$$\lim_{c_t^y \to 0} U_1(c_t^y, c_{t+1}^o) = \infty \quad \text{for } c_{t+1}^o > 0,$$

$$\lim_{c_{t+1}^o \to 0} U_2(c_t^y, c_{t+1}^o) = \infty \quad \text{for } c_t^y > 0.$$

(iii) Both goods c_t^y and c_{t+1}^o are normal goods.

Let m_t and d_t stand for the real value of the money and deposits demand per young agent measured in units of the output good, respectively. When deciding about the composition of their savings, consumers take the pair of gross return rates on deposits and real balances (R_t^d, R_t^m) as given. With money being held purely on speculative grounds, the demand for real balances will

---

[3]More specifically, for the seigniorage mechanism to work, injections of the additional units of money have to take place before the other markets open.

[4]For a more detailed discussion of the properties mentioned under assumption (A 3), see Galor/Ryder (1989).

[5]Using standard notation, $U_1(c_t^y, c_{t+1}^o)$ stands for the partial derivative of the function $U(c_t^y, c_{t+1}^o)$ with respect to the first argument.

50

vanish if R_t^d exceeds R_t^m. To allow also for non-monetary equilibria, we assume with respect to return rates at this stage:

(A 4) Return rates satisfy the condition:

$$R_t^d > 0 \quad \text{and} \quad R_t^d \geq R_t^m$$

The combined consumption and portfolio decision problem of young agents can now be stated as:

$$\max_{c_t^y, c_{t+1}^o, d_t, m_t} : \quad U(c_t^y, c_{t+1}^o) + \lambda_t \cdot (w_t - c_t^y - d_t - m_t) + \nu_t \cdot (R_t^d \cdot d_t + R_t^m \cdot m_t - c_{t+1}^o)$$

(4.5)

As it is well known from consumer theory, for w_t, p_t, and p_{t+1} being positive and finite, assumptions (A 3) and (A 4) ensure that there exists a uniquely determined, optimal consumption bundle. Furthermore, both goods will be demanded in positive amounts, and by non-satiation budget constraints in both periods will be binding.

Differentiating with respect to the choice variables c_t^y, c_{t+1}^o, d_t, and m_t yields the set of first order conditions:

$$U_1(c_t^y, c_{t+1}^o) = \lambda_t \tag{4.6}$$

$$U_2(c_t^y, c_{t+1}^o) = \nu_t \tag{4.7}$$

$$\nu_t \cdot R_t^d - \lambda_t = 0 \tag{4.8}$$

$$\nu_t \cdot R_t^m - \lambda_t \leq 0, \quad [\nu_t \cdot R_t^m - \lambda_t] \cdot m_t = 0 \tag{4.9}$$

Rearranging terms, one obtains:

$$\frac{U_1(c_t^y, c_{t+1}^o)}{U_2(c_t^y, c_{t+1}^o)} = R_t^d \tag{4.10}$$

$$[R_t^d - R_t^m] \cdot m_t = 0 \tag{4.11}$$

Equation (4.10) simply says that the marginal rate of substitution between present and future consumption needs to be equal to the relevant intertemporal price ratio, i.e. to the real interest factor. Equally suggestive, equation (4.11) restates that a positive demand for real balances requires that money is not return-dominated by deposits. Evidently, in such a situation the portfolio composition with respect to deposits and real balances will be indeterminate from the consumer's perspective.

In summary, our assumptions ensure that consumption plans and associated overall savings s_t are uniquely determined, and by normality of the goods c_t^y and c_{t+1}^o reaction patterns are as following:

$$c_t^y = c^y(w_t, R_t^d) \quad \text{with:} \quad c_w^y > 0 \tag{4.12}$$

$$s_t = m_t + d_t = s(w_t, R_t^d) \quad \text{with:} \quad s_w > 0 \tag{4.13}$$

4.2 Equilibrium conditions

In a competitive equilibrium, all agents take prices as given and choose actions which are both individually optimal and mutually consistent. Despite the primitive treatment of profit maximizing behaviour in the production sphere, it is fairly obvious that a competitive matching of investment projects and savings requires that the following condition needs to be satisfied:

$$R_t^d = f'(k_{t+1}) + 1 - \delta \qquad (4.14)$$

Moreover, note that the gross return rate on real balances is simply given by the inverse of the expected inflation factor:

$$R_t^m = \frac{p_t}{p_{t+1}} = \frac{M_{t+1}/p_{t+1}}{(1+\mu) \cdot M_t/p_t} = \frac{1}{1+\mu} \cdot \frac{m_{t+1}}{m_t} \qquad (4.15)$$

Thus, the complementary slackness condition (4.11) governing the demand for real balances takes in equilibrium the form:

$$[f'(k_{t+1}) + 1 - \delta - \frac{1}{1+\mu} \cdot \frac{m_{t+1}}{m_t}] \cdot m_t = 0 \qquad (4.16)$$

The economy starts to operate in $t = 0$, and we assume that there exists initially a generation of old agents. Each member of this generation is endowed with M_{-1} units of money and owns k_0 units of physical capital. Members of this generation simply seek to maximize old age consumption c_0^o.

Given these initial conditions, a competitive equilibrium is defined as:

Definition 1 *Given the initial capital stock k_0 and the initial money stock M_{-1}, a competitive equilibrium is given by a sequence of quantities $\{m_t, d_t, g_t, c_0^o, c_t^y, c_{t+1}^o, k_{t+1}\}$ and a sequence of prices $\{p_t, w_t, R_t^d\}$ such that for all periods $t = 0, 1, 2...$:*

(a) competition ensures that factors get paid their marginal products according to (4.1),(4.2),

(b) given (4.3), the budget constraint (4.4) of the government is satisfied,

(c) given the price sequence, agents solve optimally the decision problem (4.5),

(d) investments and savings are competitively matched according to (4.14),

(e) the evolution of money balances satisfies (4.16),

(f) all markets clear with the equilibrium conditions being as following:[6]

---

[6]Note the asymmetrical treatment of the labour market which clears always at the full employment level according to equation (4.2). Furthermore, by Walras' law the three remaining market clearing conditions mentioned under (f) are not independent: for example,

Money market: $m_t = \frac{M_t}{p_t}$

Capital market: $d_t = k_{t+1}$

Goods market: $f(k_t) + (1 - \delta) \cdot k_t = g_t + c_t^y + c_t^o + k_{t+1}$

To simplify the analysis we distinguish in the following between *inside* and *outside money equilibria:* inside money equilibria are associated with a situation in which all savings take the form of deposits and, accordingly, outside money balances are zero. In contrast, outside money equilibria are associated with positive outside money balances.

After rearranging the relevant equilibrium conditions, for the two regimes the dynamics can be summarized as following:[7]

Inside money equilibria:

$$k_{t+1} = s[w(k_t), f'(k_{t+1}]$$ (4.17)

With government spending being reduced to zero, inside money equilibria seem to be of limited interest in this context. However, without a careful analysis of equation (4.17) not much can be said about the existence of equilibria for the outside money regime.

Outside money equilibria:

$$g_t = \frac{\mu}{1 + \mu} \cdot m_t$$ (4.18)

$$k_{t+1} = s[w(k_t), f'(k_{t+1}] - m_t$$ (4.19)

$$f'(k_{t+1}) + 1 - \delta = \frac{1}{1 + \mu} \cdot \frac{m_{t+1}}{m_t}$$ (4.20)

Outside money equilibria are characterized by a three-dimensional, non-linear dynamical system in k_t, m_t, and g_t. Reflecting our prime interest in the effects of monetary policy, we take for the rest of the discussion g_t as being

---

assume that both the money and capital market clear. Then, adding up over all budget constraints shows that the goods market needs to clear as well:

$$g_t = \frac{\mu}{1 + \mu} \cdot m_t$$

$$c_t^o = (\frac{1}{1 + \mu} \cdot \frac{m_t}{m_{t-1}}) \cdot m_{t-1} + (f'(k_t) + 1 - \delta) \cdot k_t$$

$$c_t^y = w_t - m_t - k_{t+1}$$

$$g_t + c_t^o + c_t^y = w_t + f'(k_t) \cdot k_t + k_t \cdot (1 - \delta) - k_{t+1}$$

$$= y_t + k_t \cdot (1 - \delta) - k_{t+1}$$

---

[7]To save on notation, we suppress in (4.17) the dependency of k_{t+1} on the constant parameter δ.

endogenously determined.[8] Due to the recursive structure of the system under this specification, dynamics of the outside money regime are then entirely described by equations (4.19) and (4.20), which constitute a system in k_t and m_t. While in period t the capital stock k_t is predetermined by last period's investment decision, real balances m_t are freely determined through forward-looking behaviour. Accordingly, the system (4.19) - (4.20) is made up of the state variable k_t (with initial condition k_0) and the forwardlooking, 'jumping' variable m_t with a free initial condition.

To compare the standard Diamond system with the refined versions of the ensuing chapters, we will introduce the benchmark classification of equilibrium conditions as given by Azariadis/Smith (1996). According to this classification, the outside money version of the Diamond model with production consists of a single *accumulation equation* (4.19) and a single *arbitrage relation* (4.20).

Following common practice, we begin the analysis of (4.17) and (4.18)-(4.20) with a discussion of steady state equilibria.

Steady state equilibria: Since we have not specified a growth promoting mechanism, in any steady state equilibrium all variables need to be constant over time.

Inside money steady states:

Dropping time subscripts in (4.17), the steady state condition for inside money equilibria with $m = 0$ is given by:

$$k = s[w(k), f'(k)] \qquad (4.21)$$

To start with, we exploit the fact that savings of young agents are bounded by their wage income. Thus, since $f(0) = w(0) = 0$ by (A2), (4.21) is trivially solved by $k = 0$. Yet as argued in detail by Galor/Ryder (1989), assumptions (A 1)-(A 3) are not sufficient to secure the existence of a non-trivial inside money steady state with $k > 0$. In particular, restrictions need to be imposed with respect to the interaction of preferences and technology. Moreover, even if a non-trivial steady state should exist under (A 1)-(A 3), it does not need to be unique.

For the following discussion it will be helpful to establish a set of sufficient conditions which ensure the existence of a unique non-trivial inside money

---

[8]Thus, despite the rudimentary structure of the government's budget constraint, we simply say that the conduct of monetary policy takes precedence over all fiscal matters. Technically, under this specification the rate of monetary expansion μ becomes an exogenous variable for the remaining system (4.19)-(4.20). For a more detailed discussion of how to resolve the standard coordination problem between monetary and fiscal policy measures in a similar context, see Gale (1983).

54

steady state. To this end, we make with respect to preferences the additional
assumption:

(A 5) Savings are a non-decreasing function of the interest rate:

$$\frac{\partial s(w_t, R_t^d)}{\partial R_t^d} \geq 0 \text{ for all } (w_t, R_t^d) \geq 0$$

Evidently, under (A 5) the income effect of a rise in the interest rate never
dominates the substitution effect. This in turn ensures that there exists implicitly a single-valued, increasing savings function $k_{t+1} = \phi(k_t)$ in equation
(4.17). For further reference, note that the derivative of the function $\phi(k_t)$ is
given by: $\frac{d k_{t+1}}{d k_t} = \phi'(k_t) = \frac{-s_w \cdot k_t \cdot f''(k_t)}{1 - s_R \cdot f''(k_{t+1})} > 0$.

Furthermore, we modify the Inada-condition (A 2) as required for our purposes. Also, we assume that $\phi(k_t)$ is a strictly concave function:[9]

(A 2*) The interaction of preferences and technology is such that:

(i) $\phi(0) > 0 \ \vee \ \lim_{k \to 0} \frac{-s_w \cdot k \cdot f''(k)}{1 - s_R \cdot f''(k)} > 1$,

(ii) $\lim_{k \to \infty} \frac{w(k)}{k} < 1$,

(iii) $\phi'(k) > 0, \phi''(k) < 0$ for all $k > 0$.

Allowing for these modifications, the desired proposition can now be stated
as following:

Proposition 1 *Under the assumptions (A 1), (A 2*), (A 3), and (A 5)
the overlapping generations economy with production exhibits a unique, non-
trivial inside money steady state with $k^{In} > 0, m^{In} = 0$.*

Proof: For details, see Galor/Ryder (1989). However, we use figure 4.2 to
sketch the proof diagrammatically: due to (A 5) the function $\phi(k_t)$ is single-
valued, part (i) of (A 2*) ensures that $\phi(k_t) > k_t$ at least for some k_t, part (ii)

---

[9]Both part (i) and (ii) of (A 2*) deviate slightly from the corresponding assumptions
made by Galor/Ryder (1989). First, in part (i) of (A 2*) we drop the assumption $f(0) = 0$
maintained by Galor/Ryder (1989), since we are not interested in the existence of trivial
inside money steady states with $k = 0$. Clearly, whenever $\phi(0) > 0$ the condition $f(0) > 0$
needs to be satisfied. For an appropriate example satisfying $f(0) > 0$, see the discussion
at the end of the chapter. However, figure 4.2 is drawn for the case $f(0) = 0$.

Second, part (ii) of (A 2*) is slightly less restrictive than the corresponding assumption
$lim_{k \to \infty} f'(k) = 0$ maintained by Galor/Ryder (1989). Note that $lim_{k \to \infty} f'(k) = 0$
implies $lim_{k \to \infty}[w(k)/k] = 0 < 1$, since $w(k)$ is bounded from above by $f(k)$. However,
as we will argue in the discussion at the end of this chapter, one easily finds (standard)
examples with $lim_{k \to \infty}[w(k)/k] < 1$ and $lim_{k \to \infty} f'(k) \neq 0$, and we prefer therefore the
less restrictive specification.

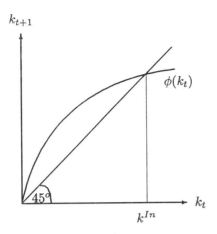

Figure 4.2: *Base model - Non-trivial inside money steady state: existence*

of (A 2*) guarantees that $\phi(k_t)$ intersects the 45°-line (since: $\phi(k_t) \leq w(k_t)$), and part (iii) of (A 2*) establishes uniqueness of the intersection by concavity of $\phi(k_t)$.[10] q.e.d.

Outside money steady states:

By (4.19) and (4.20), steady states of the outside money regime need to satisfy:

$$k = s(w(k), f'(k)) - m \tag{4.22}$$

$$f'(k) + 1 - \delta = \frac{1}{1+\mu} \tag{4.23}$$

For a unique outside money steady state to exist, it is a well-known result that the previous proposition needs to be augmented as following:

Proposition 2 *Assume there exists a unique, non-trivial inside money steady state with associated capital stock $k^{In} > 0$. Then, a unique outside money steady state with associated capital stock $k^{Out} > 0$ exists if the following restriction holds:*

$$f'(k^{In}) < \delta + \frac{1}{1+\mu} - 1 \tag{4.24}$$

---

[10]Galor/Ryder (1989) construct an example in which under (A 1), (A 2), (A 3), and (A 5) no steady state equilibrium exists. Essentially, this is due to the fact that part (ii) of (A 2) is not strong enough to guarantee that $\phi'(0) > 1$ will be satisfied. Thus, part (i) of (A 2*) strengthens the Inada-condition for $k \to 0$ in the appropriate way.

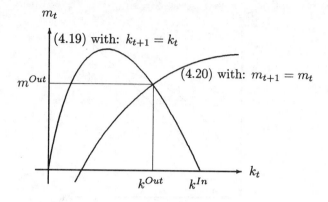

Figure 4.3: *Base model - Outside money steady state: existence*

Proof: Again, we sketch only the outline of the proof.[11] Any steady state combination $(k^{Out}, m^{Out}) > 0$ needs to satisfy the accumulation equation (4.19) evaluated at $k_{t+1} = k_t$. Evidently, this locus reflects which part of savings needs to be absorbed by real balances for the capital stock to stay constant over time. Given our discussion of equation (4.17), it is clear that the accumulation equation with $k_{t+1} = k_t$ is uniquely solved by some $m_t > 0$ if $\phi(k_t) > k_t$. In contrast, no positive solution for m_t exists for $\phi(k_t) \leq k_t$. Thus, $k^{Out} < k^{In}$ needs to hold. However, irrespective of m the solution for k needs to satisfy as well equation (4.23), and condition (4.24) follows trivially from the concavity of $f(k)$ as stated in (A 1). q.e.d.

Graphically, the outside money steady state can be represented as shown in figure 4.3.[12] In any steady state, the two phaselines as drawn in figure 4.3 need to intersect. As argued above, the shape of the accumulation equation with $k_t = k_{t+1}$ is closely related to the shape of the function $\phi(k_t)$ in figure 4.2, i.e. $m_t = \phi(k_t) - k_t$ needs to be satisfied. To establish the locus of the arbitrage relation with $m_t = m_{t+1}$ in m_t-k_t-plane one needs to replace k_{t+1} in (4.20) with the expression $\phi(k_t) - m_t$. Note that equation (4.20) with $m_t = m_{t+1}$ fixes $\phi(k_t) - m_t$ at a uniquely determined level. Clearly, k_{t+1} depends on k_t and m_t as following: $\frac{\partial k_{t+1}}{\partial k_t} = \phi'(k_t) > 0$ and $\frac{\partial k_{t+1}}{\partial m_t} = -1 < 0$. Thus, the arbitrage relation with $m_t = m_{t+1}$ slopes upward in m_t-k_t-plane.

Condition (4.24) reflects the well-known fact that for the Diamond version of

---

[11]For details, see Tirole (1985).

[12]We choose this particular representation since it can also be used to indicate the dynamics of the system as to be shown below.

the overlapping generations model with production the existence of an outside money steady state is tied to the 'dynamical inefficiency' of the non-trivial inside money steady state. To see why, note that in the context presented here, because of the absence of population growth and technological progress, the 'golden rule' level of the capital stock (i.e. the level of the capital stock that maximizes per capita steady state consumption) is defined by the condition: $f'(k^{GR}) = \delta$. Thus, for $\mu > 0$ condition (4.24) implies that the existence of an outside money steady state is ultimately linked to the condition $f'(k^{In}) < f'(k^{GR})$, i.e. to a constellation in which the inside money steady state is dynamically inefficient. The intuition underlying this result is straightforward: Consider a constellation in which the marginal productivity of capital falls short of δ in steady state, and hence a negative real interest rate net of depreciation obtains. In such a constellation, all generations can be made better off by introducing some non-interest bearing outside asset that is traded between members of different generations: essentially, the existence of the outside asset prevents agents from transferring wealth over time by undertaking marginally unproductive, intragenerational investment projects. Instead, agents can invest in the outside asset at a higher return rate and exploit more productive intergenerational trading opportunities.

In contrast, in a situation with $f'(k^{In}) \geq \delta$ (i.e. in a situation in which the inside money steady state is dynamically efficient) real balances would have to grow over time according to (4.20) for money to be held on purely speculative grounds. However, given the stationary specification of our environment, ever increasing real balances are not compatible with individual wealth constraints in long run equilibrium. Under rational expectations, this inconsistency is perfectly anticipated and outside money will therefore not be valued.

In our context, with money being the only outside asset, the intertemporal inefficiency associated with marginally 'unproductive' investment projects could be entirely removed by means of a policy of a constant money stock ($\mu = 0$). In contrast, in outside money steady states with an expanding money stock ($\mu > 0$) and a positive level of inflation taxation, the economy is less efficient than in the golden rule equilibrium. Yet, for such a constellation to occur, the non-trivial inside money steady state needs to be dynamically inefficient in the first place.[13]

---

[13]For $\mu > 0$, we have $f'(k) - \delta < 0$, i.e. in steady state a negative real interest rate net of depreciation obtains. However, in overlapping generations models that grow over time, the bubbly view on money is perfectly consistent with a positive level of the real net interest rate: assume, for example, that the population and the aggregate money stock grow with the constant growth factors $1 + n$ and $1 + \mu$, respectively. Then, the steady state inflation factor $1 + \pi$ is determined by the relation $1 + \mu = (1 + n) \cdot (1 + \pi)$, and the arbitrage relation takes the form:

$$\frac{1}{1+\pi} = \frac{1+n}{1+\mu} = f'(k) + 1 - \delta$$

For $\mu = 0$, the golden rule for growing economies $f'(k) = n + \delta$ obtains. Again, for $\mu > 0$ the economy is less efficient than in the golden rule equilibrium, but the term $f'(k) - \delta$ may

However, contrary to the original version of the Diamond model with bonds, we think that in the framework presented here efficiency considerations should not be overemphasized. In the original approach, government activity serves the exclusive function, whenever appropriate, to remove the dynamical inefficiency of the economy by running a scheme of intergenerationally traded bonds: essentially, the maintenance of this scheme over time defines the role assigned to the government. In contrast, the framework presented here acknowledges that beyond the question of intertemporal efficiency there are genuine government activities that are costly and need to be financed. Thus, despite the primitive treatment of the government sector it is implicitly assumed that these activities are so vital for the way the economy operates that welfare comparisons with a constellation without any government spending are meaningless.

4.3 Policy effects

Comparative statics: The simple structure of outside money steady states as given by (4.22)-(4.23) is perfectly geared to reproduce the mechanics of the Tobin effect. More specifically, the arbitrage relation (4.23) ensures that real balances and capital act as perfect substitutes. Accordingly, the long run effect of a shift to a more expansionary monetary policy is as following:

Proposition 3 *Assume that the rate of monetary expansion μ is permanently raised. Then, in the new outside money steady state the capital stock will be higher than before, i.e. the Tobin effect prevails.*

Proof: Straightforward comparative statics analysis in (4.22)-(4.23) yields:

$$\frac{\partial k^{Out}}{\partial \mu} = -\frac{1}{(1+\mu)^2 \cdot f''(k)} \tag{4.25}$$

Obviously, by (A 1), the coefficient is positive. q.e.d.

As illustrated in figure 4.4, equation (4.25) reflects that the policy change leaves the accumulation equation (4.22) unaffected, but disturbs the arbitrage relation (4.23) by lowering the return on real balances via increased inflation taxation. To rebalance the arbitrage relation, the composition of the portfolios of agents needs to readjust in favour of capital. As a result, with long run inflation being equal to the rate of monetary expansion μ, in

---

well be positive. Clearly, this requires $0 < \mu < n$ and $\pi < 0$, i.e. a situation of ongoing deflation. Thus, as summarized by Tirole (1985), the bubbly view on money taken in the overlapping generations literature can well account for a positive real interest rate net of depreciation, but not in connection with a positive inflation rate.

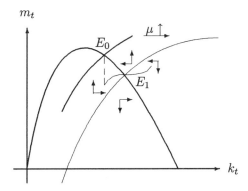

Figure 4.4: *Base model - Outside money steady state: policy effects*

the new steady state equilibrium E_1 both the capital stock and the inflation rate will be higher than before.[14]

Dynamics: To assess the dynamical adjustment behaviour of the system off-steady state, we proceed in two steps. First, we indicate qualitatively adjustment patterns for the outside money steady state by constructing the appropriate phase diagram. In a second step, we classify dynamical properties of inside and outside money steady states in a rigorous manner by employing standard tools as summarized in appendix II.

Dynamics of the outside money steady state are governed by the equations (4.19) and (4.20) which constitute a two-dimensional system of first-order, non-linear difference equations in k_t and m_t.[15]

As argued above, by virtue of the implicit function theorem equation (4.19) can locally be solved for k_{t+1} as following:

$$k_{t+1} = \phi(k_t) - m_t \quad \text{with:} \quad \frac{\partial k_{t+1}}{\partial k_t} = \phi'(k_t) > 0, \quad \frac{\partial k_{t+1}}{\partial m_t} = -1 \qquad (4.26)$$

Inserting (4.26) into (4.20) yields:

$$k_{t+1} = s[w(k_t), f'(k_{t+1}) - m_t \qquad (4.27)$$

---

[14]One easily confirms that the effect on steady state real balances m is ambiguous. To have a positive effect on m, the initial impact effect that tends to reduce real balances needs to be outweighed by the income effect that is induced by the increased level of capital formation.

[15]Note that the rational expectations assumption implies that markets continue to clear at every instant along any path off-steady state.

$$f'[\phi(k_t) - m_t] + 1 - \delta \;=\; \frac{1}{1 + \mu} \cdot \frac{m_{t+1}}{m_t} \tag{4.28}$$

Upon this modification, one easily establishes, at least qualitatively, dynamical properties of the system in the neighbourhood of the outside money state. By (4.27), k_t evolves off-steady state according to:

$$k_{t+1} \geq k_t \;\Leftrightarrow\; m_t = s[w(k_t), f'(k_{t+1}] - k_{t+1} \leq s[w(k_t), f'(k_t] - k_t \tag{4.29}$$

Using (4.29), the following proposition in terms of figure 4.4 is obvious:

Proposition 4 *For points below (above) the graph of the accumulation equation(4.27) with $k_{t+1} = k_t$, the capital stock evolves according to: $k_{t+1} > (<)k_t$.*

Similarly, real balances m_t evolve according to:

$$m_{t+1} \geq m_t \;\Leftrightarrow\; f'[\phi(k_t) - m_t] \geq \delta + \frac{1}{1 + \mu} - 1 \tag{4.30}$$

Summarizing the information provided by (4.30) in terms of figure 4.4 yields:

Proposition 5 *For points to the right of (left of) the graph of (4.28) at equality, real money balances evolve according to: $m_{t+1} < (>)m_t$.*

In the light of the previous two propositions figure 4.4 suggests that local dynamics around the outside money steady state are saddlepath stable: well in accordance with the rational expectations approach, it seems that there exists, at least for small perturbations of the system, a unique level of real balances that leads the system back into the new outside money steady state E_1. In other words, the fundamentals of the economy are informative enough to rule out indeterminate behaviour of the system in the neighbourhood of the outside money steady state.[16]

As shown in the appendix to this chapter, this rather intuitive assessment of dynamical properties can be made rigorous by inspection of the Jacobian matrix of equations (4.19)-(4.20). Similarly, the dynamics associated with the inside money steady states can also be rigorously classified as reflected in the following proposition:

---

[16]Strictly speaking, the continuous time representation of the system in figure 4.4 is not the appropriate way to handle a system with discrete dynamics. Neverthelss, it gives an intuitive idea of the dynamics involved.

Proposition 6 *Local adjustment behaviour around steady states follows the pattern:*

i) The outside money steady state is saddlepath stable and subject to monotone adjustment.

ii) The trivial inside money steady state with $k = 0$ is a source, i.e. entirely unstable.

iii) The non-trivial inside money steady state with $k^{in} > 0$ is a sink, i.e. adjustment is locally indeterminate, and the dominant eigenvalue induces monotone adjustment.

Proof: see appendix.

4.4 Discussion

We conclude the chapter with a brief discussion of how to assess the 'restrictiveness' of the set of sufficient conditions (A 1), (A 2*), (A 3), and (A 5), ensuring under proposition 1 the existence of a unique inside money steady state. In general, the interaction of preferences and technology as specified in (A 2*) makes it difficult to answer this question for arbitrary functional forms of utility and production functions. However, as the following remarks illustrate, appropriate examples can easily be constructed by combining standard functional forms.

For the sake of simplicity, let us assume that the intertemporal utility function is of Cobb-Douglas type: $U(c_t^y, c_{t+1}^o) = \beta \cdot \ln(c_t^y) + (1 - \beta) \cdot \ln(c_{t+1}^o)$. Clearly, this function satisfies (A 3). It is a standard property of this type of preferences that the income and substitution effects resulting from a change in the interest rate exactly offset each other, i.e.: $\partial s(w_t, R_t^d)/\partial R_t^d = 0$ obtains. Thus, assumption (A 5) is also satisfied. Furthermore, savings are simply determined as a linear function of wage income: $\phi(k_t) = (1 - \beta) \cdot w(k_t)$. Consequently, if combined with Cobb-Douglas preferences, any neoclassical production function subject to (A 1) is admissible that has an associated profile of wage income $w(k_t)$ satisfying (A 2*). For $w(k_t)$ to be strictly concave as required by (A 2*), assumptions need to be made with respect to the third derivative of the production function $f(k_t)$.[17] While standard theory places a priori no restrictions on the sign of this derivative, we show in appendix I at the end of the book that the function $w(k_t)$ is strictly concave, for example, for any Cobb-Douglas production function and any CES

---

[17]Remember that the function $F(K_t, L_t)$ is assumed to exhibit constant returns to scale. Hence, wage income $w(k_t)$ is given by $w(k_t) = f(k_t) - k_t \cdot f'(k_t)$, and $w''(k_t)$ is therefore linked to $f'''(k_t)$.

production function with elasticity of substitution no less than one.[18] Also in appendix I, we demonstrate that for these functions the modified Inada-conditions as stated in part i) and ii) of (A 2*) are met.[19] Hence, combining Cobb-Douglas preferences with either of the two production functions yields the desired result.

However, the literature knows various short cuts which avoid the use of narrowly specified functional forms, but break nevertheless the awkward interdependence of preferences and technology. In particular, the entire analysis gets considerably simplified if agents have a constant savings rate or, even more drastically, if one assumes that agents save their entire wage income because they derive no utility from first period consumption. More formally, consider the following modified conditions:

(A 2**) The function $f(k)$ admits the following behaviour of $w(k)$:

(i) $w(0) > 0 \quad \vee \quad w'(0) > 1$,

(ii) $\lim\limits_{k \to \infty} \frac{w(k)}{k} < 1$,

(iii) $w'(k) > 0$, $w''(k) < 0$ for all $k > 0$.

(A 3*) The function $U(c_t^y, c_{t+1}^o)$ has the properties:

$$U(c_t^y, c_{t+1}^o) = u(c_{t+1}^o) \quad \text{with: } u'(c_{t+1}^o) > 0 \quad \text{for all } c_{t+1}^o \geq 0.$$

In the light of the preceding discussion one easily confirms that the simplified set of conditions (A 1), (A 2**), and (A 3*) can be used interchangeably for the purposes of proposition 1. Thus, we state without proof:

Proposition 7 *Given assumptions (A 1), (A 2**), and (A 3*), there exists a unique, non-trivial steady state solution k^{In} to equation (4.21) with $k^{In} > 0$.*

According to (A 3*) the entire wage income will always be saved, i.e. intertemporal substitution effects are entirely removed from the now trivial

---

[18] As derived in appendix I, for CES production functions with elasticity of substitution less than one the function $w(k_t)$ is no longer globally concave. As a consequence, the equation $k_t = (1 - \beta) \cdot w(k_t)$ may well be solved by two non-trivial inside money steady states.

[19] In appendix I, we show that for any CES production function with elasticity of substitution no less than one $f(0) > 0$ and, hence, $\phi(0) > 0$ holds. Thus, in this case there exists no trivial inside money state with $k = 0$. Moreover, we establish for this type of function in appendix I the limits: $\lim_{k \to \infty} f'(k) > 0$, $\lim_{k \to \infty} [w(k)/k] = 0 < 1$. Hence, as suggested above, this type of function satisfies our mild specification of part (ii) of (A 2*), while it fails to meet the corresponding, but more restrictive requirement in Galor/Ryder (1989), p. 372.

savings decision. However, in the following chapters we will analyze at various stages effects which result from changes in the composition of savings rather than from changes in the overall level of savings. Thus, to isolate these effects in a transparent manner, we will frequently invoke the alternative set of sufficient conditions as stated in proposition 7.

4.5 Appendix

Proof of proposition 6:

To assess the dynamical behaviour of the system, we employ the standard technique described in appendix II at the end of the book. The relevant system to be analyzed can be rewritten as:

$$k_{t+1} = s[w(k_t), f'(k_{t+1})] - m_t \qquad (4.31)$$

$$\frac{1}{1+\mu} \cdot m_{t+1} = [f'(k_{t+1}) + 1 - \delta] \cdot m_t \qquad (4.32)$$

Totally differentiating (4.31)-(4.32) yields:

$$[1 - s_R \cdot f''(k)] \cdot d\,k_{t+1} = s_w \cdot w'(k) \cdot d\,k_t - d\,m_t$$

$$\frac{1}{1+\mu} \cdot d\,m_{t+1} - f''(k) \cdot m \cdot d\,k_{t+1} = [f'(k) + 1 - \delta] \cdot d\,m_t$$

Let the matrix J be defined as:

$$J = \begin{bmatrix} \phi'(k) & -\frac{1}{1-s_R \cdot f''(k)} \\ (1+\mu) \cdot \phi'(k) \cdot f''(k) \cdot m & (1+\mu) \cdot [f'(k) + 1 - \delta - \frac{f''(k) \cdot m}{1-s_R \cdot f''(k)}] \end{bmatrix}$$

Then, rearranging terms gives:

$$[\begin{matrix} d\,k_{t+1} \\ d\,m_{t+1} \end{matrix}] = J \cdot [\begin{matrix} d\,k_t \\ d\,m_t \end{matrix}] \qquad (4.33)$$

By inspecting the Jacobian matrix J of equation (4.33), equilibria can be classified as in proposition 6:

i) Outside money steady state: $k^{Out} > 0$, $m^{Out} > 0$.

At the outside money steady state needs to hold: $f'(k^{Out}) + 1 - \delta = 1/(1+\mu)$. Thus: $Det(J) = \phi'(k^{Out})$, $Tr(J) = 1 + Det(J) - [1+\mu] \cdot \frac{f''(k^{Out}) \cdot m}{1-s_R \cdot f''(k^{Out})}$, $p(1) = 1 + Det(J) - Tr(J) = [1+\mu] \cdot \frac{f''(k^{Out}) \cdot m}{1-s_R \cdot f''(k^{Out})}$. By (A 2*), terms can be signed as: $Det(J) > 0$, $p(1) < 0$. Thus, in terms of figure A.4 in appendix II, region 1a is reached, and eigenvalues follow therefore the pattern: $0 < \lambda_1 < 1 < \lambda_2$. Accordingly, the steady state is a saddle with monotone adjustment.

ii) Trivial inside money steady state: $k = 0$, $m = 0$.

Evaluating $Det(J)$ at $k = m = 0$ gives rise to the expression: $Det(J) = [lim_{k \to 0}\phi'(k)] \cdot [1 + \mu] \cdot [f'(0) + 1 - \delta]$. Moreover, one obtains: $Tr(J) = lim_{k \to 0}\phi'(k) + [1 + \mu] \cdot [f'(0) + 1 - \delta]$. By virtue of Vieta's theorem, eigenvalues are given by: $\lambda_1 = lim_{k \to 0}\phi'(k)$ and $\lambda_2 = [1 + \mu] \cdot [f'(0) + 1 - \delta]$. By (A 2*), $lim_{k \to 0}\phi'(k) > 1$. Thus, we have: $\lambda_1 > 1$. Moreover, since $k^{Out} > 0$ we have: $f'(0) > f'(k^{Out}) = \delta + 1/(1 + \mu) - 1$. Therefore, $\lambda_2 > 1$ needs to hold, and the steady state is a source.

iii) Diamond inside money steady state: $k^{In} > 0$, $m = 0$.

One obtains for $Det(J)$ and $Tr(J)$: $Det(J) = \phi'(k^{In}) \cdot [1 + \mu] \cdot [f'(k^{In}) + 1 - \delta]$, $Tr(J) = \phi'(k^{In}) + [1 + \mu] \cdot [f'(k^{In}) + 1 - \delta]$. Again, by Vieta's theorem: $\lambda_1 = \phi'(k^{In})$ and $\lambda_2 = [1 + \mu] \cdot [f'(k^{In}) + 1 - \delta]$. Since $k^{Out} > k^{In}$ and by concavity of $\phi(k)$, we have: $0 < \phi'(k^{In}) < 1$. Thus, we have: $0 < \lambda_1 < 1$. Similarly, the existence of the outside money steady state implies: $f'(k^{In}) < \delta + 1/(1 + \mu) - 1$. Hence, $0 < \lambda_2 < 1$ needs to be satisfied and, according to figure A.4 in appendix II, the steady state falls in region 7b, i.e. the steady state is a sink. Since we have two stable eigenvalues and only one state variable, adjustment towards the steady state will be indeterminate. Moreover, the dominant eigenvalue is positive. Thus, adjustment will ultimately be monotone. q.e.d.

Chapter 5

Variation 1: Imperfect credit markets and asymmetric information

It is a key feature of the base model introduced in the previous chapter that intermediation between savings and investment projects comes about in a smooth and entirely frictionless way. Yet, Azariadis/Smith (1996) show that this is not an innocuous assumption. In fact, the authors demonstrate that the mechanics of the Diamond model with outside money change dramatically, once a simple information asymmetry in the credit market is introduced that creates an adverse selection problem. However, to isolate the effects which arise from the information problem in the credit market, Azariadis/Smith (1996) retain the 'bubbly' view on money, i.e. they assume that money balances and financial assets are perfect substitutes with identical return rates. In this chapter, we summarize the essential features of the work of Azariadis/Smith (1996) and, in particular, we reproduce the effects that lead to a reversal of the results of the base model.

To allow for an informational friction, Azariadis/Smith (1996) introduce some heterogeneity among agents, and it is assumed that agents have private information about their own type. More specifically, the authors present a framework in which potential borrowers have projects with different qualities, and via the associated adverse selection problem inflation is shown to have a potentially detrimental impact on capital formation.[1] In particular, each generation is made up of two types of agents: On the one hand, there are

---

[1] The formulation of the adverse selection problem follows Rothschild/Stiglitz (1976). For the standard discussion of the adverse selection problem in credit markets, see Stiglitz/Weiß (1981). For a closely related treatment of adverse selection effects, although in a non-monetary version of a Diamond-type economy, see also Azariadis/Smith (1998).

genuine producers with 'legitimate' investment projects. On the other hand, there are potential savers who can misrepresent their type and turn into 'illegitimate' borrowers. In contrast to legitimate entrepreneurs, illegitimate borrowers misuse borrowed funds and invest them in an unproductive 'storage' technology with an exogenously specified constant return rate. When exercising this 'outside option', illegitimate borrowers go underground, and it is assumed that loans never get repaid.

The mechanics that reverse the Tobin effect hinge crucially on the idea that the value of the outside option of potential savers depends positively on the inflation rate. By reducing the return on properly saved (i.e. intermediated) wage income, a higher inflation rate makes it for potential savers more attractive to misrepresent their type and to turn into illegitimate borrowers. As a result, a higher inflation rate exacerbates the problem of intermediaries to induce a proper self-selection among borrowers. Exploiting this mechanism, the model shows that for sufficiently high inflation rates the dynamics of the standard model get reversed if intermediaries react to the incentive problem of potential savers by imposing a regime of credit rationing.

As to be discussed below in detail, once the 'private information regime of credit rationing' controls the dynamics of the system, real balances and physical capital cease to be close substitutes as expressed by the arbitrage relation of the base model. Instead, intermediaries respond to higher inflation rates by reducing the loan size per entrepreneur in order to rebalance the incentive constraint that prevents the misuse of funds by 'illegitimate' borrowers. Thus, in contrast to the base model, under the 'private information regime of credit rationing' the level of investment is positively correlated with yields on financial assets. As a result, inflation has a detrimental impact on capital formation and the Anti-Tobin effect prevails. Moreover, equilibrium dynamics may well become indeterminate and exhibit endogenous fluctuations in the neighbourhood of the monetary steady state.

Basically, Azariadis/Smith (1996) emphasize strongly that situations of ongoing high inflation rates reduce the incentives of agents to invest in intermediated investment projects and make it rather more profitable for agents to exercise less productive outside options. As pointed out by the authors, in the context of their model the outside option is best to be thought of as the 'investment' in consumption inventories. However, while this narrow interpretation of the outside option merely reflects the highly special nature of the assumptions underlying the model, the authors make in fact a far more general point. To the extent that high inflation rates indicate a situation of high uncertainty with respect to the course of future policies, agents will find it in general less attractive to commit themselves to 'productive' investment projects with a typically long gestation period. Thus, in more general versions of the model it would be attractive to include additional outside options of potential investors, such as the decision to engage in capital flight or to take on a wait-and-see attitude as discussed by Dixit/Pindyck (1994).

As shown in chapter 2, theoretical work needs to address the stylized fact that for 'high' inflation economies the level of real activity and the level of the inflation rate are negatively correlated, while this relationship is potentially different in 'very low' inflation regimes. Moreover, there is strong evidence that high inflation economies suffer from a poor performance of financial systems. We think that the model presented by Azariadis/Smith (1996) addresses this evidence in a promising way by establishing a negative link between inflation and the size of intermediated funds beyond a certain threshold value of the inflation rate. Moreover, results with respect to equilibrium dynamics hint at the empirically plausible fact that activities in money and financial markets are a potential source both of indeterminacies and endogenous volatility. In particular, the uncontroversial fact that inflation rates correlate strongly with the variability of inflation is well accounted for by the model. Finally, the authors show convincingly that it is not the bubbly view on money per se that is responsible for the results of the base model.

Similar results are obtained in closely related work by Boyd/Smith (1998). Also addressing the issue of imperfect credit markets in the context of the Diamond model, Boyd/Smith (1998) present a setting that gives rise to a moral hazard problem on the side of entrepreneurs and admits the possibility of multiple monetary steady state equilibria with rich dynamics. We think that the work of Boyd/Smith (1998) complements the study of Azariadis/Smith (1996) in a highly productive way, and we discuss therefore briefly some of the results at the end of the chapter. However, we now turn to the model of Azariadis/Smith (1996) in more detail.

5.1 The model

In contrast to the base model, it is assumed that each generation is made up of two distinct types of agents: with $\lambda \in (0,1)$, a fraction λ of agents per generation is born as (potential) *savers* and a fraction $1 - \lambda$ is born as *producers*. The composition of generations is assumed to be constant over time.

Characteristics of agents: Both types of agents consume only when old, and preferences are simply described by a linear utility function.

(A 1) For both types of agents, preferences can be represented by the utility function:

$$u(c_t, c_{t+1}) = c_{t+1}$$

Savers have one unit of labour when being young and no labour when old. It is assumed that they have access to a storage technology that transforms one unit of time t output into $x > 0$ units of time $t + 1$ output. Thus, when deciding about the composition of their savings, savers can choose between storage on the one hand and holdings of deposits or real balances on the other hand.

Producers have no labour when young and one unit of labour in their old age, and they have access to an investment technology that converts one unit of time t output into one unit of time $t + 1$ capital goods. In their old age, producers combine their capital and their own labour endowment with the labour supply offered by young savers and produce the single output good of the economy. Producers have no access to the storage technology. Conversely, savers lack the know-how to run the production process.

In addition, it is assumed that each member of the initial old generation is endowed with one unit of labour and K_0 and M_{-1} units of capital and nominal money balances, respectively.

Information structure: The information structure is simple: the age of agents and all market transactions like working and borrowing are observable, but agents have private information about their own type. Thus, a producer cannot claim to be a saver since he receives no wage income when being young. Conversely, potential savers can misrepresent their type and borrow from intermediaries. When doing so, they supply no labour in their youth and store the illegitimately borrowed funds since they have no access to the investment technology. However, with storage being specified as an underground activity, there is no way how intermediaries could recover loans from illegitimate borrowers. Finally, note that producers never misuse funds since they have no access to the storage technology.[2]

To simplify the following exposition we assume directly that a separating equilibrium obtains, i.e. the constellation is assumed to be such that all loans are 'legitimately' handed out to producers and all potential savers work when young. As we will show below, non-trivial equilibria (i.e. constellations in which the economy is actually getting off the ground) always require that all potential borrowers are induced to truthfully reveal their type.

Government: Slightly deviating from Azariadis/Smith (1996), we specify government activities for the sake of easy comparison as in the base model.[3]

---

[2]Clearly, the assumptions regarding the characteristics of agents are rather special. However, they are simply motivated by the idea to present the adverse selection mechanism in a most transparent setting.

[3]In the version given in Azariadis/Smith (1996), government expenditures take the form of lump-sum subsidies to young producers, i.e. things are arranged such that newly printed money directly subsidizes the process of capital accumulation. Thus, to illustrate the fragility of the Tobin effect Azariadis/Smith (1996) deliberately choose a framework that makes the "...strongest possible case for money growth to have a *positive* effect on

Hence, the nominal money supply follows the rule:

$$M_t = (1 + \mu) \cdot M_{t-1} \quad \text{with: } \mu > 0 \tag{5.1}$$

Let g_t denote government expenditures per young agent. Then, the budget constraint of the government is given by:

$$g_t = \frac{M_t - M_{t-1}}{p_t} \tag{5.2}$$

Production: Let b_{t-1} denote the real value of borrowing per young producer in period $t-1$. With all borrowing being invested to produce capital goods, the period t capital stock per old producer will be given by $K_t = b_{t-1}$. Moreover, let L_t stand for the amount of labour hired per old producer in period t. Then, in a separating equilibrium labour market clearing requires:

$$(1 - \lambda) \cdot L_t = \lambda \quad \Leftrightarrow \quad L_t = \frac{\lambda}{(1 - \lambda)} \tag{5.3}$$

Let k_t denote the capital-labour ratio. As in the base model, production occurs according to a standard neoclassical production function $F(K, L)$ with constant returns and diminishing marginal products.

(A 2) The function $f(k)$ is twice continuously differentiable, positive, increasing, and strictly concave:

$$\text{(i) } f(k) > 0, \quad \text{(ii) } f'(k) > 0 \quad \text{(iii) } f''(k) < 0 \text{ for } k > 0.$$

Moreover, the production function satisfies the requirements:[4]

(A 3) The function $f(k)$ admits the following behaviour of $w(k)$:

(i) $w(0) > 0$, $\frac{1+\mu}{1-\lambda} \cdot x > \frac{1}{\lambda}$ $\vee$ $w'(0) > \frac{1+\mu}{1-\lambda} \cdot x > \frac{1}{\lambda}$,

(ii) $\lim\limits_{k \to \infty} \frac{w(k)}{k} = 0$,

(iii) $w'(k) > 0$, $w''(k) < 0$ for all $k > 0$.

---

the capital stock" (p. 331). However, as our analysis will show, this specification is by no means critical for the results.

[4] Assumption (A 3) reflects the heterogeneity among agents and the existence of an outside option, and, for reasons to become transparent below, it is therefore slightly more restrictive than assumption (A 2**) of the previous chapter. However, as shown in appendix I at the end of the book, assumptions with respect to technology are still satisfied, for example, by the Cobb-Douglas function and by any CES function with elasticity of substitution no less than one.

With constant returns to scale and producers being endowed with unit one of labour when being old, output per producer will be given by the term $F(K_t, L_t+1) = (L_t+1) \cdot f(k_t)$. By (5.3), the capital-labour ratio is given as:

$$k_t \equiv \frac{K_t}{L_t+1} = (1-\lambda) \cdot K_t \qquad (5.4)$$

For simplicity, capital is assumed to depreciate entirely within the production process. Then, by perfect competition and constant returns to scale, the wage rate w_t and the rate of return on capital ρ_t are given in standard fashion by:

$$\rho_t = f'(k_t) \qquad (5.5)$$
$$w_t = f(k_t) - k_t \cdot f'(k_t) = w(k_t) \qquad (5.6)$$

Savings: With money playing no distinctive role compared to other assets, savers treat real balances and deposits as perfect substitutes. Moreover, it is assumed that storage is strictly return-dominated by financial assets.

(A 4) Storage is strictly return-dominated:

$$R_t^d = R_t^m > x$$

Evidently, (A 4) ensures that wage income will never be stored. Moreover, it follows from (A 4) that the composition of savings between deposits and real balances will be indeterminate from the perspective of savers. Since all wage income will be saved according to (A 1), capital market clearing requires:

$$\lambda \cdot w(k_t) = (1-\lambda) \cdot b_t + m_t = k_{t+1} + m_t \qquad (5.7)$$

Loan contracts: Let R_t^l denote the loan rate that is charged for loans handed out in period t and to be repaid in period $t+1$. When announcing loan contracts (R_t^l, b_t), intermediaries are assumed to be engaged in Nash competition. On the deposit side intermediaries behave competitively, i.e. they take the return rate R_t^d on deposits as given. In a separating equilibrium potential savers have no incentive to misreport their type, and the following incentive compatibility constraint needs therefore to hold:

$$R_t^d \cdot w(k_t) \geq x \cdot b_t \qquad (5.8)$$

With intermediation being subject to free entry, any spread between loan rates and deposit rates will vanish in equilibrium:

$$R_t^l = R_t^d \qquad (5.9)$$

Moreover, by Nash competition between intermediaries the size of the loan b_t must be chosen in a way such that the consumption level of old producers will be maximized. In general, the consumption of old producers is given by:

$$c_{t+1} = (L_{t+1}+1) \cdot f(k_{t+1}) - L_{t+1} \cdot w_{t+1} - R_t^l \cdot b_t \qquad (5.10)$$

Inserting (5.3), (5.4), (5.6), and (5.9) into (5.10) yields:

$$c_{t+1} = (f'(k_{t+1}) - R_t^d) \cdot b_t + w_{t+1} \qquad (5.11)$$

In period t, intermediaries will maximize (5.11) over b_t such that the incentive constraint (5.8) holds.[5] In any non-trivial equilibrium the optimizing choice of b_t must be positive and finite. Furthermore, a positive demand for loans on the side of producers requires:

$$f'(k_{t+1}) \geq R_t^d \qquad (5.12)$$

Thus, in any separating equilibrium both the incentive constraint (5.8) and the arbitrage relation (5.12) need to hold, with at least one of them holding as strict equality.

To ensure that the separating loan contract constitutes indeed a genuine Nash equilibrium, further restrictions need to be imposed. In particular, as indicated by the proposition given below, a high frequency of potential savers makes it, ceteris paribus, more likely for a separating Nash equilibrium to exist. Moreover, one easily shows that pooling loan contracts can never occur in a non-trivial equilibrium. In summary, with the proofs being delegated to the appendix at the end of the chapter, we state:

Proposition 1 *Separating loan contracts* $(R_t^l = R_t^d, b_t^*)$, *where both (5.8) and (5.12) are satisfied and at least one of the two constraints holds as strict equality, constitute a Nash equilibrium if the following condition holds:*

$$R_t^d \leq f'(k_{t+1}) \leq \frac{R_t^d}{1 - \lambda} \qquad (5.13)$$

Proposition 2 *Pooling loan contracts occur only in a trivial equilibrium with* $k_t = 0$ *for all periods.*

Proofs: see appendix.

For the remainder of this chapter we take it for granted that the critical condition (5.13) is satisfied.

5.2 Equilibrium conditions

As shown in the discussion of the base model, the return rate on money can be rewritten as:

$$R_t^m = \frac{p_t}{p_{t+1}} = \frac{1}{1 + \mu} \cdot \frac{m_{t+1}}{m_t} \qquad (5.14)$$

---

[5]More precisely, when maximizing over (5.11) intermediaries take prices including w_{t+1} as given. However, by anticipating labour market competition as given by (5.6) one period ahead, any expectation of w_{t+1} is directly linked to some expectation of k_{t+1}.

Then, upon rearranging the relevant conditions, competitive equilibria evolve over time according to the following system of equations in k_t and m_t:

$$k_{t+1} = \lambda \cdot w(k_t) - m_t \tag{5.15}$$

$$f'(k_{t+1}) \geq \frac{1}{1+\mu} \cdot \frac{m_{t+1}}{m_t} \tag{5.16}$$

$$k_{t+1} \leq \frac{1}{1+\mu} \cdot \frac{m_{t+1}}{m_t} \cdot (1-\lambda) \cdot \frac{1}{x} \cdot w(k_t) \tag{5.17}$$

Essentially, competitive equilibria are governed by a particularly simple version of the standard accumulation equation (5.15) and by the pair of arbitrage and incentive constraints as given by (5.16) and (5.17). However, as argued above, at least one of the constraints (5.16) and (5.17) needs to hold as strict equality. Abstracting from the rare case where both (5.16) and (5.17) are strictly binding, Azariadis/Smith (1996) propose the following classification of equilibrium outcomes: a situation in which the arbitrage relation is strictly binding (as in the base model) is called a 'Walrasian equilibrium'. In contrast, a situation in which the incentive constraint is tight and credit rationing obtains is called a 'private information' equilibrium. Drawing on this distinction, we turn now to a discussion of steady state equilibria.

Steady state equilibria: In the following, Walrasian equilibria will be indicated by starred variables, while hat variables will be used for private information equilibria. Let the function $\Omega(k)$ be defined as $\Omega(k) \equiv k/w(k)$. Then, steady state conditions can be summarized as:

Walrasian steady states:

$$k^* = \lambda \cdot w(k^*) - m \tag{5.18}$$

$$f'(k^*) = \frac{1}{1+\mu} \tag{5.19}$$

$$\Omega(k^*) < \frac{1}{1+\mu} \cdot \frac{1}{x} \cdot (1-\lambda) \tag{5.20}$$

Note that equations (5.18) and (5.19) are virtually identical to those that describe the steady state behaviour of the base model. Moreover, as argued in detail in the previous chapter, the simple shape of the savings function in (5.18) facilitates the analysis considerably, and we assume directly that the system (5.18)-(5.19) has a unique outside money steady state.[6]

---

[6]In particular, as shown in the preceding chapter, for an outside money steady state to exist, we need to assume that the unique inside money steady state implied by (A 3) is dynamically inefficient, i.e. $f'(k^{In}) < 1/(1+\mu)$ needs to be satisfied.

73

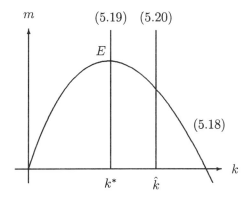

Figure 5.1: *Variation 1 - Steady state: existence*

Private information steady states:

$$\widehat{k} = \lambda \cdot w(\widehat{k}) - \widehat{m} \tag{5.21}$$

$$\Omega(\widehat{k}) = \frac{1}{1+\mu} \cdot \frac{1}{x} \cdot (1-\lambda) \tag{5.22}$$

$$f'(\widehat{k}) > \frac{1}{1+\mu} \tag{5.23}$$

For private information steady states the following proposition is readily verified:

Proposition 3 *Given our assumptions, there exists a unique and strictly positive pair of real balances and capital $(\widehat{m}, \widehat{k})$ solving the equation system (5.21)-(5.22).*

Proof: Note that $\Omega'(k) > 0$ is implied by concavity of $w(k)$. From the first part of (A 3), we have: $\Omega(0) < \frac{1-\lambda}{(1+\mu)\cdot x}$. Furthermore, $lim_{k\to\infty}\Omega(k) = \infty$ follows from the second part of (A 3). Thus, by continuity of $\Omega(k)$, there exists a unique and positive value $\widehat{k}$ that solves (5.22). Rearranging (5.21) and (5.22) yields: $\widehat{m} = \widehat{k} \cdot [\lambda \cdot (1+\mu) \cdot x/(1-\lambda) - 1]$. Then, it follows from the first part of (A 3) that monetary balances $\widehat{m}$ associated with $\widehat{k}$ are strictly positive. q.e.d.

But which of the two regimes will prevail ? In figure 5.1 we graph the accumulation equation (5.18) and both the arbitrage relation (5.19) and the incentive constraint (5.20) as strict equalities. Note that any value of k that

74

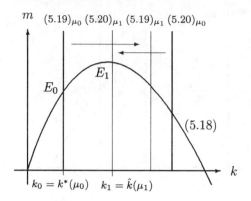

Figure 5.2: *Variation 1 - Steady state: comparative statics, $\mu_1 > \mu^{Cr} > \mu_0$*

exceeds k^* violates the arbitrage constraint. Similarly, values of k exceeding $\hat{k}$ are not consistent with the incentive constraint. Thus, the steady state value of the capital stock is given by $k = \min[k^*, \hat{k}]$. Accordingly, figure 5.1 represents a Walrasian equilibrium.[7]

5.3 Policy effects

Comparative statics: Again, we want to establish how a permanent shift to a more inflationary policy impacts on the steady state level of capital formation. As argued in the previous chapter, solutions k^* of the Walrasian system depend positively on the rate of monetary expansion μ, i.e. the Tobin effect obtains. In contrast, since $\Omega'(k) > 0$, solutions $\hat{k}$ of the private information system are negatively linked to μ, i.e. the Anti-Tobin effect prevails. Thus, as indicated in figure 5.2, the steady state interaction of the two regimes makes it likely that for sufficiently 'low' inflation rates the Walrasian solution obtains. However, a high inflation policy exacerbates the task of intermediaries to induce a proper self-selection among borrowers. Hence, beyond some critical threshold level μ^{cr}, the private information regime becomes effective and the Anti-Tobin effect prevails. We summarize this reasoning without proof in the subsequent proposition:[8]

---

[7]To make sure that a constellation with $\hat{k} < k^*$ satisfies the separating equilibrium condition (5.13), the inequality $f'(\hat{k}) \leq \frac{1}{(1+\mu)\cdot(1-\lambda)}$ needs to hold.

[8]The upper bound for μ results from assumption (A 4) which ensures that savers have no incentive to store their wage income.

Proposition 4 *A permanent shift to a more inflationary policy induces the following reaction of the steady state capital stock:*

$$\frac{\partial k}{\partial \mu} = \begin{cases} > 0 \;\; for: & 0 < \mu < \mu^{cr} \\ < 0 \;\; for: & \mu^{cr} < \mu < (1-x)/x \end{cases}$$

Dynamics: From (5.15)-(5.17) one quickly obtains the relevant conditions that determine locally the dynamical adjustment behaviour of the system over time. Again, we present the two regimes in turn.[9]

Walrasian equilibria:

$$k_{t+1} = \lambda \cdot w(k_t) - m_t \tag{5.24}$$

$$f'(\lambda \cdot w(k_t) - m_t) = \frac{1}{1+\mu} \cdot \frac{m_{t+1}}{m_t} \tag{5.25}$$

As already shown for the slightly more general version of the base model, the outside money steady state is a saddle, i.e.: monetary equilibria are locally determinate and subject to monotone adjustment. Thus, with the incentive constraint being slack, dynamics can graphically be represented as in figure 4.4 of the previous chapter.

Private information equilibria:

$$k_{t+1} = \lambda \cdot w(k_t) - m_t \tag{5.26}$$

$$\lambda \cdot w(k_t) - m_t = \frac{1}{1+\mu} \cdot \frac{m_{t+1}}{m_t} \cdot (1-\lambda) \cdot \frac{1}{x} \cdot w(k_t) \tag{5.27}$$

According to (5.26), dynamics of k_t evolve according to:

$$k_{t+1} \geq k_t \;\; \Leftrightarrow \;\; m_t \leq \lambda \cdot w(k_t) - k_t \tag{5.28}$$

With $k_{t+1} = k_t$, equation (5.26) can be graphed as shown in figure 5.3. Then, by (5.28), the following proposition is straightforward:

Proposition 5 *For points below (above) the graph of (5.26) with $k_{t+1} = k_t$, the capital stock evolves according to: $k_{t+1} > (<)k_t$.*

Note that equation (5.27) with $m_{t+1} = m_t$ simplifies to:

$$m_t = [\lambda - \frac{1}{1+\mu} \cdot (1-\lambda) \cdot \frac{1}{x}] \cdot w(k_t) \tag{5.29}$$

---

[9]We make for the rest of this section the simplifying assumption that dynamics are caused by policy changes that do not lead to a regime switch. Otherwise, one would have to analyze all three equations of the system (5.15)-(5.17) simultaneously. For a more detailed treatment, see Azariadis/Smith (1996).

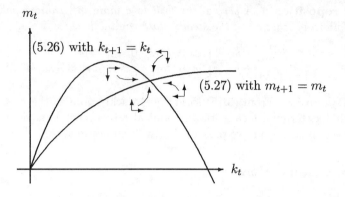

Figure 5.3: *Variation 1 - Steady state: dynamics*

Then, due to assumption (A 3), the graph of (5.27) with $m_{t+1} = m_t$ can be drawn as indicated in figure 5.3. From (5.27), one easily establishes that dynamics of m_t obey:

$$m_{t+1} \geq m_t \;\; \Leftrightarrow \;\; m_t \leq [\lambda - \frac{1}{1+\mu} \cdot (1-\lambda) \cdot \frac{1}{x}] \cdot w(k_t) \qquad (5.30)$$

Obviously, the relations given in (5.30) imply:

Proposition 6 *For points to the right (left) of the graph of (5.27) with $m_{t+1} = m_t$, real balances evolve according to: $m_{t+1} > (<)m_t$.*

Combining propositions 5 and 6, figure 5.3 reproduces the local force field that predominates in the neighbourhood of private information steady states. While figure 5.3 suggests that private information steady states are indeterminate, a rigorous analysis of the dynamics leads to the following, more accurate classification:

Proposition 7 *For a wide range of parameter values, private information steady states are a sink, i.e. adjustment behaviour is locally indeterminate. Moreover, adjustment behaviour may well be subject to endogenous volatility.*

Proof: see appendix.

In summary, under the Walrasian, frictionless regime the assumptions with respect to preferences and technology are sufficiently strong to ensure a

uniquely determined, smooth adjustment behaviour of the system with valued fiat money. However, under the private information regime this feature
may well get lost. Transient dynamics towards the steady state may no
longer be uniquely determined. Moreover, adjustment may well be subject
to endogenously arising volatility. Thus, high inflation regimes may well give
rise to dynamics where both real balances and the inflation rate fluctuate
strongly when approaching the steady state. To substantiate this claim, we
construct in the appendix a simple parametrized example in a Cobb-Douglas
framework.

5.4 Discussion

In closely related work, Boyd/Smith (1998) demonstrate that the explicit
treatment of frictions in the capital market may not only change the nature
of the monetary steady state in the Diamond model, but also allow for the
possibility of multiple monetary steady states. Evidently, this finding is an
additional important modification of the base model, since it shows that non-
convergence phenomena across otherwise similar economies may result from
differences with respect to activities in money and financial markets. Thus,
we conclude this chapter briefly with an informal discussion of the modified
version of the Diamond model presented by Boyd/Smith (1998).

As in the base model, Boyd/Smith (1998) present a setting in which agents
work only when being young. Yet, agents differ with respect to their entrepreneurial abilities. In particular, a certain fraction of agents has access to a
stochastic investment technology that converts current output into next period's capital, while all remaining agents, so-called 'lenders', lack this ability.
The investment technology is assumed to be indivisible, and the minimum
scale of inputs at which the technology can be operated is supposed to exceed
the wage income of young agents. Thus, when undertaking an investment
project, entrepreneurs use not only internal funds stemming from their first
period wage income, but also external funds obtained from lenders.

Moreover, it is assumed that the outcome of investment projects is private
information of entrepreneurs. Lenders know only the probability distribution
over outcomes which is identical across projects. Yet, outcomes can be observed by lenders against a fixed monitoring cost. Thus, Boyd/Smith (1998)
consider a version of an information asymmetry between entrepreneurs and
lenders that leads to a 'costly state verification problem' as analyzed, for
example, by Townsend (1979). Given the information asymmetry, contract
terms under which entrepreneurs obtain funds from lenders clearly need to
address the moral hazard problem on the side of entrepreneurs to misreport
successful project outcomes. In particular, drawing on a well-known result
of the literature, Boyd/Smith (1998) argue that in equilibrium entrepreneurs
will announce contract terms that take the form of standard debt contracts,

i.e. terms are such that entrepreneurs either repay the borrowed amount plus a fixed sum of interest or else default. In the case of default, lenders monitor the project and retain the proceeds of the project net of monitoring costs.

Importantly, the authors assume that financial assets and outside money balances are perfect substitutes. Thus, like Azariadis/Smith (1996) the authors endorse the bubbly view on money and obtain thereby a simple macroeconomic closure of the model. Under this specification, in any equilibrium with valued outside money returns to lenders must be identical to the return on money.

Finally, as shown by Bernanke/Gertler (1989), the amount of internal financing decides about the severity of the costly state verification problem. It is this feature that is crucial for the possibility of multiple monetary steady states. In particular, it can be shown that two steady state equilibria with different levels of activity and identical return rates to lenders may well coexist. More specifically, the high level equilibrium will be characterized by a high capital stock, leading both to a low gross interest rate (due to a low marginal product of capital) and to small monitoring costs (due to the high level of internal financing associated with a high wage income). Similarly, in the low level equilibrium these effects will be reversed: Now, the gross interest rate will be high (due to a high marginal product of capital), but monitoring costs will also be high (due to the severity of the state verification problem associated with a low level of internal financing), and this makes it possible that the return to lenders net of monitoring costs will be identical for the two equilibria.

Not surprisingly, the rich structure of the model permits a broad range of results, as far as the effectiveness of monetary policy is concerned. In particular, it can be shown that the low level equilibrium is a saddle with monotone adjustment behaviour, and that at this equilibrium the Tobin effect prevails. In contrast, the high level equilibrium is of Anti-Tobin nature and dynamics may well be indeterminate and subject to endogenous volatility. In summary, the results established by Boyd/Smith (1998) correspond closely to those given by Azariadis/Smith (1996), and both studies show convincingly that with the introduction of informational frictions in the capital market monetary policy plays a far more interesting role than suggested by the base model.

5.5 Appendix

Proof of proposition 1:

Let $\xi \in [0,1]$ denote the fraction of young potential savers who receive 'illegitimately' loans and default. Then, the average gross return on loans is given by the term: $R_t^l \cdot (1 - \lambda)/(1 - \lambda + \lambda \cdot \xi)$. For contracts with $(R_t^l = R_t^d, b_t^*)$ to constitute a Nash equilibrium, deviating to any alternative contract $(\widetilde{R}_t^l, \widetilde{b}_t)$ must not be profitable. Consider the following cases:

i) $\widetilde{R}_t^l = R_t^d, \widetilde{b}_t \neq b_t^*$: Clearly, deviating to a contract of this type does not increase profits.

ii) $\widetilde{R}_t^l > R_t^d$ and $f'(k_{t+1}) = R_t^d$: No such contract will be accepted by young producers. Hence, there is no incentive to offer it.

iii) $\widetilde{R}_t^l > R_t^d$ and $f'(k_{t+1}) > R_t^d$: Assume $\widetilde{R}_t^l \in (R_t^d, \frac{R_t^d}{1-\lambda})$. For intermediaries to break even, $\xi \in [0,1)$ needs to hold. This in turn implies that the incentive constraint (5.8) needs to be satisfied. Thus, $\widetilde{b}_t \leq b_t^*$ has to hold, i.e. borrowers are charged a higher loan rate with no increase in the loan size. Hence, deviating to the contract $(\widetilde{R}_t^l, \widetilde{b}_t)$ does not attract any young producers and therefore it cannot be profitable. Assume now that the restriction (5.13) holds: $R_t^d \leq f'(k_{t+1}) \leq R_t^d/(1 - \lambda)$. Then, deviating to a loan rate larger than $f'(k_{t+1})$ is clearly not profitable since it attracts no young producers and proposition 1 follows immediately. On the contrary, if (5.13) does not hold, there exists a complete pooling contract that dominates the separating contract (R_t^d, b_t^*) and no separating equilibrium exists. q.e.d.

Proof of proposition 2:

i) Consider contracts $(\widetilde{R}_t^l, \widetilde{b}_t)$ with $\widetilde{R}_t^l \in (R_t^d, \frac{R_t^d}{1-\lambda})$. As argued above this admits (partial) pooling with $\xi \in (0,1)$. However, deviating to a contract that offers a lower interest rate and reduces the loan size by an infinitesimally small amount is profitable: clearly, the contract will appeal to legitimate borrowers, but no 'illegitimate' borrowers will feel attracted since they care only about the loan size dimension of the contract. Thus, no (partial) pooling equilibrium exists for $\widetilde{R}_t^l \in (R_t^d, \frac{R_t^d}{1-\lambda})$.

ii) Consider complete pooling contracts $(\widetilde{R}_t^l, \widetilde{b}_t)$ with $\widetilde{R}_t^l \geq \frac{R_t^d}{1-\lambda}$ such that $\xi = 1$. For such contracts to be profitable, clearly restriction (5.13) must be violated. With all potential savers turning into 'illegitimate' borrowers no savings will be realized. Thus, $b_t = K_t = 0$ for all periods. q.e.d.

Proof of proposition 7:

Rearranging equation (5.27), the system (5.26)-(5.27) can be expressed as:

$$k_{t+1} = \lambda \cdot w(k_t) - m_t \tag{5.31}$$

$$m_{t+1} = \frac{\lambda}{1-\lambda} \cdot (1+\mu) \cdot x \cdot m_t - (1+\mu) \cdot \frac{x}{1-\lambda} \cdot \frac{m_t^2}{w(k_t)} \tag{5.32}$$

Following the procedure outlined in appendix II at the end of the book, the Jacobian matrix of the system (5.31)-(5.32) is given by:

$$J = \begin{bmatrix} \lambda \cdot w'(\widehat{k}) & -1 \\ \frac{(1+\mu)\cdot x}{1-\lambda} \cdot w'(\widehat{k}) \cdot (\frac{\widehat{m}}{w(\widehat{k})})^2 & \frac{\lambda}{1-\lambda} \cdot (1+\mu) \cdot x - \frac{2 \cdot (1+\mu) \cdot x}{1-\lambda} \cdot \frac{\widehat{m}}{w(\widehat{k})} \end{bmatrix}$$

Invoking (A 3), we define the constant:

$$A = \frac{\lambda}{1-\lambda} \cdot (1+\mu) \cdot x > 1 \tag{5.33}$$

Using (5.21) and (5.22), one can establish: $\widehat{m}/w(\widehat{k}) = \lambda \cdot (1 - 1/A)$. Then, the Jacobian matrix J can be rearranged to:

$$J = \begin{bmatrix} \lambda \cdot w'(\widehat{k}) & -1 \\ w'(\widehat{k}) \cdot \frac{1-\lambda}{x \cdot (1+\mu)} \cdot (A-1)^2 & 2 - A \end{bmatrix}$$

Next, the determinant and the trace of the Jacobian are given by:

$$Det = w'(\widehat{k}) \cdot \lambda \cdot \frac{1}{A} \tag{5.34}$$

$$Tr = 2 - A + \lambda \cdot w'(\widehat{k}) = 2 + A \cdot (Det - 1) \tag{5.35}$$

Note that in steady state the following relation holds: $\widehat{k}/w(\widehat{k}) = \lambda/A$. Thus, by exploiting the concavity of the function $w(k)$, the determinant satisfies:

$$0 < Det = w'(\widehat{k}) \cdot \frac{\widehat{k}}{w(\widehat{k})} < 1 \tag{5.36}$$

Moreover, combining (5.33),(5.35), and (5.36) yields:

$$Tr < 1 + Det \tag{5.37}$$

Note that in terms of the classification of equilibria as presented in figure A.4 in appendix II, (5.36) and (5.37) admit combinations of the trace and the determinant that give rise to a saddle (region 3a) or a sink (regions 6, 7a, and 7b). However, the following condition is necessary and sufficient to rule out the case of a saddle:

$$Det > -1 - Tr \quad \Leftrightarrow \quad \frac{3 + Det}{1 - Det} > A \tag{5.38}$$

Thus, private information steady states with a parameter constellation satisfying requirement (5.38) are subject to indeterminate and potentially fluctuating adjustment behaviour.[10]

To illustrate that condition (5.38) is indeed satisfied by a wide parameter range, we conclude by presenting a simple parametrized example. In particular, parameters are chosen such that adjustment behaviour is subject to endogenous fluctuations.

Example: Assume production is of Cobb-Douglas-type: $f(k) = c \cdot k^{\alpha}$. Let parameters be given by:

$$\alpha = 0.3, \ c = 2, \ \lambda = 0.75, \ x = 0.5, \ 1 + \mu = 1.2$$

For the case of a Cobb-Douglas function, $w(k)$ is a strictly concave function, $lim_{k \to \infty} w(k)/k = 0$, and $lim_{k \to 0} w'(k) = \infty$. By (5.33), $A = 1.8 > 1$. Thus, assumption (A 3) is satisfied. As required by assumption (A 4), financial assets return-dominate storage: $1/(1 + \mu) = 0.83 > x = 0.5$. By equations (5.21) and (5.22), the private information steady state needs to satisfy for the Cobb-Douglas case:

$$\frac{1}{(1 - \alpha) \cdot c} \cdot \widehat{k}^{1-\alpha} = \frac{1}{1 + \mu} \cdot \frac{1}{x} \cdot (1 - \lambda) \tag{5.39}$$

$$\widehat{m} = \lambda \cdot (1 - \alpha) \cdot c \cdot \widehat{k}^{\alpha} - \widehat{k} \tag{5.40}$$

Solving for $\widehat{k}$ and $\widehat{m}$ yields: $\widehat{k} = 0.46$, $\widehat{m} = 0.37$. Comparing the yields on real balances and capital, one readily establishes that money is strictly return-dominated by capital, i.e. condition (5.23) holds as strict inequality and credit rationing obtains in equilibrium: $f'(\widehat{k}) = 1.03 > 1/(1 + \mu) = 0.83$. Furthermore, the second part of the inequality of (5.13) is equally satisfied, i.e.: separating loan contracts give indeed rise to a Nash equilibrium: $f'(\widehat{k}) = 1.03 < [(1 + \mu) \cdot (1 - \lambda)]^{-1} = 3.33$. By virtue of (5.36), the determinant of the Jacobian matrix turns out to be constant for the Cobb-Douglas case: $Det = \alpha$. Next, indeterminacy of equilibrium is ensured since (5.38) holds: $(3 + Det)/(1 - Det) = (3 + \alpha)/(1 - \alpha) = 4.7 > A = 1.8$. One easily verifies that the value of the trace is given by: $Tr = 0.74$. Finally, the dynamics need to be fluctuating since the eigenvalues of the Jacobian matrix are conjugate complex: $Tr^2 - 4 \cdot Det = -0.65 < 0$. q.e.d.

---

[10]For the adjustment path to be fluctuating, eigenvalues need to be complex, i.e. in addition to requirement (5.38) the condition $Tr^2 - 4 \cdot Det < 0$ needs to be satisfied.

Chapter 6

Variation 2: Random liquidity needs

The models presented so far have been silent on why money is commonly held by agents despite being dominated in return by other assets. Instead, the whole issue has been simply defined away by virtue of the untenable assumption that all assets have equal rates of return. To treat the issue of return-dominance in such a way is hardly satisfactory, and, therefore, we turn now to a version of the Diamond model due to Schreft/Smith (1997) in which assets are no longer uniquely characterized by their return rates. Instead, Schreft/Smith (1997) present a framework with an elaborate timing of events that stresses the liquidity aspects of assets. Due to different degrees of liquidity, interest-bearing assets and money cease to be perfect substitutes, and as in the previous chapter this changes the mechanics of the base model in a significant way. Moreover, Schreft/Smith (1997) assume that the government issues not only money, but also illiquid, interest-bearing bonds which compete with capital in the portfolios of agents. Thus, compared to the base model, Schreft/Smith (1997) present a framework with a rich financial structure, and this makes it more rewarding to analyze the interaction of monetary policy and financial markets. Otherwise things are arranged in a conventional manner: capital markets operate smoothly, and trades in all markets are settled according to some centralized, frictionless trading scheme in Walrasian manner.

Broadly speaking, Schreft/Smith (1997) show that due their modifications multiple monetary steady states may well exist and that the effects of monetary policy depend crucially on the mix of interest-bearing assets, i.e. on the mix of government bonds and private capital. In particular, the authors derive a constellation in which the low level equilibrium is of Anti-Tobin nature because of a comparatively inefficient operation of financial markets. We think that this result addresses the stylized facts presented in chapter 2 in an instructive way and concentrate therefore in our summary of the model of Schreft/Smith (1997) on this constellation.

To create a genuine demand for money resulting from its high degree of liquidity, Schreft/Smith (1997) present a setting that specifies a mismatch of the time horizon between potentially short run liquidity needs of savers and a 'long' gestation period of investment projects in physical capital. Drawing on work by Diamond/Dybvig (1983), it is assumed that agents are individually subject to random liquidity needs. However, there is no uncertainty with respect to liquidity needs at the aggregate level. Agents seek to insure against these needs, and it turns out that agents prefer to insure themselves with the help of intermediaries ('banks'), rather than to rely on self-insurance through holdings of money at the individual level. With no uncertainty at the aggregate level, banks can exploit the law of large numbers and face therefore a perfectly predictable demand for liquidity. Thus, as in studies by Bencivenga/Smith (1991,1992), banks help the economy to economize on holdings of liquid, but unproductive assets and avoid the premature liquidation of productive, but illiquid investments in capital formation.[1] With all savings being intermediated, banks hold two types of assets: on the one hand, reserves to meet the withdrawal demand of agents in need of liquidity and, on the other hand, interest-bearing investments in physical capital and government bonds, both being perfect substitutes.

The existence of two outside assets, interest-bearing government bonds and interest-free fiat money, naturally leads the authors to address the coordination problem between monetary and fiscal policy measures as discussed in detail, for example, by Gale (1983) or Sargent/Wallace (1981). However, reflecting their interest in the interaction of money and capital formation, Schreft/Smith (1997) concentrate exclusively on a regime in which fiscal policy is fully subordinated to monetary policy. In particular, monetary policy

---

[1]In related work, also incorporating varying degrees of liquidity of assets, Bencivenga/Smith (1991) present a framework that discusses more broadly the growth promoting role of financial intermediaries in the context of a Romer-type endogenous growth model. In particular, Bencivenga/Smith (1991) show that even for a constant savings rate a higher growth rate of the economy may result from a more productive composition of savings due to the activity of intermediaries. While in Bencivenga/Smith (1991) the specific nature of the liquid asset of the economy remains unclear, Bencivenga/Smith (1992) extend the base version by specifying outside money as the single liquid asset of the economy. Furthermore, the budget constraint of the government is explicitly addressed, with outside money entering the constraint as tax base for the inflation tax. In summary, Bencivenga/Smith (1992) argue that the observed reluctance in many developing countries to liberalize capital markets may well be rationalized from a (short-run) public finance perspective: while intermediation helps the economy as a whole to economize on the demand for real balances from an insurance perspective, this may well conflict with the interest of the government to have a large tax base for the inflation tax. Moreover, by taking into account the effects of (binding) legal reserve requirements, the model of Bencivenga/Smith (1992) works in favour of the Anti-Tobin effect. However, since both versions use an overlapping generations framework with three-period lived agents a discussion within the context of the Diamond model is elusive.

is specified as a regime with an exogenously given, constant growth rate of the money stock, while the profile of bonds and interest-rates is endogenously determined within the model.

Under particular conditions discussed below, Schreft/Smith (1997) show that this specification of monetary policy in a non-trivial financial system gives rise to the existence of exactly two monetary steady-states. In particular, the low level equilibrium with a low capital stock is shown to be associated with a high value of outstanding government bonds and a high interest rate, signalling the rather inefficient operation of the financial system. At this equilibrium, the Anti-Tobin effect prevails and local dynamics are saddlepath stable with monotone adjustment behaviour towards the steady state. In contrast, the high level equilibrium displays a high level of physical capital and a low interest rate. The level of government bonds is also low - in fact, the government turns into the position of a net lender to the banking system. Reflecting the beneficial role of monetary policy, the high level equilibrium is shown to be of Tobin-nature. Moreover, local dynamics are indeterminate and adjustment behaviour towards the steady state may well be subject to endogenous volatility.

Commenting on these findings, Schreft/Smith (1997) give the following interpretation:

"...Not only are financial markets a source of indeterminacy of dynamical equilibria, but with multiple steady states, development trap phenomena are ubiquitous. In particular, economies with very similar - or even identical - initial capital stocks may, depending on their endogenous initial nominal interest rates, follow the saddlepath to the low capital stock steady state or one of the many paths approaching the high capital stock steady state. Economies that have high initial nominal interest rates will suffer the former fate, while economies that have low initial nominal interest rates will avoid it."[2]

Thus, the modified version of the Diamond model by Schreft/Smith (1997) suggests convincingly that the stance of monetary itself is a poor indicator of the growth prospects of an economy. Clearly, for the growth prospects of an economy it should make a difference whether the banking system is a large-scale investor in capital or whether it holds predominantly government debt. Similarly, a policy of comparatively tight money and stable prices, if not accompanied by a sufficient wave of optimism among private investors, might well be inferior to a rather loose monetary policy in a climate conducive to investment projects. In any case, the possibility of multiple equilibria signals that it is only of limited value to have knowledge of the current stance of the monetary policy of an economy. Instead, the entire package of fiscal and monetary measures needs to be addressed in a comprehensive manner, with

---

[2]Schreft/Smith (1997), p. 160.

particular attention being paid to the question how much credibility these measures find with the private sector.

For the remainder of this chapter we turn now to a more detailed discussion of the model of Schreft/Smith (1997) and reproduce its main results.

6.1 The model

Following Townsend (1980) and Mitsui/Watanabe (1989), the economy has a distinct spatial arrangement that allows money to act as a transferable store of value across otherwise strictly separated locations. More specifically, the economy is assumed to consist of two different locations, and each location contains a continuum of young agents with unit mass. Between the two locations, there is no trade or communication, and at the beginning of each period transactions in goods, labour, and asset markets occur autarkically within each location. However, after all markets are closed a constant random fraction $\pi \in (0, 1)$ of young agents gets relocated to the other location. Relocations between islands are symmetric, i.e. the size of the population on each island remains unaffected by the relocations.

As in the base model, all new-born agents are identical. Agents are endowed with one unit of labour when being young and have no labour endowment in their old age. Agents consume only when being old, and preferences are represented by a logarithmic utility function.

(**A 1**) Preferences of agents are given by:

$$u(c_t, c_{t+1}) = \ln(c_{t+1})$$

Reflecting the restrictions on trade, only currency can be moved between locations. In particular, arrangements are such that there is no way how relocated agents could transfer private credit instruments or government bonds across locations.[3] Thus, the random assignment of agents to locations simply serves the purpose to create a demand for the unique liquidity services offered by money. Due to the random nature of the relocations at the individual level, there is a genuine role for banks to offer insurance against the liquidity shocks. As a consequence, all savings will be intermediated and agents who

---

[3] While the first assumption simply stands for the absence of communication across locations, the second assumption is clearly more restrictive. Reflecting Wallace's argument on legal restrictions as summarized in chapter 3, Schreft/Smith (1997) acknowledge that "...the notion that bonds cannot be used in interlocational exchange could be motivated by the assumption that they are issued in large denominations and hence must be intermediated" (p. 162).

86

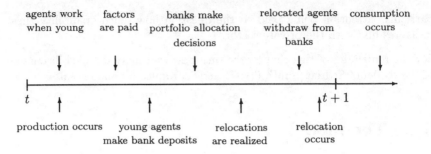

Figure 6.1: *Variation 2 - Timing of events*

get relocated will liquidate their entire savings. In short, the timing of events follows the pattern summarized in figure 6.1.[4]

Government: Let M_t denote in each location the stock of outside money per young agent in period t. Then, for all periods $t \geq 0$, in each location the money supply per capita follows the law of motion:

$$M_{t+1} = (1 + \mu) \cdot M_t \quad \text{with: } \mu > 0 \tag{6.1}$$

To simplify matters, the government is assumed to levy no taxes and to have no non-interest related expenditures.[5] Bonds are simply one-period bonds. Let b_t represent in each location the real amount of bonds per young agent in period t, paying gross real interest R_t^b in period $t+1$. Then, the government's budget constraint in t is given by:

$$R_{t-1}^b \cdot b_{t-1} = \frac{M_t - M_{t-1}}{p_t} + b_t \tag{6.2}$$

The right-hand side of (6.2) reflects that government revenues result from seigniorage and newly issued bonds, while the term on the left-hand side simply says that the government needs to honour the debt issued one period before.[6] However, since the path of bonds is assumed to be endogenously determined, the government might well become a net lender in the following analysis, i.e. b_t might well take on a negative value.

---

[4]Figure 6.1 is adapted from Schreft/Smith (1997), p. 162.

[5]As summarized by Azariadis (1993, ch. 20), multiple equilibria become possible in the standard Diamond model if the government is allowed to run a primary deficit. Here, the primary budget is assumed to be balanced. Clearly, this specification helps to identify sources of multiple equilibria which are specific to the arrangement proposed here.

[6]Appropriate initial conditions for the stocks of money and bonds are discussed below.

Production: Production takes place autarkically within each location. Again, production occurs according to a standard production function with constant returns to scale and diminishing marginal products. In particular, using the notation introduced above, the intensive form version of the production function satisfies the conditions:[7]

(A 2) The function $f(k)$ is twice continuously differentiable, positive, increasing, and strictly concave:

$$\text{(i) } f(k) > 0, \quad \text{(ii) } f'(k) > 0 \quad \text{(iii) } f''(k) < 0 \text{ for } k > 0.$$

(A 3) The function $f(k)$ admits the following behaviour of $w(k)$:

(i) $\lim_{k \to 0} f'(k) = \infty$, $w(0) > 0 \lor \lim_{k \to 0} f'(k) = \infty$, $w'(0) > \frac{1}{1-\pi}$,

(ii) $\lim_{k \to \infty} f'(k) < 1 \land \lim_{k \to \infty} \frac{w(k)}{k} = 0$,

(iii) $w'(k) > 0$, $w''(k) < 0$ for all $k > 0$.

Capital is assumed to depreciate entirely within the production process. Then, assuming that the market of the output good is perfectly competitive, the wage rate w_t and the rate of return on capital ρ_t are given by:

$$\rho_t = f'(k_t) \tag{6.3}$$
$$w_t = f(k_t) - k_t \cdot f'(k_t) = w(k_t) \tag{6.4}$$

Banks and asset markets: The banking sector is assumed to be subject to competition and free entry. Thus, when deciding upon the (per capita) composition of their portfolios between real balances (m), bonds (b), and investments in real capital (i), banks take the triple of corresponding gross rates of return $(p_t/p_{t+1}, R_t^b, \rho_{t+1})$ as given. On the deposit side, banks offer pairs of gross return rates (d_t^N, d_t^M), with d_t^M being paid in the case that agents need to 'move' (because of getting dislocated) and d_t^N being paid to 'non-moving' agents. Banks are Nash competitors and, when announcing pairs of return rates (d_t^N, d_t^M), they take the announcements of competing banks as given.

To ensure that money is indeed return-dominated, the nominal interest factor is assumed to exceed unity:

---

[7]Due to the Inada-type conditions mentioned under part (i) and (ii) of (A 3), assumptions (A 2) and (A 3) are slightly more restrictive than those stated in the previous chapter. However, the assumptions are still satisfied, for example, by the Cobb-Douglas function. Moreover, for any CES function with elasticity of substitution no less than one all assumptions apart from part (ii) of (A 3) are always satisfied, and parameter values satisfying part (ii) of (A 3) are easily found. For details, see appendix I at the end of the book.

(A 4) Money is strictly return-dominated:

$$R_t^b \cdot \frac{p_{t+1}}{p_t} > 1$$

Clearly, with (A 4) being satisfied, banks hold no reserves in excess of the perfectly anticipated withdrawal demands. Under competition, banks will be forced to maximize the expected utility of the representative depositor as given by:

$$\pi \cdot \ln[d_t^M \cdot w_t] + (1 - \pi) \cdot \ln[d_t^N \cdot w_t] \tag{6.5}$$

However, when maximizing over (6.5), banks are subject to a couple of constraints. Obviously, the balance sheet requires:

$$m_t + b_t + i_t \le w_t \tag{6.6}$$

With a predictable fraction π of depositors withdrawing prematurely, the return rate d_t^M offered to 'movers' needs to satisfy the constraint:

$$\pi \cdot d_t^M \cdot w_t \le p_t/p_{t+1} \cdot m_t \tag{6.7}$$

Correspondingly, for d_t^N needs to hold:

$$(1 - \pi) \cdot d_t^N \cdot w_t \le R_t^b \cdot b_t + \rho_{t+1} \cdot i_t \tag{6.8}$$

Furthermore, investments in real capital and reserve holdings per depositor are required to be non-negative:[8]

$$m_t \ge 0, \quad i_t \ge 0 \tag{6.9}$$

Given the logarithmic specification of the utility function, maximization of (6.5) over d_t^M, d_t^N, m_t, b_t, and i_t under the constraints (6.6)-(6.9) leads to the convenient solution, assuming that banks behave competitively:

$$m_t = \pi \cdot w(k_t) \tag{6.10}$$

With income and substitution effects exactly offsetting each other, (6.10) requires that banks choose optimally a reserve ratio $m/w(k)$ that does not respond to changes in return rates and equals the constant withdrawal probability π.[9]

---

[8] As mentioned above, no such restriction is made with respect to b_t, since we do not want to rule out a situation with $b_t < 0$ where the government turns into the position of a net lender towards the banking system.

[9] Clearly, the logarithmic specification of the utility function leads to a considerable simplification of the analysis. Note from (6.7) that (6.10) implies: $d_t^M = p_t/p_{t+1}$. Similarly, with $R_t^b = \rho_{t+1}$ holding via arbitrage, one obtains: $d_t^N = R_t^b$. In the discussion at the end of the chapter we indicate briefly how results change if this specification is relaxed.

6.2 Equilibrium conditions

With government bonds and real capital being perfect substitutes, arbitrage requires that we have in any competitive equilibrium:

$$R_t^b = \rho_{t+1} = f'(k_{t+1}) \tag{6.11}$$

Since capital depreciates entirely within the production process next period's capital stock will be given by $k_{t+1} = i_t$. Then, consolidation of the relevant constraints yields the following system of equations, describing how competitive equilibria evolve over time:[10]

$$k_{t+1} = (1-\pi) \cdot w(k_t) - b_t \tag{6.12}$$

$$b_{t+1} = f'(k_{t+1}) \cdot b_t - \frac{\mu}{1+\mu} \cdot \pi \cdot w(k_{t+1}) \tag{6.13}$$

$$f'(k_{t+1}) > p_t/p_{t+1} = \frac{1}{1+\mu} \cdot \frac{m_{t+1}}{m_t} \tag{6.14}$$

The system (6.12)-(6.14) lends itself nicely to a simple classification: while equation (6.12) assumes the role of the accumulation equation, equation (6.13) simply restates the budget constraint of the government. Finally, the relation (6.14) guarantees that money is return-dominated by all interest-bearing assets. Note that with (6.14) holding as strict inequality, equations (6.12) and (6.13) describe a two-dimensional system in k_t and b_t.

As far as initial conditions are concerned, we assume that each member of the initial old generation is endowed with k_0 units of capital and M_{-1} units of money, i.e. both k_0 and M_{-1} are taken as being predetermined. Moreover, at $t = 0$ the stock of bonds b_0 must satisfy:

$$\frac{M_0 - M_{-1}}{p_0} + b_0 = 0 \quad \Leftrightarrow \quad b_0 = M_{-1}/p_0 - \pi \cdot w(k_0) \tag{6.15}$$

With M_{-1} being predetermined, b_0 will be fixed for a fixed value of M_0 (since $p_0 = M_0 \cdot [\pi \cdot w(k_0)]^{-1}$), while b_0 will be free if M_0 is taken as endogenously determined.[11] However, as we will show below, under a more general utility function the reserve ratio chosen by banks will no longer be constant, and a fixed value of M_0 will therefore no longer suffice to determine b_0 by initial conditions. Thus, it seems reasonable to take the stock of bonds as a jumping variable with a free initial condition.

---

[10]Compared to (6.2), the budget constraint in (6.13) has been updated by one period. We also use the identity: $[M_{t+1} - M_t]/p_{t+1} = m_{t+1} \cdot \mu/(1+\mu)$.

[11]Endogeneity of M_0 is to be understood as a policy where the government satisfies in period 0 the entire demand for money at the going interest rate.

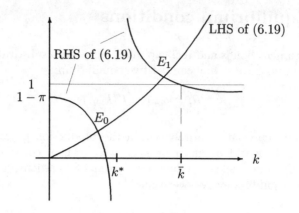

Figure 6.2: *Variation 2 - Steady state: existence*

Steady state equilibria: With all variables being constant over time, rearranging (6.12)-(6.14) yields the steady state conditions:

$$b = (1 - \pi) \cdot w(k) - k \tag{6.16}$$

$$b = \frac{\mu}{1 + \mu} \cdot \pi \cdot w(k) \cdot \frac{1}{f'(k) - 1} \tag{6.17}$$

$$f'(k) > 1/(1 + \mu) \tag{6.18}$$

As in the previous chapter we define: $\Omega(k) = k/w(k)$. Then, after eliminating b the system simplifies to:

$$\Omega(k) = (1 - \pi) - \frac{\frac{\mu}{1+\mu} \cdot \pi}{f'(k) - 1} \tag{6.19}$$

$$f'(k) > 1/(1 + \mu) \tag{6.20}$$

To prove the existence of multiple steady state equilibria of the system (6.19)-(6.20), we proceed in two steps.[12]

Proposition 1 *Equation (6.19) has exactly two solutions with $k > 0$.*

Proof: Concavity of $w(k)$ as given by part (iii) of (A 3) implies $\Omega'(k) > 0$. Thus, the LHS of (6.19) is strictly upward sloping as displayed in figure 6.2. By part (ii) of (A 3), $\Omega(k)$ tends to infinity for $k \to \infty$, while we have by

---

[12]To keep the analysis in line with the following discussion of dynamical properties of the system, our proof deviates from the proof given in Schreft/Smith (1997).

part(i) of (A 3): $0 \leq \lim_{k \to 0} \Omega(k) < 1 - \pi$.[13] It is straightforward to see that the graph of the RHS of (6.19) is made up of two downward sloping branches, with the discontinuity occurring at $k^* = (f')^{-1}[1]$. The following limits are readily established: by part(i) of (A 3), $\lim_{k \to 0} RHS(k) = 1 - \pi$. Similarly, by part (ii) of (A 3), $0 < \lim_{k \to \infty} RHS(k) < \infty$. Furthermore, one obtains: $\lim_{k \uparrow k^*} RHS(k) = -\infty$ and $\lim_{k \downarrow k^*} RHS(k) = \infty$. Thus, the two sides of equation (6.19) can be graphed as in figure 6.2 with exactly two intersections. q.e.d.

Proposition 2 *For a sufficiently large value of μ, there exist exactly two steady state equilibria solving the system (6.19)-(6.20).*

Proof: Two steady state equilibria will exist, if the larger value of k solving (6.19) satisfies: $k < \overline{k} = (f')^{-1}[1/(1 + \mu)]$. Note that the RHS of (6.19) evaluated at $\overline{k}$ yields unity. Furthermore, by raising μ the graph of the RHS of (6.19) shifts upward for $k > k^*$, while $\Omega(k)$ remains unaffected. Clearly, since $\lim_{k \to \infty} f'(k) < 1$ by virtue of part (ii) of (A 3), there must exist a high level equilibrium with $k^* < k < \overline{k}$ for μ being sufficiently large. q.e.d.

Multiple equilibria can emerge in this context because the net lending position of the government substantially differs between steady states. The low level equilibrium has a high interest rate and a positive amount of outstanding bonds, thereby crowding out investment in real capital. In contrast, the high level equilibrium is associated with a low interest rate. In fact, the real interest rate is negative, and, as equation (6.17) confirms, this ensures that the government becomes a net lender to the banking system. Thus, at this equilibrium the creation of additional money acts like a subsidy to capital formation since banks can finance further investment projects by borrowing additional money from the government.[14]

---

[13]In figure 6.2, we simply assume: $\Omega(0) = 0$. Thus, the graph corresponds, for example, to the case of a Cobb-Douglas function.

[14]However, this strong result vanishes if the primary budget is allowed to be unbalanced. Then, two equilibria, both with the government being a net borrower, are conceivable.

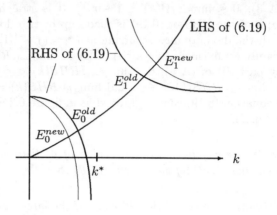

Figure 6.3: *Variation 2 - Steady state: comparative statics*

6.3 Policy effects

Comparative statics: Drawing on the proof of the preceding proposition, it is straightforward to classify the reaction of the capital stock to changes in the rate of monetary expansion μ in steady state comparison. As illustrated in figure 6.3, reaction patterns are as following:

Proposition 3 *Assume that the government increases permanently the rate of monetary expansion μ. Then, at the high level equilibrium the Tobin effect prevails, while the low level equilibrium is of Anti-Tobin nature.*

Proof: Totally differentiating (6.19) yields the reaction coefficient:

$$\frac{dk}{d\mu} = \frac{\pi}{1 - f'(k)} \cdot \frac{1}{(1+\mu)^2 \cdot [\Omega'(k) - \frac{\mu}{1+\mu} \cdot \frac{f''(k)\cdot\pi}{(f'(k)-1)^2}]}$$

Given our assumptions with respect to technology, the sign of the reaction coefficient is given by: $sign[\frac{dk}{d\mu}] = sign[1 - f'(k)]$. However, from the preceding section we know that the two steady states straddle $k^* = (f')^{-1}[1]$. q.e.d.

Dynamics: Following closely the analysis given in Schreft/Smith (1997), we indicate the local dynamics of equilibria, at least qualitatively, by establishing the appropriate phase diagram for the relevant equations (6.12) and (6.13). Throughout, it is assumed that a regime with exactly two steady states prevails.

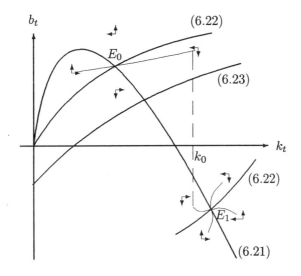

Figure 6.4: *Variation 2 - Steady state: dynamics*

According to (6.12), the evolution of k_t off-steady state satisfies $k_{t+1} \geq k_t$ iff:

$$(1 - \pi) \cdot w(k_t) - k_t \geq b_t \qquad (6.21)$$

Qualitatively, equation (6.21) at equality can be graphed as in figure 6.4, and the following proposition is straightforward:[15]

Proposition 4 *For points below (above) the graph of (6.21) at equality, the capital stock evolves according to:* $k_{t+1} > (<)k_t$.

Inserting (6.12) into (6.13), one easily verifies that the off-steady state behaviour of b_t satisfies $b_{t+1} \geq b_t$ iff:

$$\{f'[(1 - \pi) \cdot w(k_t) - b_t] - 1\} \cdot b_t \geq \pi \cdot \frac{\mu}{1 + \mu} \cdot w[(1 - \pi) \cdot w(k_t) - b_t] \quad (6.22)$$

The analysis of (6.22) is more involved and proceeds in three steps. First, to get a better grasp of (6.22) at equality, we define the locus:

$$b_t = (1 - \pi) \cdot w(k_t) - (f')^{-1}[1] \qquad (6.23)$$

---

[15] As in the previous section, we simply draw a graph as it corresponds, for example, to a Cobb-Douglas function.

The graph of (6.23) slopes upward in b_t-k_t-plane and intersects the horizontal axis at the uniquely defined value given by $(1 - \pi) \cdot w(k_t) = (f')^{-1}[1]$. Also, it is easily seen that for pairs of (k_t, b_t) above (below) the graph of (6.23) the marginal product, evaluated at the steady state, exceeds (falls short of) unity. Thus, for pairs of (k_t, b_t) above (below) the graph of (6.23), equation (6.22) at equality can only be satisfied for a positive (negative) level of bonds b_t.

Second, by virtue of (6.23), we can state the following two lemmata, describing the location and the slope of (6.22) at equality.

Lemma 1 *Consider values of k_t, satisfying $(1 - \pi) \cdot w(k_t) > (f')^{-1}[1]$. For each such k_t, there exist at least two values of b_t that satisfy (6.22) at equality. In particular, there is at least one positive and one negative value of b_t satisfying this condition.*

Lemma 2 *At both steady states, the graph of (6.22) at equality slopes upward.*

Proofs: see appendix.

Third, with the additional information provided by the two lemmata, one obtains easily a comprehensive classification, at least qualitatively, of the off-steady state behaviour of b_t. We summarize this classification in the following proposition:

Proposition 5 *In a neighbourhood of the steady state with $b_t > 0$, the stock of bonds evolves at points below (above) the graph of (6.22) at equality according to: $b_{t+1} < (>)b_t$. In contrast, in a neighbourhood of the steady state with $b_t < 0$, points below (above) the graph of (6.22) at equality have: $b_{t+1} > (<)b_t$.*

Proof: see appendix.

Given propositions 4 and 5, the dynamics of the system can be indicated by phase lines as shown in figure 6.4. With k_0 being given and b_0 being subject to a free initial condition, figure 6.4. suggests that the low level equilibrium is a saddle, while the high level equilibrium might well be a sink. However, as demonstrated in Schreft/Smith (1997), to confirm this conjecture further restrictions need to be imposed, and the exact proof, though standard, is rather tedious. Therefore, we conclude this section by reproducing the dynamical classification of equilibria as given by Schreft/Smith (1997) without proof:

Proposition 6 *Consider a constellation with two monetary steady states.*

a) Assume that the condition $\mu \leq \pi/(1-\pi)$ is satisfied. Then, any high level equilibrium is a sink, i.e. local adjustment behaviour towards the steady state is indeterminate. Moreover, adjustment may well be subject to endogenous volatility.

b) Assume that the production function is of Cobb-Douglas type: $f(k) = k^{\alpha}$, $\alpha \in (0,1)$. Then, any low level equilibrium is a saddle, and local adjustment behaviour of b_t and k_t towards the steady state is monotone.

Proof: see Schreft/Smith (1997, p. 173ff.).

Finally, note that figure 6.4. confirms the possibility of development trap phenomena as indicated in the quoted passage in the introduction. If the (predetermined) value of the capital stock k_0 of some economy and its rate of monetary expansion μ are common knowledge, this does not suffice, in the context of the model presented here, to pin down the path of further development. Instead, two economies with similar initial conditions may well end up on divergent paths. In other words, the fundamentals of the economy may not be informative enough to rule out self-fulfilling paths of divergent development.

6.4 Discussion

As indicated above, the analysis becomes more involved, once the special assumption of a logarithmic utility function is relaxed. Yet, this issue is addressed in related work by Bhattacharya/Guzman/Huybens/Smith (1997) and Schreft/Smith (1998). In particular, both studies use the framework introduced in Schreft/Smith (1997), but employ a CRRA utility function:

$$u(c_{t+1}) = \frac{1}{1-\varepsilon} \cdot c_{t+1}^{1-\varepsilon} \quad \varepsilon > 0, \varepsilon \neq 1 \tag{6.24}$$

As to be expected, the optimal reserve ratio chosen by banks is upon this modification no longer invariant to return rates. In particular, with the nominal interest factor I_t being the relevant return premium of capital and bonds over money, the solution of the decision problem (6.5) subject to the constraints (6.6)-(6.9) yields now for the optimal reserve ratio:

$$\gamma(I_t) = \frac{m_t}{w(k_t)} = \frac{1}{1 + \frac{1-\pi}{\pi} \cdot I_t^{\frac{1-\varepsilon}{\varepsilon}}} \tag{6.25}$$

With the reserve ratio being given by (6.25), binding equilibrium conditions are now governed by a three-dimensional system in k_t, b_t, and m_t. Yet, to re-establish a two-dimensional system along the lines of Diamond (1965), both

Schreft/Smith (1998) and Bhattacharya/Guzman/Huybens/Smith (1997) concentrate on a joint regime of fiscal and monetary policy that fixes by means of open market operations the ratio of bonds to real balances at a constant level:[16]

$$\frac{b_t}{m_t} = \beta \quad \nabla t \tag{6.26}$$

Under the modified policy rule (6.26), Schreft/Smith (1998) address the behaviour of the system for a high degree of risk aversion, i.e. for the parameter range $\varepsilon > 1$.[17] For this case, it is straightforward to see from (6.25) that the reserve ratio will be increasing in the interest factor, i.e. one obtains: $\gamma'(I) > 0$. It is this feature that establishes a close similarity of the modified equilibrium conditions to those discussed in the main section. In particular, Schreft/Smith (1998) show that multiple monetary steady states may well occur due to the following mechanism: for a given value of β, assume that the level of bonds b is 'high', leading to a 'high' degree of crowding out of investment in real capital. Thus, the interest rate will be 'high', and with $\gamma'(I) > 0$ this will prompt a 'high' demand for reserves. In contrast, assume now that the level of b is 'low'. Then, with little crowding out taking place, investment in real capital will be 'high', leading to a 'low' interest rate and a 'low' demand for reserves. Thus, the same level of β may well be associated with different levels of real balances, bonds, and real capital, and multiple monetary steady states may well exist.

In contrast, Bhattacharya/Guzman/Huybens/Smith (1997) address the case of risk loving agents with $\varepsilon < 1$. Now, the substitution effect dominates over the income effect, and the reserve ratio chosen by banks is therefore a declining function of the interest factor, i.e. one obtains $\gamma'(I_t) > 0$. This implies that the above sketched mechanism no longer works, and, indeed, the authors show that for this case multiple monetary steady states no longer exist.

---

[16]Under this specification, a change in β can be interpreted as a variation in the 'tightness' of open market operations.

[17]Equivalently, the case of $\varepsilon > 1$ represents a constellation in which consumption opportunities in the states of 'relocation' and 'no-relocation' are regarded as gross complements, with the income effect dominating over the substitution effect.

6.5   Appendix

Proof of Lemma 1:

The proof proceeds in two steps.

i) First, we prove that for any fixed k_t with $(1 - \pi) \cdot w(k_t) > (f')^{-1}[1]$ there exists a value for b_t with $b_t > 0$, solving (6.22) at equality. Let $b_t = (1 - \pi) \cdot w(k_t)$. Then the LHS of (6.22) tends to infinity while the RHS approaches the finite value $\pi \cdot \frac{\mu}{1+\mu} \cdot w(0)$. Correspondingly, let now $b_t = (1 - \pi) \cdot w(k_t) - (f')^{-1}[1]$. In this case, the LHS becomes zero while the RHS attains the positive value $\pi \cdot \frac{\mu}{1+\mu} \cdot w[(f')^{-1}[1]]$. Thus, by continuity of both sides in b_t and the intermediate value theorem, there must exist a positive value of b_t that solves (6.22) at equality. q.e.d.

ii) Second, we prove now that for any fixed k_t with $(1 - \pi) \cdot w(k_t) > (f')^{-1}[1]$ there exists a value for b_t with $b_t < 0$, solving (6.22) at equality. Rearranging of (6.22) at equality yields:

$$1 - f'[(1 - \pi) \cdot w(k_t) - b_t] = -\pi \cdot \frac{\mu}{1+\mu} \cdot \frac{w[(1 - \pi) \cdot w(k_t) - b_t]}{b_t} \qquad (6.27)$$

Let $b_t \to 0$ with $b_t < 0$. Then, the LHS of (6.27) approaches some value $\theta_1 \in (0, 1)$ while the RHS of (6.27) tends to infinity. Next, consider the case $b_t \to -\infty$. While the LHS of (6.27) tends to some value $\theta_2 \in (0, 1]$, we rearrange the RHS slightly before we establish the limit. Exploiting the identity $w(k) = f(k) - f'(k) \cdot k$, the RHS can be alternatively written as: $\pi \cdot \frac{\mu}{1+\mu} \cdot \{f[.]/(-b_t) + [(1 - \pi) \cdot w(k_t)/b_t - 1] \cdot f'[.]\}$. Then, by the rule of L'Hôpital, for $b_t \to -\infty$ the RHS tends to zero. Again, by continuity of both sides in b_t and the intermediate value theorem, there must exist a negative value of b_t that solves (6.22) at equality. q.e.d.

Proof of Lemma 2:

Differentiating (6.22) yields:

$$\frac{d\,b_t}{d\,k_t} = \frac{(1 - \pi) \cdot w'(k_t) \cdot \{\pi \cdot \frac{\mu}{1+\mu} \cdot w'[.] - b_t \cdot f''[.]\}}{f'[.] - 1 + \pi \cdot \frac{\mu}{1+\mu} \cdot w'[.] - b_t \cdot f''[.]} \qquad (6.28)$$

For the low level equilibrium with $f'[.] > 1$ and $b > 0$, both the denominator and the numerator will be unambiguously positive. Thus, (6.22) slopes upward at the low level equilibrium.

Things are less obvious for the high level equilibrium with $f'[.] < 1$ and $b < 0$. However, as we will show below, at the high level equilibrium the following condition holds:

$$\pi \cdot \frac{\mu}{1+\mu} \cdot w'[.] < b_t \cdot f''[.] \qquad (6.29)$$

98

Note that (6.29) is a sufficient condition for (6.22) to slope upward at the high level equilibrium. To establish that (6.29) is indeed satisfied, we use again the identity $w'(k) = -f''(k) \cdot k$. Remember that the omitted term in brackets is given by: $[.] = (1 - \pi) \cdot w(k_t) - b_t$. Thus, rearranging terms in (6.29) yields: $\pi \cdot \frac{\mu}{1+\mu} \cdot (1-\pi) \cdot w(k) < (\pi \cdot \frac{\mu}{1+\mu} - 1) \cdot b$. From (6.17), one obtains: $b = \frac{\mu}{1+\mu} \cdot \pi \cdot w(k)/[f'(k) - 1]$. After manipulating terms, one sees that (6.29) holds iff: $f'(k) > \pi/[(1 + \mu) \cdot (\pi - 1)]$. Note that $\pi/[(1 + \mu) \cdot (\pi - 1)] < 0$ will always be satisfied, while $f'(k)$ is positive by assumption. Thus, at the high level equilibrium (6.29) is satisfied. q.e.d.

Proof of proposition 5:

The proposition follows immediately from Lemma 2. The first part of the proposition will be true if the denominator in (6.28) is positive. As argued above, this will be the case at the low level equilibrium. In contrast, the second part of the proposition will hold, if the denominator in (6.28) is negative. At the high level equilibrium, with (6.29) being satisfied as shown above, this will be the case. q.e.d.

Chapter 7

Variation 3: Standard cash-in-advance constraint and endogenous savings

In our presentation up to this point no attempt has been made to address explicitly the transactions role of money. In contrast, in this and the following chapters we discuss various aspects related to this role in more detail. As a common theme, we replace in all these chapters the 'bubbly' view on money as developed in the base model with versions of the alternative, 'fundamentalist' view on money, which asserts that money is ultimately held because certain transactions need to be settled by payment via money. Despite its strong emphasis on transaction-related aspects of money, the fundamentalist view does not dispute the importance of the store of value function of money, i.e. the transactions and the store of value function are by no means considered as being mutually exclusive. Yet, following Tirole (1985), the fundamentalist view denies the idea that money is a pure store of value which is held exclusively for speculative reasons, as stressed in the overlapping generations literature in the spirit of Samuelson (1958), Diamond (1965), and Wallace (1980). Instead, it is argued that there is a fundamental value attached to money since its use is 'essential' for the settlement of certain transactions, and this value allows money to be a widely accepted store of value despite being return-dominated by interest-bearing assets.

It is the purpose of this chapter to show that the results obtained for the base model can be easily reversed once the transactions role of money is adequately addressed. To this end, we present a framework that adds to the narrow overlapping generations friction a version of a standard cash-in-advance constraint which accounts for the transactions services offered by money in a particularly simple manner. Drawing on recent work by Hahn/Solow (1995),

100

we assume that the cash-in-advance constraint applies only to old agents.[1] Accordingly, we take it as given that due to a legal restriction an exogenously fixed fraction of old age consumption needs to be carried out by payment in cash. We readily admit that the imposition of this type of constraint has a strong ad-hoc element and we do not attempt to rationalize it from first principles. Instead, this specification simply serves the purpose to challenge the plausibility of the Tobin effect from a fundamentalist perspective with a minimum of effort, i.e. our discussion proceeds closely along the lines of the base model as presented in chapter 4. However, being aware of the shortcomings of the version presented here, we leave it for the following chapter to develop a more plausible framework that endogenizes the use of money in an environment with truly competing means of payment, which are characterized by distinct survival values in the spirit of Fama (1983).

Reflecting the nature of the cash-in-advance constraint, young agents will hold a certain fraction of their savings in the form of real balances, even if money is strictly return-dominated by interest-bearing assets. Importantly, the cash-in-advance specification removes the substitutability assumption with respect to capital and money. To illustrate this point, assume that due to some policy change young agents expect (correctly) a higher inflation rate. Ceteris paribus this has the effect that both the value of real balances in the second period and the share of real balances in overall second period income will be lower than before. However, to restore liquidity in the second period as required by the cash-in-advance constraint, young agents will have to rearrange their portfolios by shifting from capital to money holdings for any given level of savings. This negative effect on capital formation will be even more pronounced if present and future consumption goods are gross substitutes: since the higher inflation rate translates into a lower effective return on overall savings, agents will reduce under gross substitutability the level of savings as well, i.e. for this specification both the portfolio and the savings effect work in the same direction.

In short, due to the introduction of the cash-in-advance constraint the mechanics of the model work now strongly in favour of the Anti-Tobin effect. Also, we establish that dynamics of the economy are no longer as in the base model, i.e. monetary steady states cease to be saddlepath stable. We demonstrate that further restrictions need to be imposed to rule out that steady states are entirely unstable. Yet, further investigating this issue in a set-up with Cobb-Douglas-type preferences and a Cobb-Douglas production

---

[1]Hahn/Solow (1995) use a monetary version of an overlapping generations framework to demonstrate broadly that monetary production economies, as envisaged by Keynes, may well be inherently unstable despite perfectly competitive markets with flexible wages and prices. Consequently, the model is designed to produce an economy in which, contrary to the new-classical proposition of policy ineffectiveness, some sort of active stabilization policy at the macroeconomic level is shown to be the adequate response to shocks. Here, we extract for our purposes only the set-up of the cash-in-advance constraint.

function, we show that now the unique monetary steady state will always be entirely stable, with adjustment behaviour towards the steady state being monotone, though indeterminate.

7.1 The model

Apart from the cash-in-advance constraint imposed on old agents, the model is virtually identical to the base model. Thus, without commenting on the details, we restate now briefly the essential elements as described in chapter 4.

Production: Production occurs according to a standard neoclassical production function with constant returns to scale and the familiar properties in intensive form:

(A 1) The function $f(k)$ is twice continuously differentiable, positive, increasing, and strictly concave:

(i) $f(k) > 0$, (ii) $f'(k) > 0$ (iii) $f''(k) < 0$ for $k > 0$.

All markets are subject to perfect competition. For simplicity, we assume that the capital stock depreciates entirely in the production process. Thus, for $\delta = 1$, factor returns are given by:

$$\rho_t = f'(k_t) \tag{7.1}$$
$$w_t = f(k_t) - f'(k_t) \cdot k_t = w(k_t) \tag{7.2}$$

Moreover, for reasons to become transparent below, we assume with respect to the overall income received by capital:[2]

(A 2) The function $f(k)$ satisfies the condition:

(i) $\lim_{k \to 0} f'(k) \cdot k = 0$ (ii) $\dfrac{d\,f'(k) \cdot k}{k} > 0$ for $k > 0$.

Government: Money is the only outside asset of the economy and grows over time at a constant rate μ:

$$M_t = (1 + \mu) \cdot M_{t-1} \quad \text{with: } \mu > 0 \tag{7.3}$$

---

[2]Assumption (A 2) is not very restrictive. We show in appendix I at the end of the book that it is satisfied, for example, by any Cobb-Douglas function and any CES function with elasticity of substitution no less than one.

In period t, the government is assumed to consume g_t units of the output good per young agent. Seigniorage is the only revenue source of the government and the budget constraint of the government is given by:

$$g_t = \frac{M_t - M_{t-1}}{p_t} = \frac{\mu}{1+\mu} \cdot \frac{M_t}{p_t} \qquad (7.4)$$

Consumers: Agents want to consume positive amounts of the single output good in both periods of their life. More specifically, preferences can be represented by an intertemporal utility function in the following manner:

(A 3) The function $U(c_t^y, c_{t+1}^o)$ has the standard properties:

(i) The function $U(c_t^y, c_{t+1}^o)$ is twice continuously differentiable, strictly quasiconcave, and increasing in both arguments on the interior of the consumption set R_+^2.

(ii) Starvation is avoided in both periods:

$$\lim_{c_t^y \to 0} U_1(c_t^y, c_{t+1}^o) = \infty \quad \text{for } c_{t+1}^o > 0,$$

$$\lim_{c_{t+1}^o \to 0} U_1(c_t^y, c_{t+1}^o) = \infty \quad \text{for } c_t^y > 0.$$

(iii) Both goods c_t^y and c_{t+1}^o are normal goods.

In period t, young agents allocate their savings s_t between real balances m_t and deposits d_t. Again, deposits represent a claim to the return on capital and they are issued by competitively operating intermediaries. When deciding about the composition of their portfolios, young agents know in advance that a certain fraction of second period consumption needs to be financed by payment in cash. Let $1/\xi$ denote this fraction, with $\xi > 1$. Moreover, let R_t^d and R_t^m denote the gross return rates on deposits and real balances, respectively. Thus, the cash-in-advance constraint on old age consumption takes the form:

$$R_t^m \cdot m_t \geq \frac{1}{\xi} \cdot [R_t^d \cdot d_t + R_t^m \cdot m_t] \qquad (7.5)$$

We assume throughout that money is weakly return-dominated by deposits:

(A 4) Deposits weakly return-dominate money:

$$R_t^d \geq R_t^m \text{ for all } t$$

Let R_t denote the effective return rate on overall savings. Clearly, for $R_t^d > R_t^m$ the effective return rate R_t will be less than R_t^d, and young agents will economize on money holdings such that (7.5) holds as strict equality.

Moreover, we assume for simplicity that for the degenerate case $R_t^d = R_t^m$ equation (7.5) continues to hold as a strict equality, i.e. whenever agents are indifferent between deposits and real balances they break the tie in favour of deposits.[3]

To calculate the fraction of savings to be held in real balances, we rewrite (7.5) at equality as:

$$\xi \cdot R_t^m \cdot m_t = R_t^d \cdot s_t - (R_t^d - R_t^m) \cdot m_t \qquad (7.6)$$

Rearranging (7.6) yields:

$$m_t = \frac{R_t^d}{R_t^d + (\xi - 1) \cdot R_t^m} \cdot s_t \qquad (7.7)$$

The effective return rate R_t needs to satisfy the equation:

$$\xi \cdot R_t^m \cdot m_t = R_t \cdot s_t \qquad (7.8)$$

Then, combining (7.8) with (7.7) yields for R_t:

$$R_t = \frac{\xi}{\frac{\xi-1}{R_t^d} + \frac{1}{R_t^m}} \qquad (7.9)$$

Note that for $\xi \to \infty$ the cash-in-advance constraint vanishes, i.e. $R_t \to R_t^d$ and all savings will be deposited with $m_t \to 0$. Conversely, for $\xi \to 1$ all second period purchases need to be cash-financed. Thus, all savings will be held as real balances $(m_t \to s_t)$ and $R_t \to R_t^m$.

With the composition of savings being governed by (7.7), the decision problem of young agents can be stated as:

$$\max_{c_t^y, s_t, c_{t+1}^o} U(c_t^y, c_{t+1}^o) + \lambda_t \cdot (w_t - c_t^y - s_t) + \nu_t \cdot (R_t \cdot s_t - c_{t+1}^o) \qquad (7.10)$$

By assumption (A 3), there exists a uniquely defined solution (c_t^y, s_t, c_{t+1}^o) of optimizing values depending on (w_t, R_t). In order to obtain clear-cut comparative statics results, we assume as in chapter 4 that the income effect of a rise in R_t never dominates the substitution effect:[4]

(A 5) Savings are a non-decreasing function of the effective interest rate:

$$\frac{\partial s(w_t, R_t)}{\partial R_t} \geq 0 \text{ for all } (w_t, R_t^d) \geq 0$$

---

[3]For a more detailed discussion of the degenerate situation of 'portfolio indifference', see Hahn/Solow (1995), p. 20.

[4]Note that for $\frac{\partial s(w_t, R_t)}{\partial R_t} > 0$ present and future consumption goods are gross substitutes. We will return to such a constellation below.

Upon this additional assumption, optimal consumer behaviour can be summarized as:

$$c_t^y = c^y(w_t, R_t) \quad \text{with: } c_w^y > 0, c_R^y \leq 0 \qquad (7.11)$$

$$s_t = m_t + d_t = s(w_t, R_t) \quad \text{with: } s_w > 0, s_R \geq 0 \qquad (7.12)$$

7.2 Equilibrium conditions

Equilibrium conditions can be derived in close analogy to the procedure presented in chapter 4. In particular, the zero profit condition on the side of intermediaries implies that the conditions $d_t = k_{t+1}$ and $f'(k_{t+1}) = R_t^d$ need to be satisfied. Combining equations (7.1)-(7.12), yields the set of dynamical equilibrium conditions:

$$g_t = \frac{\mu}{1+\mu} \cdot m_t \qquad (7.13)$$

$$R_t^d = f'(k_{t+1}) \geq R_t^m = \frac{1}{1+\mu} \cdot \frac{m_{t+1}}{m_t} \qquad (7.14)$$

$$R_t = \frac{\xi}{\frac{\xi-1}{f'(k_{t+1})} + (1+\mu) \cdot \frac{m_t}{m_{t+1}}} \qquad (7.15)$$

$$k_{t+1} + m_t = s(R_t, w(k_t)) \qquad (7.16)$$

$$m_{t+1} = \frac{1+\mu}{\xi-1} \cdot f'(k_{t+1}) \cdot k_{t+1} \qquad (7.17)$$

Equation (7.13) restates the budget constraint of the government. As in the previous chapters, we treat g_t as being endogenously determined. Thus, our analysis concentrates exclusively on the system (7.14)-(7.17) which describes the evolution of k_t and m_t over time. Equation (7.14) restates assumption (A 3), implying that the cash-in-advance constraint will always bind. Equation (7.15) follows from (7.9) and defines the effective return on savings in terms of the equilibrium return rates on deposits and real balances. Equation (7.16) represents the accumulation equation of the system. Finally, the version of the cash-in-advance constraint given in (7.17) follows immediately from (7.5) and replaces the arbitrage relation of the base model.

Steady state equilibria: Again, we begin our analysis of the equilibrium conditions by considering the special case of steady state equilibria. In steady state, equations (7.14)-(7.17) can be rewritten as:

$$f'(k) \geq \frac{1}{1+\mu} \qquad (7.18)$$

$$R(k,\mu) = \frac{\xi}{\frac{\xi-1}{f'(k)} + 1 + \mu} \qquad (7.19)$$

$$k + m = s(R(k,\mu), w(k)) \qquad (7.20)$$

$$m \;=\; \frac{1+\mu}{\xi-1}\cdot f'(k)\cdot k \tag{7.21}$$

As discussed extensively in chapter 4, the interaction of preferences and technology in equation (7.20) makes it unpleasant to establish conditions which ensure the existence of a steady state equilibrium. Here, this difficulty is exacerbated by the fact that the nature of the cash-in-advance constraint renders the notion of a pure inside money equilibrium with $m = 0$ entirely meaningless. However, the existence of a pair $(k, m) > 0$ solving equations (7.19)-(7.21) is clearly a necessary condition for the existence of a steady state solution of the entire system (7.18)-(7.21). Thus, to secure the existence of such a pair we state now a modified version of assumption (A 2*) of chapter 4.[5]

(A 6) The savings function $s(R(k,\mu), w(k))$ and the income received by capital as given by the term $f'(k)\cdot k$ have the properties:

(i) $\lim\limits_{k\to 0} \frac{\partial s(R(k,\mu),w(k))}{\partial k} > 1 \;\vee\; \lim\limits_{k\to 0} s(R(k,\mu), w(k)) > 0,$

(ii) $\lim\limits_{k\to\infty} \frac{s(R(k,\mu),w(k))}{k} < 1,$

(iii) $\frac{\partial s(R(k,\mu),w(k))}{\partial k} > 0,\; \frac{\partial^2 s(R(k,\mu),w(k))}{\partial k^2} < 0,$ for $k > 0$, i.e. $s(k,\mu)$ is strictly concave,

(iv) $\lim\limits_{k\to 0} \frac{\partial s(R(k,\mu),w(k))}{\partial k} > \frac{1+\mu}{\xi-1}\cdot \lim\limits_{k\to 0} \frac{\partial f'(k)\cdot k}{\partial k} \;\vee\; \lim\limits_{k\to 0} s(R(k,\mu), w(k)) > 0.$

Essentially, as the following proposition reflects, assumption (A 6) helps to generate candidate solutions for a steady state equilibrium:

Proposition 1 *a) Assume that the overlapping generations economy with a cash-in-advance constraint as characterized by assumptions (A 1)-(A 5) satisfies also assumption (A 6). Then, there exists a pair $(k, m) > 0$ that solves equations (7.20) and (7.21).*

b) Any pair (k, m) derived under a) that satisfies the return-dominance condition (7.18) constitutes a monetary steady state equilibrium.

Proof: Ad a): Parts (i)-(iii) of (A 6) guarantee that the accumulation equation (7.20) can be drawn as in figure 7.1: (i) ensures that $m > 0$ at least near the origin, (ii) guarantees that $m(k)$ is a strictly concave function, and by part (iii) there exists a unique, positive solution $k^{max} > 0$ which solves the equation $k = s(R(k,\mu), w(k))$. Correspondingly, we have $m(k) < 0 \Leftrightarrow k > k^{max}$.

---

[5]Deviating from assumption (A 2*) of chapter 4, assumption (A 6) operates not only with the accumulation equation, but also with the arbitrage relation as given by the cash-in-advance constraint (7.21).

106

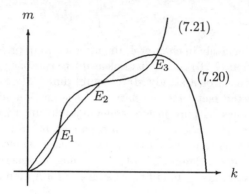

Figure 7.1: *Variation 3 - Steady state: multiple equilibria*

Due to (A 2), the cash-in-advance constraint (7.21) satisfies $m(0) = 0$ and
increases in m-k-plane. Finally, part (iv) of (A 6) ensures that both loci have
an intersection in the positive orthant. Ad b): The argument in a situation
with $f'(k) \geq \frac{1}{1+\mu}$ is obvious. In contrast, assume that the solution found
under a) satisfies: $f'(k) < \frac{1}{1+\mu}$. Then, young agents have no incentive to
invest in deposits, resulting in $k = 0$. However, by construction $(k, m) > 0$.
Thus, such a solution is not consistent with a perfect foresight equilibrium.
q.e.d.

How restrictive is assumption (A 6) in combination with the return-dominance
condition (7.18) ? We will demonstrate below that it is not difficult to find
parametrized versions of our economy that admit the existence of a unique
steady state. However, as indicated in figure 7.1, the assumptions made so
far are not strong enough to rule out the possibility of multiple steady states:
while in the base model the nature of the arbitrage relation ensured a unique
outside money steady state, in the version presented here the cash-in-advance
constraint may well lead to a situation with multiple steady states.

7.3   Policy effects

Comparative statics: Again, we want to establish how a permanent change
in the rate of monetary expansion μ affects in steady state comparison the
capital stock, and hence the overall level of economic activity.

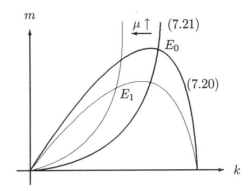

Figure 7.2: *Variation 3 - Steady state: comparative statics* $(s_R > 0)$

Proposition 2 *Assume that the rate of monetary expansion μ is permanently raised. Moreover, assume that the economy exhibits a unique steady state. Then, in the new steady state equilibrium the capital stock will be lower than before, i.e. the Anti-Tobin effect prevails.*

Proof: Combining (7.20) and (7.21), one obtains:

$$s(R(k,\mu), w(k)) - k = \frac{1+\mu}{\xi - 1} \cdot f'(k) \cdot k \tag{7.22}$$

Differentiating yields:

$$\frac{\partial k}{\partial \mu} = \frac{\frac{1}{\xi-1} \cdot f'(k) \cdot k - s_R \cdot \frac{\partial R}{\partial \mu}}{[s_R \cdot \frac{\partial R}{\partial k} + s_w \cdot \frac{\partial w}{\partial k} - 1] - [\frac{1+\mu}{\xi-1} \cdot (f''(k) \cdot k + f'(k))]} \tag{7.23}$$

From equation (7.19), we have: $\frac{\partial R}{\partial \mu} < 0$ and $\frac{\partial R}{\partial k} < 0$. Thus, by assumptions (A 2) and (A 5), the numerator of (7.23) is unambiguously positive. In the denominator, the terms in brackets represent the slopes of the accumulation equation (7.20) and the cash–in–advance constraint (7.21) in m-k-plane, respectively. As to be inferred from figure 7.2, the slope of the cash-in-advance constraint, evaluated at the equilibrium, must exceed the slope of the accumulation equation in a situation with a unique steady state. Thus, the denominator is negative, and the Anti-Tobin effect needs to prevail. q.e.d.

Evidently, assumption (A 5) needs to be invoked in order to obtain an unambiguous result. This can be interpreted as following: assume that present and future consumption goods are gross substitutes, i.e. consider the case $s_R > 0$. Then, an increase in μ induces not only a portfolio shift away from capital for any given level of savings (as expressed in the leftward shift of the cash-in-advance constraint in figure 7.2), but also a reduction in overall savings because of the decline of the effective return rate R (as expressed in the downward shift of the accumulation equation in figure 7.2). Thus, both the portfolio and the savings level effect work in the same direction and reduce the level of capital formation. Clearly, if present and future consumption goods were to be gross complements both effects would work in opposite directions and the overall effect would be a priori indeterminate.

Similarly, it is straightforward to show that in a situation with a unique steady state the relaxation of the cash-in-advance constraint leads to a higher steady state capital stock:

Proposition 3 *Assume that the cash-in-advance constraint is relaxed, i.e. ξ increases. Moreover, assume that the economy exhibits a unique steady state where money is strictly return-dominated with $f'(k) > \frac{1}{1+\mu}$. Then, in the new steady state the capital stock will be higher than before.*

Proof: Differentiating (7.22) yields:

$$\frac{\partial k}{\partial \xi} = \frac{-\frac{1+\mu}{(\xi-1)^2} \cdot f'(k) \cdot k - s_R \cdot \frac{\partial R}{\partial \xi}}{[s_R \cdot \frac{\partial R}{\partial k} + s_w \cdot \frac{\partial w}{\partial k} - 1] - [\frac{1+\mu}{\xi-1} \cdot (f''(k) \cdot k + f'(k))]} \qquad (7.24)$$

Differentiating (7.19), one easily shows: $f'(k) > \frac{1}{1+\mu} \Rightarrow \frac{\partial R}{\partial \xi} > 0$. Thus, the numerator of (7.24) is negative. However, in a constellation with a unique steady state the denominator is also negative, as shown in the proof of proposition 2. Hence, the reaction coefficient in (7.24) is unambiguously positive. q.e.d.

To illustrate the results we have established so far, we present now a particularly simple parametrization of the economy.

Example:

$$y = f(k) = k^\alpha, \quad \alpha \in (0,1) \qquad (7.25)$$
$$U(c_t^y, c_{t+1}^o) = \beta \cdot \ln(c_t^y) + (1-\beta) \cdot \ln(c_{t+1}^o), \quad \beta \in (0,1) \qquad (7.26)$$

One easily verifies that the functions satisfy the assumptions (A 1), (A 2), (A 3), and (A5). In particular, for Cobb-Douglas-type preferences the income and substitution effect with respect to a change in R are exactly offsetting, i.e. $s_R = 0$ obtains. Moreover, savings are a constant fraction $1 - \beta$ of wage income, which is given by the expression $w(k) = (1 - \alpha) \cdot k^\alpha$. In summary, the accumulation equation (7.20) and the cash-in-advance constraint (7.21) are now given by:

$$k + m \ = \ s = (1 - \beta) \cdot (1 - \alpha) \cdot k^\alpha \tag{7.27}$$

$$m \ = \ \frac{1 + \mu}{\xi - 1} \cdot \alpha \cdot k^\alpha \tag{7.28}$$

As demonstrated in appendix I at the end of the book, one readily shows that parts (i)-(iii) of (A 6) are satisfied. However, since both curves pass through the origin, part (iv) of (A 6) requires that the slope of the accumulation equation exceeds the slope of the cash-in-advance constraint at $k = 0$. Thus, the following condition needs to be met:

$$[(1 - \beta) \cdot (1 - \alpha) - \frac{1 + \mu}{\xi - 1} \cdot \alpha] \cdot \alpha \cdot \lim_{k \to 0} k^{\alpha - 1} > 0 \tag{7.29}$$

Clearly, condition (7.29) is satisfied if and only if the term in brackets is positive. Rearranging equations (7.27) and (7.28) yields the unique value of the capital stock which qualifies for a candidate steady state solution:

$$k = \left[(1 - \beta) \cdot (1 - \alpha) - \frac{1 + \mu}{\xi - 1} \cdot \alpha \right]^{\frac{1}{1 - \alpha}} \tag{7.30}$$

However, one easily selects 'plausible' parameter values such that condition (7.29) is satisfied and k as given by (7.30) is indeed an admissible solution. For example, let: $\beta = 0.7$, $\alpha = 0.25$, $\mu = 0.05$ and $\xi = 10$. Then, (7.29) is clearly satisfied, and steady state values of k and m are given by: $k = 0.11$, $m = 0.02$. One readily verifies that $f'(k) > 1/(1+\mu)$ as required by condition (7.18) holds as well. Finally, confirming propositions 2 and 3, the solution given by (7.30) has the property that k declines in μ and increases in ξ.

Dynamics: We conclude this chapter by pointing out that the differences in terms of comparative statics results between the economy presented here and the economy of the base model also translate into different dynamical properties. While for the base model local adjustment behaviour around the outside money steady state was shown to be saddlepath stable, results are less clear-cut for the economy with a cash-in-advance constraint. In fact, without imposing further restrictions we cannot rule out the unpleasant situation of steady states being entirely unstable. However, for the example presented in the previous section the ambiguity vanishes and the unique steady state will always be stable:[6]

---

[6]The classification given in proposition 4 holds only for steady state constellations in which money is strictly return dominated. In boundary regimes with $f'(k) = 1/(1 + \mu)$ the relevant approximations are no longer valid and dynamics will therefore be different.

110

Proposition 4 *Consider the economy with Cobb-Douglas-type preferences and a Cobb-Douglas production function as specified in (7.25) and (7.26). Furthermore, assume that money is strictly return-dominated, i.e. $f'(k) > 1/(1+\mu)$ holds. Then, the unique steady state will be locally stable and adjustment behaviour will be monotone, though indeterminate.*

Proof: see appendix.

Undoubtedly, the way we have addressed in this chapter the transactions role of money has been rather primitive and by no means 'realistic'. However, due to the simple arrangement of the economy, we have been able to indicate in a transparent manner that the mechanics of the base model are seriously at risk, once the pure store of value function of money is abandoned. And not surprisingly, we reach a similar conclusion in the following chapter in which we present a richer (and potentially more 'realistic') framework.

7.4 Appendix

Proof of proposition 4:

Rewriting equations (7.15)-(7.17), dynamics of the system are given by:

$$R_t = \frac{\xi}{\frac{\xi-1}{f'(k_{t+1})} + (1+\mu) \cdot \frac{m_t}{m_{t+1}}} \tag{7.31}$$

$$k_{t+1} + m_t = s(R_t(k_{t+1}, m_t, m_{t+1}), w(k_t)) \tag{7.32}$$

$$m_{t+1} = \frac{1+\mu}{\xi-1} \cdot f'(k_{t+1}) \cdot k_{t+1} \tag{7.33}$$

Note that the system has a simple recursive structure, since in equation (7.33) m_{t+1} depends only on k_{t+1}.[7] Because of this special structure the Jacobian matrix J of the system is not invertible (i.e. $Det(J) = 0$), and the procedure outlined in appendix II to classify equilibrium dynamics is therefore not appropriate. Instead, we employ a procedure which exploits directly the recursive structure of the system. To this end, we replace m_t and m_{t+1} in (7.32) with expressions related to k_t and k_{t+1} as given by (7.33) and arrive thereby at the first-order, non-linear difference equation in k_t:

$$k_{t+1} + \frac{(1+\mu) \cdot f'(k_t) \cdot k_t}{\xi-1} \tag{7.34}$$

$$= s(R_t[k_{t+1}, \frac{(1+\mu) \cdot f'(k_t) \cdot k_t}{\xi-1}, \frac{(1+\mu) \cdot f'(k_{t+1}) \cdot k_{t+1}}{\xi-1}], w(k_t))$$

---

[7]According to assumption (A 2), the term $f'(k) \cdot k$ is strictly increasing in k. Thus, for any k_{t+1} there exists a uniquely defined value m_{t+1}.

To assess the dynamical properties of (7.34), we investigate its linear expansion around the steady state. Thus, differentiating (7.34) yields:

$$d\,k_{t+1} = \frac{(s_R \cdot R_2 - 1) \cdot \frac{1+\mu}{\xi-1} \cdot (f''(k) \cdot k + f'(k)) + s_w \cdot w'(k)}{1 - s_R \cdot [R_1 + R_3 \cdot \frac{1+\mu}{\xi-1} \cdot (f''(k) \cdot k + f'(k))]} \cdot d\,k_t \quad (7.35)$$

According to (7.35) the system will be stable if and only if the coefficient associated with $d\,k_t$ is of absolute value less than one. However, depending on the magnitudes of the derivatives involved, stability of the system cannot be taken for granted. In particular, stability requires that the intertemporal income effect $w'(k)$ resulting from the readjustment of the portfolios of agents needs to be sufficiently small.

We turn now to the specific example given in the text. First, for the special case of Cobb-Douglas-type preferences one obtains: $s_w = 1 - \beta$ and $s_R = 0$. Thus, equations (7.32) and (7.33) take now simply the form:

$$k_{t+1} + m_t = (1 - \beta) \cdot w(k_t) \quad (7.36)$$

$$m_{t+1} = \frac{1+\mu}{\xi - 1} \cdot f'(k_{t+1}) \cdot k_{t+1} \quad (7.37)$$

Correspondingly, this simplifies (7.35) considerably:

$$d\,k_{t+1} = [(1 - \beta) \cdot w'(k) - \frac{1+\mu}{\xi - 1} \cdot (f''(k) \cdot k + f'(k))] \cdot d\,k_t \quad (7.38)$$

Note that the term $w'(k)$ can be rearranged as:

$$w'(k) = -f''(k) \cdot k \quad (7.39)$$

Thus, using (7.39), (7.38) further simplifies to:

$$d\,k_{t+1} = [-(f''(k) \cdot k) \cdot (1 - \beta + \frac{1+\mu}{\xi - 1}) - \frac{1+\mu}{\xi - 1} \cdot f'(k)] \cdot d\,k_t \quad (7.40)$$

Second, for a Cobb-Douglas production function the expressions $-f''(k) \cdot k$ and $f'(k)$ are given by:

$$-f''(k) \cdot k = \alpha \cdot (1 - \alpha) \cdot k^{\alpha-1}, \quad f'(k) = \alpha \cdot k^{\alpha-1} \quad (7.41)$$

Inserting (7.41) into (7.40) yields, after some tidying up:

$$d\,k_{t+1} = \alpha \cdot k^{\alpha-1} \cdot [(1 - \beta) \cdot (1 - \alpha) - \frac{1+\mu}{\xi - 1} \cdot \alpha] \cdot d\,k_t \quad (7.42)$$

However, from (7.30) we know that the steady state capital stock is given by:

$$k = \left[(1 - \beta) \cdot (1 - \alpha) - \frac{1+\mu}{\xi - 1} \cdot \alpha \right]^{\frac{1}{1-\alpha}} \quad (7.43)$$

112

Substituting (7.43) into (7.42) yields:

$$d\,k_{t+1} = \alpha \cdot d\,k_t \qquad\qquad (7.44)$$

Thus, since $\alpha \in (0,1)$ by assumption, the unique steady state will always be stable. Remember that in period t the capital stock is a predetermined variable, resulting from last period's investment decision, while the level of real balances m_t is freely determined through forwardlooking behaviour. Yet, for any initial choice of m_t dynamics of the system (7.36) and (7.37) will be governed by equation (7.44). Therefore, adjustment towards the steady state is indeterminate. Moreover, since $\alpha > 0$, adjustment must be monotone. q.e.d.

Chapter 8

Variation 4: Differentiated goods, multiple means of payment, and money as single outside asset

In the previous chapter we presented a simple version of a cash-in-advance framework in order to challenge the bubbly view on money from a fundamentalist perspective. In particular, we assumed in chapter 7 that a fixed fraction of purchases needed to be settled by payment in cash. Obviously, this is a questionable assumption, and certainly it is not suited to give a satisfactory account of the long run. We therefore summarize in this chapter briefly more involved specifications discussed in the cash-in-advance literature and present then a framework which permits a more subtle discussion of the superneutrality issue.

As already indicated in chapter 3, in standard specifications of the cash–in–advance constraint the use of cash is simply motivated by the idea that the range of goods being available can be rigidly divided into so-called 'cash' and 'credit' goods. This specification is exogenously imposed, and since, as a matter of definition, cash goods are only available by payment in cash, money will always be valued despite being dominated in return, as long as preferences with respect to cash and credit goods are appropriately specified.

Following Stockman's influential contribution, various authors have used versions of a cash-in-advance economy in order to address the question of money and growth.[1] Huo (1997), for example, presents a framework in which money

---

[1] For a detailed discussion of Stockman's analysis, see chapter 1.

is not superneutral, although only consumption goods are subject to a partial cash-in-advance constraint. To establish this result, Huo (1997) uses a two sector cash-in-advance economy with two consumption goods, one being a cash good and the other being a credit good. In Huo's analysis both goods are imperfect substitutes in consumption and they differ on the production side in their capital intensities. Under these specifications, the effect of inflation on capital formation reflects essentially the mechanics of the Heckscher-Ohlin framework: a higher inflation rate raises the relative price of the cash good and, hence, diverts demand from the cash good to the credit good sector. Assuming, for example, that the credit good is relatively more capital intensive, the Tobin effect will then prevail.

In related work, Jones/Manuelli (1995) differentiate between cash and credit goods in a rich Lucas-type endogenous growth setting with human capital production and link the strength of the effect to the question of whether consumers regard cash and credit goods as substitutes or complements. In the spirit of some of our results given below, Jones/Manuelli (1995) show that for goods being complements the growth rate of the economy will be negatively linked to higher inflation rates. In contrast, for goods being substitutes a positive link obtains, i.e. the Tobin effect dominates.

However, to assume a rigid distinction between cash and credit goods does not seem appropriate for an analysis of the long run. Instead, it seems desirable that specifications of the cash-in-advance constraint live up to the compelling standards of the Lucas-critique which asserts in this context, broadly speaking, that transaction patterns themselves should react to changes in the regime of monetary policy. In particular, it seems natural to account for the fact that the private sector will respond to a situation of ongoing inflation by extending the range of goods that can be bought by 'inflation-proof', private credit arrangements. Clearly, to address such a response of the private sector, one needs a framework in which the choice between money and credit, as far as transaction aspects are concerned, becomes fully endogenous, and this in turn requires a proper specification of all transaction technologies produced by the private sector.

Various authors have dealt with the question of how to derive endogenously the use of cash in an environment with multiple means of payment. King/Plosser (1984), for example, distinguish explicitly between inside and outside money in their attempt to integrate money into the real business cycles agenda in the spirit of the 'reverse causation hypothesis'.[2] Drawing

---

[2]Summarizing the key idea of the reverse causation hypothesis, King/Plosser (1984) present a framework in which "...monetary services are privately produced intermediate goods whose quantities rise and fall with real economic developments" (p. 363).

For a critical assessment of the reverse causation hypothesis, see, for example, Coleman (1996). Coleman (1996) estimates a model with an elaborate intermediation structure which allows agents to pay for goods with either cash, check, or credit. In summary, Coleman (1996) claims that his results "...pose a serious challenge to those who

on work by Fama (1980) and Fischer (1982), King/Plosser (1984) design an environment in which agents face a choice between using transaction services offered by intermediaries and paying directly in cash. And well in accordance with the reverse causation hypothesis, King/Plosser (1984) reproduce with their model close co-movements between output and inside money, while outside money remains (super)neutral.

In related work, Ireland (1994) presents an 'alternative approach to money and growth' which also addresses the passive nature of money along the lines of the 'reverse causation hypothesis'. Following Prescott (1987) and Schreft (1992), Ireland (1994) uses a framework in which infinitely lived agents incur a fixed cost when using financial services offered by intermediaries and a proportional cost when using outside money, representing the taxation of cash-based purchases at the flat rate of inflation. Furthermore, agents are supposed to have access to a Rebelo-type technology. Thus, endogenous growth obtains, and this in turn ensures that the trade-off between the fixed cost of paying via intermediaries and the proportional cost associated with the use of outside money shifts over time in favour of the money substitutes.[3] As a result, the traditional link between money and growth is in Ireland's alternative approach reversed: the Tobin effect, which establishes a causation running from portfolio behaviour to growth, is small and in the long run swamped by the effect of growth on the composition of monetary aggregates. The dominance of this reverse causation effect is clearly borne out by Ireland's simulations: over time, as the economy grows, outside money is steadily replaced with money substitutes and its share in the overall money stock reduced.

Although we feel largely sympathetic towards Ireland's work, we think nevertheless that his specifications are too much in favour of the reverse causation hypothesis. Despite the undisputed, growing importance of money substitutes we think that it is important to see that there are limits to the possibilities to substitute inside for outside money. In particular, governments can always ensure via taxation or restrictions such as reserve requirements that outside money remains an indispensable asset. More importantly, while Ireland's substitutability assumption may well be appropriate for economies with developed financial systems, we doubt it's adequacy in the context of financially less-developed economies. In these economies, close money substitutes are not, or only to a limited extent, available. Similarly, for economies

---

argue that the endogenous determination of money can, by itself, quantitatively account for the observed money-output correlations" (p.109). However, the focus of Coleman's study is on cyclical, not on long run growth patterns.

[3]To ensure a well-defined demand for money along the entire growth path, Ireland (1994) uses a cash-in-advance framework with spatially separated markets as advanced by Lucas/Stokey (1983). The fixed cost of using financial services is not uniform across goods but distance related, and the set-up is such that in finite time there is always a well-defined demand for real balances.

116

of this type the share of cash-based underground activities is typically non-negligible.

We think that these qualifications are important since, as discussed in chapter 2, the effects of inflation on real activity depend crucially on the level of financial development of economies. Thus, while Ireland's approach can indeed show why the Anti-Tobin conjecture finds no convincing support in advanced economies, it fails to explain the strong significance of the Anti-Tobin effect in financially less-developed economies.

Clearly, the Anti-Tobin effect is dominated in Ireland's model by the mechanism of the growth channel which drives outside money steadily out of circulation. To address our criticisms we adapt, therefore, in this chapter a stationary version of Ireland's 'alternative approach to money and growth' to an economy inhabited by overlapping generations. Deviating from Ireland (1994), our modifications make it possible to derive a regime with an exogenously imposed cash-in-advance constraint as a special (i.e. limiting) case of a regime which otherwise permits a fully endogenous choice between distinct means of payments. The limiting regime is simply characterized by a rigid distinction between a cash and a credit sector. Thus, in order to approximate the effects of inflation in financially less-developed economies, we return to a specification as proposed in the earlier literature. In summary, due to our joint treatment of an 'exogenous' and an 'endogenous' cash-in-advance constraint we can also account for the prevalence of the Anti-Tobin effect in constellations in which close money substitutes are not readily available.[4]

For both regimes, we analyze how changes in monetary policy impact on the process of capital formation.

For the regime with an *endogenous cash-in-advance constraint*, the set-up ensures that a two-equation system replaces the standard arbitrage equation of the Diamond model. With the choice between cash and deposits being unrestricted, it turns out that the Tobin effect has strong support. Corresponding equilibria are shown to be saddlepath stable and adjustment behaviour towards the steady state will be monotone.

For the regime with an *exogenous cash-in-advance constraint*, we demonstrate that comparative statics results and dynamical properties depend under standard specifications crucially on whether cash and credit goods are, at the margin, substitutes or complements from the consumers' perspective. As in our discussion of the base model we derive a two-dimensional system in which

---

[4] A similar technique, although in a different context, is employed by Marquis/Reffett (1995) with respect to financing constraints on investment goods. In particular, Marquis/Reffett (1995) show that superneutrality can be derived as a limiting case in a set-up similar to Stockman's, if it is assumed that transaction costs associated with private arrangements for investement purchases are finite. Then, beyond a certain treshold value of the inflation rate, all investment purchases are credit financed and money becomes superneutral.

money balances and capital evolve over time. The accumulation equation is standard. However, borrowing from consumer theory, we obtain a simple arbitrage relation which says that the price ratio of cash and credit goods needs to be equal to the marginal rate of substitution between the two types of goods. If goods are substitutes the Tobin effect obtains and steady states are saddlepath stable, displaying monotone adjustment behaviour. Yet, if goods are complements the Anti-Tobin effect obtains and steady states can be either a saddle or a sink. Saddlepath stable Anti-Tobin steady states have monotone orbits. If Anti-Tobin steady states are a sink adjustment behaviour will ultimately be either monotone or oscillatory, depending on the sign of the dominant eigenvalue.

However, we show for both regimes that results may well get reversed if the substitution effect is dominated by some intertemporal income effect. Also due to the intertemporal income effect, we can construct for both regimes constellations with multiple steady states.

8.1 The model

We consider a version of the base model with a distinct spatial arrangement loosely along the lines of Ireland (1994). Each generation consists of an infinite amount of identical agents with unit mass. When being young, agents have a fixed labour endowment of $L = 1$ units of labour, and agents have no labour endowment when being old. Preferences are such that all wage income received by young agents is saved. Thus, deviating from the previous chapter, we concentrate in this chapter exclusively on intratemporal aspects of a cash-in-advance constrained economy. Once more, agents have two distinct financial instruments at their disposal to transfer income into the second period of their life. In particular, wage income can be deposited with an intermediary who has access to the physical investment opportunities of the economy or it can be sold intergenerationally against fiat money to members of the old generation.

The production of output occurs in a centralized manner, and with respect to the production process we maintain the convenient assumption of a one good economy. However, once output has been produced, it is sold in the form of differentiated goods in spatially separated shops. These shops are symmetrically lined up along a street of unit length, and goods are assumed to differ across shops due to some cost-free attribute such as the product name or packaging. As a result, goods are not homogenous from the consumers' perspective. Tastes of old agents reflect the variety of available goods, and we simply assume that preferences are symmetrical with respect to all goods. In other words, the spatial arrangement of the economy forces old agents to turn into 'shoppers', and preferences of shoppers are such that they will visit all shops along the street in order to get a bit from everywhere.

The peculiar spatial arrangement of the economy serves the purpose to accommodate the coexistence of two distinct means of payment. In general, consumers can use either outside money (*cash*) or checks to be drawn on their deposit accounts (*credit*). However, whenever consumers pay by check they are charged a fixed processing cost for the use of the accounting system of exchange offered by intermediaries.[5] Processing costs are a smooth function of the distance along the street up to a critical shop where the function makes a discontinuous jump. This jump is assumed to be sufficiently large such that beyond the critical shop payment by check is no longer affordable. On the other hand, at the beginning of the street processing costs are sufficiently small such that agents always prefer to use checks.

Government activities in our model are restricted to purchases of goods which do not affect the utility of private agents. As in the base model, the government has monopoly power over issuing outside money and finances its purchases exclusively by injecting additional amounts of newly printed money.

To get a more intuitive understanding of how the economy is imagined to operate, consider the following set-up. Assume that in addition to intermediaries there are some producers and some traders, with all these groups being of negligible size (i.e. of measure zero). Producers do not sell the output directly to consumers, but rather to traders who run the decentralized system of shops and sell the final output in the form of shop-specific goods to consumers. Traders finance their outlays by means of short term (i.e. intra-period) trade credits obtained from intermediaries and sell the goods to consumers against checks or cash. When paying-off their debts, traders turn in the receipts from these sales to the intermediaries, and we assume that intermediaries treat cash and checks as perfect substitutes. However, traders know that intermediaries charge a location-specific fee for the processing of checks, and this extra cost attached to non-cash payments will be passed on to consumers. As a result, depending on the location of the shop, credit goods sell at different prices from the perspective of consumers. Thus, the spatial arrangement approximates the idea that costs associated with non-cash payments (such as the evaluation of customers and the enforcement of payment obligations through intermediaries) typically differ economywide across transactions, and the distance along the street is simply a broad measure of these costs.

Producers are capable of transforming one unit of period t output into one unit of period $t + 1$ physical capital. To preclude the possibility of self-financed investments, we simply assume that producers have no endowments and also live only for two periods. Thus, in every period new investments in

---

[5]To stay in line with the terminology as it is mostly used in models with cash-in-advance constraints, goods are labeled for the rest of the paper as either cash or credit goods. However, terminology is not uniform across the literature. In the context presented here, agents pay for credit goods by check, and the associated transfer of deposits carries an extra cost in terms of processing fees.

physical capital are entirely credit-financed, and some fraction of the output is directly sold from active to prospective producers. Similarly, the government buys some fraction of the output directly from producers through cash transfers. Wages are paid out at the beginning of every period, and producers finance wage outlays via short term (i.e. intra-period) credits. Finally, we assume that production, intermediation, and trade are all subject to perfect competition, ensuring that in equilibrium zero profits are made in all these activities. Thus, at the end of every period when all transactions have been settled, all 'old' investment credits and all intra-period credits (i.e. trade credits and credits related to wage payments) will have gone out of circulation. Correspondingly, 'new' investment credits will have been handed out and the entire stock of outside money will be carried into the next period.

We specify now in detail how the economy operates.

Production: Once more, we assume that production occurs according to a neoclassical production function $Y = F(K, L)$ with constant returns to scale and standard properties in intensive form $f(k)$:

(A 1) The function $f(k)$ is twice continuously differentiable, positive, increasing, and strictly concave:

$$\text{(i) } f(k) > 0, \quad \text{(ii) } f'(k) > 0 \quad \text{(iii) } f''(k) < 0 \text{ for } k > 0.$$

As in the previous chapter, we impose the following mild restriction with respect to the income received by capital:

(A 2) The income received by capital $f'(k) \cdot k$ satisfies the condition:

(i) $\lim_{k \to 0} f'(k) \cdot k = 0$,

(ii) $\frac{d f'(k) \cdot k}{d k} > 0$ for $k > 0$.

Factor markets are subject to perfect competition. Thus, with capital depreciating entirely during the production process, we have for all periods:

$$\rho_t = f'(k_t) \tag{8.1}$$
$$w_t = f(k_t) - \rho_t \cdot k_t = w(k_t) \tag{8.2}$$

Government: We maintain the assumption that all government income results from seigniorage. Again, the money stock per young agent grows at the constant rate $\mu = M_t/M_{t-1} - 1$. Let g_t denote the consumption of goods of the government per young agent. Then, the budget constraint in period t is given by:

$$g_t = \frac{M_t - M_{t-1}}{p_t} = \frac{\mu}{1 + \mu} \cdot \frac{M_t}{p_t} \tag{8.3}$$

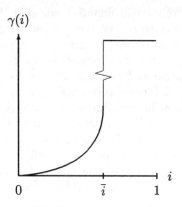

Figure 8.1: *Variation 4 - Processing costs of non-cash payments*

Problem of the representative agent: In period t, a young agent receives wage income w_t. He can transfer this income into period $t + 1$ by investing it in real deposits d_t (with gross return rate R_t^d) or real money balances m_t (with gross return rate R_t^m). The portfolio decision is driven by the prices the agent expects to prevail in period $t + 1$ with respect to credit and cash goods, respectively. Although cash and credit goods will be traded at identical producer prices, there are different costs attached to either type of good from the consumers' perspective. The relevant costs associated with cash goods are simply the opportunity costs of holding return-dominated money. These opportunity costs are proportional to the size of the purchase since there is no fixed resource cost involved when payments are made in cash. In contrast, payment by credit (i.e. the use of checks) is subject to real, distance related processing costs $\Gamma(i)$, with the location of shops along the street being indexed by $i \in [0,1]$. Moreover, as illustrated in figure 8.1, we assume that beyond a critical shop $\bar{i}$ payment by credit is no longer possible:

(A 3) Processing costs $\Gamma(i)$ are given by:

$$\Gamma(i) = \begin{cases} \Gamma + \int_0^{\bar{i}} \gamma(i) \, di & \text{for } 0 \le i \le \bar{i}, \\ \infty & \text{for } \bar{i} < i \le 1 \end{cases} \quad \text{, with:}$$

$$\Gamma \ge 0, \gamma(0) = 0, \gamma'(i) \ge 0, \Gamma(\bar{i}) < \infty$$

Note that processing costs are a non-decreasing function of the distance along the street. Moreover, at any shop with location i processing costs are fixed, i.e. they do not depend on the size of the purchase. Following Ireland (1994), we let preferences be represented by an additively separable utility function:

$$U = \int_0^1 u(c(i))\, di \qquad (8.4)$$

(A 4) The function u is assumed to be twice continuously differentiable with Inada-like properties:

$$u'(c) > 0,\, u''(c) < 0,\, u'(0) = \infty$$

Let the superscripts 0 and 1 denote cash goods (c^0) and credit goods (c^1), respectively. Furthermore, let $\tilde{i}$ denote the critical shop beyond which consumers prefer to pay in cash. Clearly, $\tilde{i} \leq \bar{i}$ needs to hold. Using this notation, the decision problem of a representative agent can be stated as:

$$\max_{c_{t+1}^0(i),\, c_{t+1}^1(i),\, m_t,\, d_t,\, \tilde{i}_{t+1}} : \int_0^{\tilde{i}_{t+1}} u(c_{t+1}^1(i))\, di \; + \int_{\tilde{i}_{t+1}}^1 u(c_{t+1}^0(i))\, di$$

$$+ \lambda_t \cdot \left(R_t^m \cdot m_t + R_t^d \cdot d_t - \Gamma(\tilde{i}_{t+1}) - \int_0^{\tilde{i}_{t+1}} c_{t+1}^1(i)\, di - \int_{\tilde{i}_{t+1}}^1 c_{t+1}^0(i)\, di \right)$$

$$+ \mu_t \cdot \left(R_t^m \cdot m_t - \int_{\tilde{i}_{t+1}}^1 c_{t+1}^0(i)\, di \right)$$

$$+ \nu_t \cdot (w_t - m_t - d_t). \qquad (8.5)$$

The multipliers λ_t, μ_t, ν_t are associated with the budget constraint in $t+1$, the additional cash constraint which applies to purchases of cash goods in $t+1$, and the portfolio constraint in t, respectively. Assuming interior solutions, differentiating with respect to $c_{t+1}^1(i)$, $c_{t+1}^0(i)$, m_t, and d_t yields the first-order conditions:

$$
\begin{aligned}
u'(c_{t+1}^1(i)) &= \lambda_t & i &\in [0, \tilde{i}_{t+1}] & (8.6)\\
u'(c_{t+1}^0(i)) &= \lambda_t + \mu_t & i &\in (\tilde{i}_{t+1}, 1] & (8.7)\\
(\lambda_t + \mu_t) \cdot R_t^m &= \nu_t & & & (8.8)\\
\lambda_t \cdot R_t^d &= \nu_t & & & (8.9)
\end{aligned}
$$

To establish that solutions will be indeed interior, we have to make sure that at $i = 0$ money will not be used.[6] Hence, we need to assume that money is return-dominated by credit net of processing costs at this location:

(A 5) Money is return-dominated:

$$R_t^d - \Gamma > R_t^m$$

---

[6] Clearly, the supposed discontinuity of processing costs at $\bar{i}$ complements the condition for an interior solution.

Furthermore, differentiating (8.5) with respect to $\widetilde{i}_{t+1}$ yields the set of complementary slackness conditions:

$$[u(c^1_{t+1}(\widetilde{i}_{t+1})) - \lambda_t \cdot (c^1_{t+1}(\widetilde{i}_{t+1}) + \gamma(\widetilde{i}_{t+1})) -$$

$$[u(c^0_{t+1}(\widetilde{i}_{t+1})) - (\lambda_t + \mu_t) \cdot c^0_{t+1}(\widetilde{i}_{t+1})]] \geq 0$$

$$\widetilde{i}_{t+1} - \bar{i} \leq 0 \qquad (8.10)$$

$$[...] \cdot [\widetilde{i}_{t+1} - \bar{i}] = 0$$

Note that by (8.6) and (8.7) the symmetrical structure of the utility function carries over into a symmetrical mix of purchases of cash and credit goods, i.e. we have: $c^1_{t+1}(i) = c^1_{t+1}$, for $i \in [0, \widetilde{i}_{t+1}]$ and $c^0_{t+1}(i) = c^0_{t+1}$, for $i \in (\widetilde{i}_{t+1}, 1]$. Combining the first order conditions with the constraints, we arrive at the system of equations:

$$w_t = m_t + d_t \qquad (8.11)$$

$$c^0_{t+1} = \frac{R^m_t \cdot m_t}{1 - \widetilde{i}_{t+1}} \qquad (8.12)$$

$$c^1_{t+1} = \frac{R^d_t \cdot d_t - \Gamma(\widetilde{i}_{t+1})}{\widetilde{i}_{t+1}} \qquad (8.13)$$

$$\frac{u'(c^0_{t+1})}{u'(c^1_{t+1})} = \frac{R^d_t}{R^m_t} \qquad (8.14)$$

$$u(c^1_{t+1}) - u'(c^1_{t+1}) \cdot (c^1_{t+1} + \gamma(\widetilde{i}_{t+1})) \geq u(c^0_{t+1}) - u'(c^0_{t+1}) \cdot c^0_{t+1} \qquad (8.15)$$

$$\widetilde{i}_{t+1} - \bar{i} \leq 0 \qquad (8.16)$$

$$[...] \cdot [\widetilde{i}_{t+1} - \bar{i}] = 0 \qquad (8.17)$$

Not much needs to be said with respect to equations (8.11)-(8.14). Essentially, we have reduced the portfolio problem of the agent to the standard choice problem of consumer theory of allocating expenditures optimally between different consumption goods. Not surprisingly, according to (8.14) the solution of the problem requires that the marginal rate of substitution in consumption needs to be equal to the price ratio of the goods as perceived by consumers. With goods being specified as cash and credit goods, this price ratio is naturally given by the nominal inflation factor.

Equally suggestive, equations (8.15)-(8.17) can be interpreted as following: first, consider a situation in which we have an interior solution for $\widetilde{i}_{t+1}$ with (8.16) holding as strict inequality. Clearly, (8.15) needs to hold then as strict equality. By (8.6) and (8.7), $u'(c^1_{t+1})$ and $u'(c^0_{t+1})$ represent the shadow values of the constraints applying to credit and cash goods, respectively. Thus, (8.15) at equality says that the unrestricted optimization over $\widetilde{i}_{t+1}$ allows agents to derive at the margin equal amounts of consumer surplus from using either cash or credit. In the following, interior solutions of this type are described as regimes with an *endogenous cash-in-advance constraint*.

Second, consider a situation in which (8.15) is slack. Then, (8.16) needs to hold as strict equality, i.e. $\tilde{i}_{t+1}$ will be given by the corner solution $\tilde{i}_{t+1} = \bar{i}$. When considering the situation of a corner solution, we assume implicitly that both $\bar{i}$ and the values of the function $\Gamma(i)$ are sufficiently small such that money is return-dominated by credit (net of processing costs) at all locations $i < \bar{i}$. Evidently, in such a situation complete arbitrage in terms of consumer surplus will not be possible due to the discontinuity in banking services at $\bar{i}$. We think that such a constellation naturally corresponds to the notion of an *exogenous cash-in-advance constraint* as traditionally discussed in the literature: due to the discontinuity in processing costs checks are simply not accepted in shops at locations $i > \bar{i}$, and optimizing agents are essentially forced to use cash in these shops.[7]

8.2 Equilibrium conditions

Arbitrage on the side of intermediaries ensures that in equilibrium zero profits will be made in production and intermediation. Thus, the marginal productivity of capital needs to be equal to the interest rate paid on deposits:

$$f'(k_{t+1}) = R_t^d \qquad (8.18)$$

Similar to the detailed discussion given in chapter 4, in equilibrium all markets need to clear for all periods $t = 0, 1, ...$, with the equilibrium conditions for the respective markets being as following:

Equilibrium conditions:

Capital market : $d_t = k_{t+1}$
Money market : $m_t = M_t/p_t$
Goods market : $y_t = \tilde{i}_t \cdot c_t^1 + (1 - \tilde{i}_t) \cdot c_t^0 + \Gamma(\tilde{i}_t) + g_t + d_t$

One easily verifies that by virtue of Walras' law the three conditions are not independent.[8]

---

[7]We abstract from the rare situation in which both (8.15) and (8.16) hold as strict equalities, i.e. a situation in which the condition for an interior solution happens to be satisfied at the margin $\bar{i}$.

[8]Assume, for example, that both the money and capital market clear. Inserting the relevant conditions into (8.3) and (8.11)-(8.13) yields:

$$\tilde{i}_t \cdot c_t^1 + \Gamma(\tilde{i}_t) = R_{t-1}^d \cdot d_{t-1} = f'(k_t) \cdot k_t$$

$$(1 - \tilde{i}_t) \cdot c_t^0 = R_{t-1}^m \cdot m_{t-1} = \frac{1}{1+\mu} \cdot m_t = \frac{1}{1+\mu} \cdot [w(k_t) - k_{t+1}]$$

124

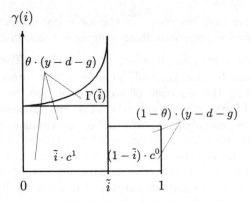

Figure 8.2: *Variation 4 - Spatial distribution of privately consumed output*

Once again, we rewrite the equilibrium return on money as:

$$R_t^m = \frac{p_t}{p_{t+1}} = \frac{M_{t+1}/p_{t+1}}{(1+\mu) \cdot M_t/p_t} = \frac{1}{1+\mu} \cdot \frac{m_{t+1}}{m_t} \qquad (8.19)$$

Note that by invoking the law of one price with respect to producer prices we implicitly assume that all markets are also locationwise in equilibrium. Thus, the spatial demand structure of privately consumed output (including shop-specific processing costs) needs to be matched, as graphed in figure 8.2, by the corresponding 'supply-side' distribution of goods across shops. More specifically, define the following fractions:

$$\theta_t = \frac{\tilde{i}_t \cdot c_t^1 + \Gamma(\tilde{i}_t)}{y_t - d_t - g_t}, \quad 1 - \theta_t = \frac{(1-\tilde{i}_t) \cdot c_t^0}{y_t - d_t - g_t}$$

Then, in equilibrium a fraction θ_t of privately consumed output will be sold in credit shops, while a fraction $1 - \theta_t$ will be sold in cash shops.

Endogenous cash-in-advance constraint: To facilitate a simple comparison of the two regimes in terms of notation, interior solutions for $\tilde{i}$ with (8.16) holding as strict inequality will be denoted by i^*. Consolidating the relevant equilibrium conditions, the regime with an endogenous cash-in-advance constraint can be compactly described by the following dynamical system in

$$g_t = \frac{\mu}{1+\mu} \cdot [w(k_t) - k_{t+1}]$$
$$d_t = k_{t+1}$$

Then, adding up the equations, one quickly establishes that the goods market needs to clear as well.

$g_t, k_t, m_t,$ and i_t^*:

$$g_t = \frac{\mu}{1+\mu} \cdot m_t \tag{8.20}$$

$$f'(k_{t+1}) - \Gamma > \frac{1}{1+\mu} \cdot \frac{m_{t+1}}{m_t} \tag{8.21}$$

$$k_{t+1} = w_t(k_t) - m_t \tag{8.22}$$

$$\frac{1}{1+\mu} \cdot \frac{m_{t+1}}{m_t} \cdot u'(c_{t+1}^0) = f'(k_{t+1}) \cdot u'(c_{t+1}^1) \tag{8.23}$$

$$u(c_{t+1}^1) - u'(c_{t+1}^1) \cdot (c_{t+1}^1 + \gamma(i_{t+1}^*)) = u(c_{t+1}^0) - u'(c_{t+1}^0) \cdot c_{t+1}^0 \tag{8.24}$$

Equilibrium consumption levels of cash and credit goods are given by the expressions:

$$c_{t+1}^0 = \frac{m_{t+1}}{(1+\mu) \cdot (1 - i_{t+1}^*)} \tag{8.25}$$

$$c_{t+1}^1 = \frac{f'(k_{t+1}) \cdot (k_{t+1}) - \Gamma(i_{t+1}^*)}{i_{t+1}^*} \tag{8.26}$$

Again, we treat g_t as being endogenously determined. Thus, due to the recursive structure of the system we can confine our analysis to equations (8.21)-(8.24) which constitute a dynamical system in k_t, m_t, and i_t^*. Following the classification introduced in chapter 4, the system exhibits the standard *accumulation equation* (8.22) of the Diamond version of the overlapping generations models with production, but the standard, single arbitrage relation is replaced with the two-equation system of *arbitrage relations* (8.23) and (8.24). Moreover, restating assumption (A 5), (8.21) says that there are always some shops where agents prefer to pay by credit, and this in turn ensures a positive level of investment in capital over time.

Exogenous cash-in-advance constraint: Similarly, consolidating the equilibrium conditions for the regime with an exogenous cash-in-advance constraint, yields the following dynamical system in g_t, k_t, and m_t, with $\bar{i}$ now being the relevant margin:

$$g_t = \frac{\mu}{1+\mu} \cdot m_t \tag{8.27}$$

$$f'(k_{t+1}) - \Gamma > \frac{1}{1+\mu} \cdot \frac{m_{t+1}}{m_t} \tag{8.28}$$

$$k_{t+1} = w_t(k_t) - m_t \tag{8.29}$$

$$\frac{1}{1+\mu} \cdot \frac{m_{t+1}}{m_t} \cdot u'(c_{t+1}^0) = f'(k_{t+1}) \cdot u'(c_{t+1}^1) \tag{8.30}$$

$$u(c_{t+1}^1) - u'(c_{t+1}^1) \cdot (c_{t+1}^1 + \gamma(\bar{i})) > u(c_{t+1}^0) - u'(c_{t+1}^0) \cdot c_{t+1}^0 \tag{8.31}$$

Accordingly, equilibrium consumption levels of cash and credit goods are given by:

$$c_{t+1}^0 = \frac{m_{t+1}}{(1+\mu) \cdot (1-\bar{i})}$$

$$c_{t+1}^1 = \frac{f'(k_{t+1}) \cdot (k_{t+1}) - \Gamma(\bar{i})}{\bar{i}}$$

Again, we let g_t being endogenously determined. Since (8.31) holds as strict inequality, the dynamics are now locally determined by the system (8.28)-(8.30). Assuming that money is strictly return-dominated as specified in (8.28), the system reduces now to a two-dimensional system in k_t and m_t. While the accumulation of capital evolves again according to (8.29), the system exhibits now, similar to the base model, a single arbitrage equation. However, arbitrage in the context presented here reflects the standard optimizing behaviour from consumer theory, and we think that due to the extreme specification of processing costs at $\bar{i}$ this modified arbitrage relation lends itself as easily to interpretations as the standard one.

We turn now to a more detailed discussion of both regimes. Since the mechanics of the regime with an exogenous cash-in-advance constraint are more transparent, our analysis treats this case first.

8.3 The regime with an exogenous cash-in-advance constraint

We are interested in steady state solutions of the system (8.28)-(8.31), with k and m being constant over time:

$$f'(k) - \Gamma > \frac{1}{1+\mu} \tag{8.32}$$

$$k = w(k) - m \tag{8.33}$$

$$\frac{1}{1+\mu} \cdot u'(c^0) = f'(k) \cdot u'(c^1) \tag{8.34}$$

$$u(c^1) - u'(c^1) \cdot (c^1 + \gamma(\bar{i})) > u(c^0) - u'(c^0) \cdot c^0 \tag{8.35}$$

Steady state consumption levels are given by:

$$c^1 = \frac{f'(k) \cdot k - \Gamma(\bar{i})}{\bar{i}}, \quad c^0 = \frac{\frac{1}{1+\mu} \cdot m}{1 - \bar{i}} \tag{8.36}$$

Existence of steady state equilibria: In general, any pair (k, m) solving the equations (8.33)-(8.34) will be a valid solution if it satisfies as well the inequalities (8.32) and (8.35). To demonstrate that such a constellation may well exist, we establish now briefly a set of appropriate conditions which are sufficient for the existence of a steady state solution. First, we assume that the function $w(k)$ has the convenient concave shape introduced in chapter 4:

(A 6) The function $f(k)$ admits the following behaviour of $w(k)$:

(i) $w(0) > 0 \ \lor \ w'(0) > 1$,

(ii) $\lim\limits_{k \to \infty} \frac{w(k)}{k} < 1$,

(iii) $w'(k) > 0$, $w''(k) < 0$ for all $k > 0$.

Clearly, (A 6) ensures that there exists a unique value $k^{\mathrm{max}} > 0$ solving the equation $w(k) = k$. Second, we assume that processing costs satisfy a strong version of (A 3). In particular, these costs are taken to be sufficiently small such that a solution $k > 0$ consistent with (A 6) becomes possible:

(A 7) Processing costs satisfy:

(i) $\Gamma > 0, \gamma(i) = 0$ for all $i \in [0, \bar{i}] \Rightarrow \Gamma(i) = \Gamma$ for all $i \in [0, \bar{i}]$

(ii) $f'(k^{\mathrm{max}}) \cdot k^{\mathrm{max}} > \Gamma$.

Finally, we assume that a particularly strong version of the return-dominance condition holds:

(A 8) At k^{max}, money is strictly return-dominated:

$$f'(k^{\mathrm{max}}) > \frac{1}{1 + \mu} + \Gamma$$

Given these additional assumptions the following proposition is straightforward:

Proposition 1 *Assume that assumptions (A 1)-(A 8) are satisfied. Then, there exists a steady state equilibrium for the regime with an exogenous cash-in-advance constraint with $(k, m) > 0$.*

Proof: We prove the proposition by referring to figure 8.3. (A 6) ensures that the accumulation equation (8.33) can be drawn as in figure 8.3. (A 1) and (A 8) guarantee that for all values $k < k^{\mathrm{max}}$ there exist some shops where money is strictly return-dominated such that $k > 0$ results from an optimal portfolio decision. By (A 2) and (A 7), there exists a unique value $k^{\mathrm{min}} > 0$, satisfying $k^{\mathrm{min}} \cdot f'(k^{\mathrm{min}}) = \Gamma(\bar{i}) = \Gamma$ and $0 < k^{\mathrm{min}} < k^{\mathrm{max}}$. Note that $\Gamma > 0$ can be made arbitrarily small in order to satisfy part (ii) of (A 7) and (A 8). Next, by (A 1), (A 2), and (A 4) the arbitrage locus (8.34) slopes

128

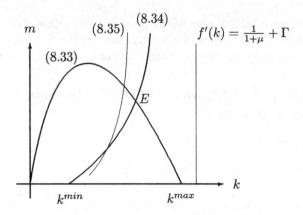

Figure 8.3: *Variation 4 - Exogenous cash-in-advance constraint*

upward in m-k-plane, and $m(k^{\min}) = 0$ needs to hold. Thus both loci must have at least one intersection with $k^{\min} < k < k^{\max}$ and $m > 0$. Finally, at any point of intersection of (8.33) and (8.34) the second arbitrage relation (8.35) holds indeed as strict inequality: since $f'(k) > \frac{1}{1+\mu}$ by (A 1) and (A 8), $c^1 > c^0$ is implied by (8.34). Note that concavity of $u(c)$ implies that the term $u(c) - u'(c) \cdot c$ rises in c. Thus, since $\gamma(\bar{\imath}) = 0$ by part (i) of (A 7), the inequality $c^1 > c^0$ ensures that (8.35) holds as strict inequality.[9] q.e.d.

Evidently, steady state solutions of (8.32)-(8.35) may well exist under less restrictive assumptions than (A 6)-(A 8). Since assumptions (A 6)-(A 8) are by no means necessary for the results to be established subsequently, we take from now on the existence of a steady state solution for granted. Thus, for the remainder of this chapter we work again with the mild set of assumptions (A 1)-(A 5).

Comparative statics: How does the system with an exogenous cash-in-advance constraint respond to a permanent change in the rate of monetary expansion μ ? Straightforward comparative statics in equations (8.33) and (8.34) yields the following classification of reaction effects:[10]

---

[9]One easily verifies that the second arbitrage locus (8.35) strictly at equality also slopes upward in m-k-plane as drawn in figure 8.3. To the south-east of this locus slackness prevails as required by (8.35). Furthermore, note that multiple steady state equilibria are well possible under (A 1)-(A 8).

[10]Note the local character of the results established in the proposition since we assume

Proposition 2 *Consider a situation with a unique steady state and assume that the rate of monetary expansion μ is permanently raised. Let $\sigma(c^0)$ denote the elasticity of substitution between cash and credit goods at the steady state equilibrium. Then, the effect on the capital stock will be given by:*

$$\frac{\partial k}{\partial \mu} = \begin{cases} > 0 & \Leftrightarrow \ \sigma(c^0) > 1 \quad \textit{Tobin effect} \\ = 0 & \Leftrightarrow \ \sigma(c^0) = 1 \quad \textit{Superneutrality} \\ < 0 & \Leftrightarrow \ \sigma(c^0) < 1 \quad \textit{Anti-Tobin effect} \end{cases}$$

Thus, the Tobin effect obtains locally if cash and credit goods, evaluated at the equilibrium, are gross substitutes. Conversely, the Anti-Tobin effect obtains if the goods are gross complements. Finally, if the cross price effect is zero superneutrality prevails.

Proof: Differentiating equations (8.33) and (8.34) yields:

$$\frac{\partial k}{\partial \mu} = \frac{\frac{\bar{i}-1}{u''(c^0)} \cdot [u''(c^0) \cdot c^0 + u'(c^0)]}{\left[\frac{(1-\bar{i}) \cdot (1+\mu)^2 \cdot [f''(k) \cdot u'(c^1) + f'(k) \cdot u''(c^1) \cdot (f''(k) \cdot k + f'(k)) \cdot \bar{i}^{-1}]}{u''(c^0)} \right] - [w'(k) - 1]} \tag{8.37}$$

Since $\bar{i} \in (0,1)$, concavity of the function u implies that the term $(\bar{i}-1)/u''(c^0)$ will be positive. The terms in brackets in the denominator of (8.37) represent the slopes of the (binding) arbitrage relation and the accumulation equation in m-k-plane, respectively. Hence, the denominator simply measures the difference between these slopes. As indicated in figure 8.3, in a situation with a unique equilibrium the arbitrage locus needs to intersect the accumulation locus from below, i.e. the denominator needs to be positive. Finally, the term in brackets in the numerator is unambiguously linked to the elasticity of substitution $\sigma(c^0)$. In particular, as shown in appendix 1, the following condition holds: $u''(c^0) \cdot c^0 + u'(c^0) > 0 \Leftrightarrow \sigma(c^0) > 1$. Using the standard classification of goods with respect to $\sigma(c^0)$, the classification of reaction effects follows then immediately. q.e.d.

We interpret this pattern of reaction effects as following: under a binding cash-in-advance constraint agents are essentially trapped at the critical margin $\bar{i}$, and the best they can do is simply to readjust the quantities to be bought of either type of good. A rise in μ makes cash goods more expensive, and since goods are assumed to be normal, agents will reduce the consumption of cash goods. However, in terms of figure 8.2 agents are without flexibility at the 'horizontal' margin, i.e. by design of the regime they are effectively

---

that both (8.32) and (8.35) continue to hold as strict inequalities in the new equilibrium.

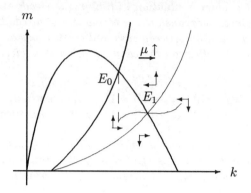

Figure 8.4: *Variation 4 - Tobin steady state* $(\sigma(c^0) > 1)$

restricted to 'vertical' adjustments in their consumption patterns. As a consequence, by knowing whether goods are substitutes or complements, we can say from a portfolio perspective which effect, Tobin or Anti-Tobin, will prevail. For example, consider a situation in which goods are at the margin gross substitutes. Then, the dominance of the Tobin effect simply reflects that capital and money enter the portfolios of agents as substitutes because, at a more primitive level, the types of goods underlying the demand for capital and money are substitutes themselves. We indicate such a constellation in figure 8.4. Note that a rise in μ leaves the accumulation locus unaffected, but it induces a downward shift of the (binding) arbitrage relation.

Similarly, if cash and credit goods are complements this translates into a situation in which capital and money balances act in a complementary manner. As illustrated in figure 8.5, a rise in μ induces now an upward shift of the (binding) arbitrage relation and the Anti-Tobin effect will therefore dominate. Finally, the special case of a zero cross price effect between the two goods makes money superneutral.

As suggested in the introduction to this chapter, the limiting case of an exogenous cash-in-advance constraint may be of considerable relevance in economies with a poorly developed financial system and a large share of cash-based informal or underground activities. In particular, for such economies it seems not implausible to argue that cash and credit goods (i.e. goods obtained in the formal vs. the informal sector of the economy) act in a complementary fashion, thereby supporting the Anti-Tobin effect.

Results are easily modified to account for a situation with multiple steady state equilibria. Of course, the signs of the reaction coefficients established in

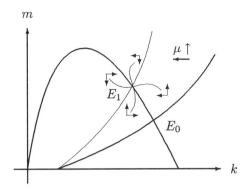

Figure 8.5: *Variation 4 - Anti-Tobin steady state $(\sigma(c^0) < \sigma^{Cr} < 1)$*

proposition 2 will be reversed whenever the locus of the (binding) arbitrage relation intersects the accumulation locus from above. Intuitively, this sign reversal has a simple explanation. At any equilibrium, the *portfolio effect* induced by changes in μ is associated with an *intertemporal income effect*, since the portfolio decision of any generation affects directly the capacity of the next generation to generate income. From this intertemporal perspective, the mechanics of the Tobin effect have clearly a self-defeating element in the sense that any (short-run) switch from money into capital makes the size of the portfolio grow over time. However, in an overall larger portfolio, despite a reduced share, real balances may well be larger than before. Thus, the signs as summarized in the previous proposition will hold as long as the portfolio effect is not dominated by the intertemporal income effect.

Dynamics: Local dynamics of the system can be assessed with standard tools for the analysis of two-dimensional systems of non-linear difference equations, as summarized in appendix II at the end of the book. Moreover, in accordance with Samuelson's correspondence principle, it can be asserted that the dynamical behaviour of the system in the neighbourhood of a steady state is directly linked to its comparative statics properties. Thus, to classify dynamical properties of the system we have to invoke again the classification of steady states given in the previous proposition:

Proposition 3 *Assume that the economy exhibits a unique steady state. Then, local equilibrium dynamics can be classified as following:*

$$\sigma(c^0) > 1 \qquad \Rightarrow \quad \textit{Steady states are a saddle: } 0 < \lambda_1 < 1 < \lambda_2$$
$$\sigma^{cr} < \sigma(c^0) < 1 \quad \Rightarrow \quad \textit{Steady states are a saddle: } \lambda_1 < -1, 0 < \lambda_2 < 1$$
$$\sigma(c^0) < \sigma^{cr} \qquad \Rightarrow \quad \textit{Steady states are a sink: } -1 < \lambda_1 < 0 < \lambda_2 < 1$$

Moreover, the critical value σ^{cr} satisfies the restriction: $0 < \sigma^{cr} < 0.5$.

Proof: see appendix 3.

Remember from chapter 4 that our system has one predetermined variable (the capital stock) and one control variable with a free initial condition (real balances). Since the number of stable (unstable) eigenvalues matches the number of state (control) variables, Tobin steady states are locally saddlepath stable. Thus, as shown in figure 8.4, for Tobin steady states choices of m_t and k_{t+1} are uniquely determined along a saddlepath which converges to the steady state. Anti-Tobin steady states are saddlepath stable if the value of the elasticity of substitution $\sigma(c^0)$ is sufficiently large. At the critical value σ^{cr}, the stability type of the system changes and a Flip bifurcation occurs. As illustrated in figure 8.5, for values of $\sigma(c^0)$ below σ^{cr} Anti-Tobin steady states metamorphose into a sink: given that now both eigenvalues are stable, choices of m_t and k_{t+1} are indeterminate, i.e. a continuum of adjustment paths converges to the steady state. At superneutral steady states (i.e. at points of transition from Tobin to Anti-Tobin steady states), off-equilibrium adjustment cannot be determined since the unstable root moves from plus to minus infinity.

Furthermore, for Tobin steady states adjustment behaviour will be monotone, since the stable eigenvalue λ_1 is positive. Similarly, saddlepath stable Anti-Tobin steady states also have monotone orbits. If Anti-Tobin steady states are a sink adjustment behaviour will ultimately be either monotone or oscillatory, depending on the sign of the dominant eigenvalue.[11]

With $\sigma(c^0)$ being in general endogenously determined, proposition 3, as it stands, needs some further comment. In particular, note that the proposition does *not* say that by changing some of the parameters it will be possible to make the system reach all the regimes mentioned in the proposition. Thus, at this level of generality the proposition seems to have little operational content.

---

[11]Again, extension of results to a situation with multiple equilibria is straightforward. Assume that the arbitrage locus intersects the accumulation locus from above. Then, as shown in appendix 3, local dynamics can be classified as following:

$$\sigma(c^0) > 1 \qquad \Rightarrow \quad \text{Steady states are a source: } 1 < \lambda_1, \lambda_2$$
$$\sigma^{cr} < \sigma(c^0) < 1 \quad \Rightarrow \quad \text{Steady states are a source: } \lambda_1 < -1, \lambda_2 > 1$$
$$\sigma(c^0) < \sigma^{cr} \qquad \Rightarrow \quad \text{Steady states are a saddle: } -1 < \lambda_1 < 0, \lambda_2 > 1$$

Note that steady states are now in the majority of cases entirely unstable.

Simulations: However, as the following simulations show, a meaningful illustration of proposition 3 can be achieved by concentrating on the special class of utility functions u with a constant elasticity of substitution σ. Thus, we parametrize the system (8.32)-(8.35) by choice of a CES utility function $u(c)$, a Cobb-Douglas production function $f(k)$, and a function $\gamma(i)$ which describes the costs of transaction services offered by intermediaries in a suitable manner. To induce a regime with an exogenous cash-in-advance constraint, things are arranged in a way that the discontinuity in processing costs materializes at a sufficiently low value $\bar{i}$. Moreover, in the first simulation functional forms are such that for all parameter constellations a unique steady state obtains.

Simulation 1:

$$u(c(i)) = \frac{1}{1-\varepsilon} \cdot c(i)^{1-\varepsilon}, \quad \varepsilon \in (0,\infty) \tag{8.38}$$

$$f(k) = A \cdot k^\alpha, \quad A > 0, \ a \in (0,1) \tag{8.39}$$

$$\gamma(i) = \begin{cases} \frac{z \cdot i}{1-i} \ for \ 0 \le i \le \bar{i}, \ with: \ z > 0 \\ \infty \ for \ \bar{i} < i \le 1 \end{cases} \tag{8.40}$$

Parameters are specified as:

$$\bar{i} = 0.7, \ \alpha = 0.4, \ \mu = 0.1, \ A = 2, \ z = 0.01$$

Note that σ is given by $\sigma = 1/\varepsilon$. Using the functions (8.38)-(8.40), we derive a parametrized version of the non-linear system (8.32)-(8.35). In particular, we consider variations in σ and hold all the other parameters constant at their specified values. To make sure that (8.32) and (8.35) hold as strict inequalities, we calculate for every choice of σ steady state values of the system (8.33) and (8.34) and check that the boundary solution at $\bar{i} = 0.7$ results indeed from optimizing behaviour. Equally, return-dominance as required by (8.32) is shown to be satisfied for all simulations.

To check the local dynamics of the system around the steady state, we approximate the equations (8.29) and (8.30) by means of first-order Taylor-expansions. As illustrated in figure A.4 in appendix II at the end of the book, the classification of the stability type of a discrete, two-dimensional system of first-order difference equations depends critically on the values of the trace and the determinant of the Jacobian matrix, evaluated at the steady state. Accordingly, we reproduce in plot 1 in appendix 4 pairwise the values of the trace and the determinant corresponding to various choices of σ. Plot 1 confirms that for sufficiently small values of σ points inside the stability triangle are reached. For the assumed parameter values the critical value σ^{cr} where the bifurcation occurs is roughly given by $\sigma^{cr} = 0.4$. The plot also

134

suggests that in the transition from a Tobin to an Anti-Tobin steady state the unstable root changes its sign. Yet, saddlepath stability is preserved.

We find it also worthwhile to reproduce simulation results that are consistent with the existence of multiple steady states. As argued above, the existence of multiple steady states requires that the intertemporal income effect is not always dominated by the portfolio effect. Thus, to obtain a more volatile shape of the function $w(k)$, we parametrize in the second simulation the production function by means of a CES function. We leave $u(c)$ unaltered, and processing costs $\gamma(i)$ are now assumed to be linear in i.

Simulation 2:

$$u(c(i)) = \frac{1}{1-\varepsilon} \cdot c(i)^{1-\varepsilon}, \quad \varepsilon \in (0,\infty) \tag{8.41}$$

$$f(k) = A \cdot [a \cdot k^{-\rho} + (1-a)]^{-\frac{1}{\rho}}, \quad \rho > -1, A > 0, a \in (0,1) \tag{8.42}$$

$$\gamma(i) = \begin{cases} p \cdot i \text{ for } 0 \leq i \leq \bar{i}, \text{ with: } p > 0 \\ \infty \text{ for } \bar{i} < i \leq 1 \end{cases} \tag{8.43}$$

Parameters are given by:

$$\rho = 0.5, \ \bar{i} = 0.553, \ \mu = 0.1, \ a = 0.3, \ A = 1, \ p = 0.3$$

For the CES production function $f(k)$ the elasticity of substitution η is given by the expression: $\eta = \frac{1}{1+\rho}$. As discussed in detail in appendix I at the end of the book, a high degree of volatility in $w(k)$ can be induced if the elasticity of substitution η is taken to be less than one.[12] Clearly, this is the case for $\rho = 0.5$. Simulation results in k-i-plane are reproduced in plot 2 in appendix 4. Note that the binding arbitrage relation is for the critical interval backward bending and has two intersections with the vertical line $i = \bar{i}$. Moreover, the flat line in plot 2 represents (8.35) at equality, and slackness of (8.35) holds in the region northwest of this line. Finally, with the elasticity of substitution being less than one ($\sigma = 0.99$), it is possible to show that in plot 2 the high level equilibrium is of Anti-Tobin nature while at the low level equilibrium the Tobin effect prevails.

---

[12]As shown in appendix I, for $\eta < 1$ part (ii) of (A 2) is not globally satisfied. However, our parameter specifications are such that this condition is in the neighbourhood of all steady states locally satisfied.

8.4 The regime with an endogenous cash-in-advance constraint

Steady state solutions of the system (8.21)-(8.24) with k_t, m_t, and i_t^* being constant over time need to satisfy the equations:

$$f'(k) - \Gamma > \frac{1}{1+\mu} \tag{8.44}$$

$$k = w(k) - m \tag{8.45}$$

$$\frac{1}{1+\mu} \cdot u'(c^0) = f'(k) \cdot u'(c^1) \tag{8.46}$$

$$u(c^1) - u'(c^1) \cdot (c^1 + \gamma(i^*)) = u(c^0) - u'(c^0) \cdot c^0 \tag{8.47}$$

Steady state consumption levels c^1 and c^0 are given by the expressions:

$$c^1 = \frac{f'(k) \cdot k - \Gamma(i^*)}{i^*}, \quad c^0 = \frac{\frac{1}{1+\mu} \cdot m}{1 - i^*} \tag{8.48}$$

As one would expect, the fact that the critical shop i^* results now from an interior solution complicates the analysis of the system (8.44)-(8.47) considerably: any candidate combination of steady solutions (k, m, i^*), as illustrated in figure 8.6, will now be given by the joint intersection of the accumulation locus (8.45) and the loci of the two binding arbitrage relations (8.46) and (8.47). In particular, with i^* resulting from an interior solution, agents will now respond to policy changes in terms of figure 8.2 both through the 'vertical' and the 'horizontal' margin. Thus, substitution effects reflect not only adjustments in terms of consumed quantities but also in terms of rearranged payment patterns, and this additional margin makes it more difficult to separate substitution effects from the intertemporal income effect.[13]

For the rest of this chapter we proceed in two steps. First, we show that it is nevertheless possible to specify constellations in which policy effects can be classified both from a comparative statics and a dynamical perspective in a meaningful way. Second, we illustrate the range of effects now being possible with results from appropriate simulations.

Comparative statics: Upon differentiating the system (8.45)-(8.47), one obtains for the effect of μ on the capital stock k an expression which has at first sight no obvious interpretation. However, it seems natural to seek for a constellation in which agents respond to a higher level of inflation by

---

[13] We do not prove the existence of a steady state equilibrium. However, as demonstrated by Ireland (1994), an appropriate specification of $\Gamma(i)$ is instrumental in establishing the proof. In particular, Ireland (1994) assumes $\Gamma(0) = 0$, $\Gamma(1) = \infty$, and $\gamma'(i) > 0$, for all $i \in (0, 1)$, and ensures thereby an interior solution $i^* \in (0, 1)$.

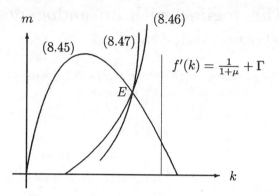

Figure 8.6: *Variation 4 - Endogenous cash-in-advance constraint*

increasing the level of privately arranged credits. We know from the previous section that the intertemporal income effect potentially offsets the substitution effect. Thus, the direction in which proposition 2 needs to be modified is obvious: the best we can hope for is some analogous proposition which says that, as long as the substitution effect dominates the intertemporal income effect, reactions of the system (8.45)-(8.47) to changes in μ are roughly in accordance with this intuition. Indeed, for steady states with a sufficiently small intertemporal income effect (i.e.: $w'(k)$ being 'small') it is possible to show:

Proposition 4 *Assume that at the steady state the restriction $w'(k) < \theta^*$ holds, with θ^* being positive and to be calculated as shown in appendix 2. Then, the system of equations (8.45)-(8.47) shows the following reaction pattern to a change in μ:*

$$\sigma(c^0) > 1 \quad \Rightarrow \quad \frac{\partial k}{\partial \mu} > 0 \quad \text{(Tobin effect)}$$
$$\sigma(c^0) = 1 \quad \Rightarrow \quad \frac{\partial k}{\partial \mu} > 0 \quad \text{(Tobin effect)}$$
$$\sigma(c^0) < 1 \quad \Rightarrow \quad \frac{\partial k}{\partial \mu} \gtreqless 0 \quad \text{(effect ambiguous)}$$

Proof: see appendix 2.

We interpret this proposition as following: if one accounts appropriately for the intertemporal income effect the regime with an endogenous cash-in-advance constraint shows strong support for the Tobin effect. However, even for a small intertemporal income effect the Tobin effect is not entirely uncontested. If consumers regard goods strongly as complements, then it is a priori not clear which effect, adjustments in terms of consumed quantities or payment patterns, will dominate at the margin.

More specifically, to see how the mechanics of the system differ from the exogenous case discussed above, consider the convenient situation of a zero cross-price effect between goods, i.e. a situation with $\sigma(c^0) = 1$. As in a situation with an exogenous cash-in-advance constraint, changes in μ leave both the accumulation equation (8.45) and the arbitrage equation (8.46) undisturbed, but now the second arbitrage equation (8.47) is critically affected: ceteris paribus, a rise in μ decreases c^0, thereby reducing the right-hand side of equation (8.47). And it turns out that a rise both in k and i^* is the dominating response to rebalance the overall system.[14]

Dynamics: Due to Samuelson's correspondence principle, ambiguity with respect to comparative statics effects makes a comprehensive dynamical classification of equilibria elusive. However, for Tobin steady states satisfying the condition $w'(k) < \theta^*$ a clear-cut characterization is readily established. Since our simulations strongly indicate that this type of equilibrium is the most likely one to occur, we find the following proposition worthwhile to be reported:

Proposition 5 *Consider a Tobin steady state with a small intertemporal income effect, i.e. the steady state satisfies: $w'(k) < \theta^*$. Then, local equilibrium dynamics are saddlepath stable, and adjustment behaviour towards the steady state is monotone.*

Proof: see appendix 2.

Simulations: We conclude this section by presenting results from two simulation exercises. In simulation 3, we choose the same functions as in simulation 1, but the discontinuity in processing costs materializes now at a sufficiently high level of $\bar{i}$ such that i^* represents an interior solution.

---

[14] Again, it is straightforward to extend results to a situation with multiple equilibria. Assume that at the steady state under consideration the intertemporal income effect is 'large', i.e. we have: $w'(k) > \theta^*$. Then, equilibria can be classified as following:

$$\sigma(c^0) > 1 \quad \Rightarrow \quad \frac{\partial k}{\partial \mu} < 0 \quad \text{(Anti-Tobin effect)}$$
$$\sigma(c^0) = 1 \quad \Rightarrow \quad \frac{\partial k}{\partial \mu} < 0 \quad \text{(Anti-Tobin effect)}$$
$$\sigma(c^0) < 1 \quad \Rightarrow \quad \frac{\partial k}{\partial \mu} \gtrless 0 \quad \text{(effect ambiguous)}$$

Simulation 3: Functional forms are as in simulation 1 and parameter values are specified as:

$$\bar{i} = 0.99, \ \mu = 0.1 \ , \alpha = 0.4, \ A = 2, \ z = 0.01$$

Substituting out for m in (8.45) yields a parametrized version of the two-equation system (8.46) and (8.47) in the two unknown variables k and i. In plots 3 (a)-(b) in appendix 4, we present for various choices of σ the corresponding graphs in k-i-plane. In all cases reported, equilibria are unique, and it turns out that even for low values of σ (i.e.: a high degree of complementarity between cash and credit goods) the Tobin effect prevails. Results are 'robust' for various parametrizations, and therefore we conclude that for standard functional forms the Tobin effect has strong support.

However, in simulation 4 we assume, similar to simulation 2, that production occurs according to a CES production function.

Simulation 4: Functional forms are as in simulation 2 and parameters are given by:

$$\rho = 0.5, \ \bar{i} = 0.99, \ \mu = 0.1 \ , \ a = 0.3, \ A = 1, \ p = 0.2$$

Note that we concentrate again on a situation in which the elasticity of substitution η of the CES function is less than one in order to induce a high degree of volatility in $w(k)$. In plots 4 (a)-(b) we present graphs corresponding to (8.46) and (8.47) in k-i-plane for varying degrees of σ. In contrast to simulation 3, constellations of multiple equilibria become now possible for low values of σ. More specifically, one easily confirms in plot 4 (b) that at the low level equilibrium, with the locus of (8.47) being flatter than the one of (8.46), the Anti-Tobin effect prevails. In contrast, at the high level equilibrium (8.47) is steeper than (8.46) and the Tobin effect dominates.

8.5 Appendix 1: Standard problem of the consumer

Standard consumer theory says that the cross-price effect between two goods will be positive whenever the goods are gross substitutes, i.e. the elasticity of substitution between the goods exceeds unity. For further reference, we reproduce this result briefly in our context by solving the standard problem from consumer theory for the special case of an additively separable utility function, with $u(c)$ being strictly concave as assumed in (A 4). For the standard problem, the critical value $\bar{i}$ is taken to be fixed.

$$\max_{c^0, c^1} \int_0^{\bar{i}} u(c^1(i))\, di + \int_{\bar{i}}^1 u(c^0(i))\, di$$

$$+ \lambda \cdot [m - \int_0^{\bar{i}} p^1 \cdot c^1(i)\, di - \int_{\bar{i}}^1 p^0 \cdot c^0(i)\, di]$$

The symmetric set-up ensures that $c^0(i)$ and $c^1(i)$ do not depend on i. First-order conditions are necessary and sufficient for an interior optimum and are given by:

$$
\begin{aligned}
u'(c^1) &= \lambda \cdot p^1 \\
u'(c^0) &= \lambda \cdot p^0 \\
m &= \bar{i} \cdot p^1 \cdot c^1 + (1 - \bar{i}) \cdot p^0 \cdot c^0
\end{aligned}
$$

Rearranging yields:

$$p^0 \cdot u'(c^1) - p^1 \cdot u'\left(\frac{m - \bar{i} \cdot p^1 \cdot c^1}{(1 - \bar{i}) \cdot p^0} \right) = 0$$

The cross-price effect is given by:

$$
\begin{aligned}
\frac{d\, c^1}{d\, p^0} &= \frac{u'(c^1) + p^1 \cdot u''(c^0) \cdot \frac{c^0}{p^0}}{(-1) \cdot [p^0 \cdot u''(c^1) + p^1 \cdot u''(c^0) \cdot \frac{\bar{i}}{1-\bar{i}} \cdot \frac{p^1}{p^0}]} \\
&= \frac{p^1}{p^0} \cdot \frac{u'(c^0) + u''(c^0) \cdot c^0}{(-1) \cdot [p^0 \cdot u''(c^1) + p^1 \cdot u''(c^0) \cdot \frac{\bar{i}}{1-\bar{i}} \cdot \frac{p^1}{p^0}]}
\end{aligned}
$$

The denominator is positive by assumption (A 4). Let the numerator be defined as: $u'(c^0) + u''(c^0) \cdot c^0 = \tau(c^0)$. Moreover, let $\varepsilon(c^0)$ denote the absolute value of the elasticity of marginal utility with respect to consumption. Note that $\varepsilon(c^0)$ is the inverse of the elasticity of substitution $\sigma(c^0)$. Rearranging the numerator yields:

$$[u'(c^0) + u''(c^0) \cdot c^0] = u'(c^0) \cdot [1 - \varepsilon(c^0)] = u'(c^0) \cdot [1 - \frac{1}{\sigma(c^0)}]$$

Thus, the cross-price effect depends on $\sigma(c^0)$, as claimed in proposition 2:

$$\frac{d\, c^1}{d\, p^0} = \begin{cases} > 0 & \Leftrightarrow \tau(c^0) > 0 \Leftrightarrow \sigma(c^0) > 1 \\ = 0 & \Leftrightarrow \tau(c^0) = 0 \Leftrightarrow \sigma(c^0) = 1 \\ < 0 & \Leftrightarrow \tau(c^0) < 0 \Leftrightarrow \sigma(c^0) < 1 \end{cases}$$

140

8.6 Appendix 2: The regime with an endogenous cash-in-advance constraint

As shown in the main section, dynamics for the regime with an endogenous cash-in-advance constraint satisfy the system of equations (8.22)-(8.24):[15]

$$k_{t+1} = w_t(k_t) - m_t \tag{8.49}$$

$$\frac{1}{1+\mu} \cdot \frac{m_{t+1}}{m_t} \cdot u'(c_{t+1}^0) = f'(w_t(k_t) - m_t) \cdot u'(c_{t+1}^1) \tag{8.50}$$

$$u(c_{t+1}^0) - u'(c_{t+1}^1) \cdot c_{t+1}^0 = u(c_{t+1}^1) - u'(c_{t+1}^1) \cdot (c_{t+1}^1 + \gamma(i_{t+1}^*)) \tag{8.51}$$

Equilibrium consumption levels of cash and credit goods are given by the expressions:

$$c_{t+1}^0 = \frac{m_{t+1}}{(1+\mu) \cdot (1 - i_{t+1}^*)} \tag{8.52}$$

$$c_{t+1}^1 = \frac{f'(w_t(k_t) - m_t) \cdot (w_t(k_t) - m_t) - \Gamma(i_{t+1}^*)}{i_{t+1}^*} \tag{8.53}$$

Totally differentiating (8.49)-(8.51) yields in matrix notation:

$$A^* \cdot \begin{bmatrix} d\,k_{t+1} \\ d\,m_{t+1} \\ d\,i_{t+1} \end{bmatrix} + h^* \cdot d\,\mu = B^* \cdot \begin{bmatrix} d\,k_t \\ d\,m_t \\ d\,i_t \end{bmatrix} \tag{8.54}$$

With all coefficients being evaluated at the steady state, the matrices A^*, B^*, and h^* are given by:

$$A^* = \begin{bmatrix} 1 & 0 & 0 \\ 0 & \alpha_1 & \alpha_2 \\ 0 & \alpha_3 & \alpha_4 \end{bmatrix}, \quad B^* = \begin{bmatrix} w'(k) & -1 & 0 \\ \beta_1 & \beta_2 & 0 \\ \beta_3 & \beta_4 & 0 \end{bmatrix}, \quad h^* = \begin{bmatrix} 0 \\ h_1 \\ h_2 \end{bmatrix}$$

$$\alpha_1 = \frac{1}{1+\mu} \cdot \frac{1}{m} \cdot [u'(c^0) + u''(c^0) \cdot c^0]$$

$$\alpha_2 = \frac{1}{1+\mu} \cdot u''(c^0) \cdot \frac{c^0}{(1-i^*)} + f'(k) \cdot u''(c^1) \cdot \frac{c^1 + \gamma(i^*)}{i^*}$$

$$\alpha_3 = -u''(c^0) \cdot c^0 \cdot \frac{1}{1+\mu} \cdot \frac{1}{(1-i^*)}$$

$$\alpha_4 = -u''(c^0) \cdot c^0 \cdot \frac{c^0}{(1-i^*)} - u''(c^1) \cdot (c^1 + \gamma(i^*)) \cdot \frac{c^1 + \gamma(i^*)}{i^*}$$
$$+ u'(c^1) \cdot \gamma'(i^*)$$

---

[15]Remember that we consider steady states where (8.21) remains slack for small perturbations of the system.

$$\beta_1 = w'(k) \cdot [f'(k) \cdot u''(c^1) \cdot \frac{d\,f'(k) \cdot k}{d\,k} \cdot \frac{1}{i^*} + f''(k) \cdot u'(c^1)]$$

$$\beta_2 = -[f'(k) \cdot u''(c^1) \cdot \frac{d\,f'(k) \cdot k}{d\,k} \cdot \frac{1}{i^*} + f''(k) \cdot u'(c^1)] + \frac{1}{1+\mu} \cdot \frac{1}{m} \cdot u'(c^0)$$

$$\beta_3 = -w'(k) \cdot u''(c^1) \cdot (c^1 + \gamma(i^*)) \cdot \frac{d\,f'(k) \cdot k}{d\,k} \cdot \frac{1}{i^*}$$

$$\beta_4 = u''(c^1) \cdot (c^1 + \gamma(i^*)) \cdot \frac{d\,f'(k) \cdot k}{d\,k} \cdot \frac{1}{i^*} = -\frac{\beta_3}{w'(k)}$$

$$h_1 = -\frac{1}{(1+\mu)^2} \cdot [u'(c^0) + u''(c^0) \cdot c^0] = -\frac{m}{1+\mu} \cdot \alpha_1$$

$$h_2 = \frac{1}{(1+\mu)^2} \cdot \frac{m}{1-i^*} \cdot u''(c^0) \cdot c^0 = -\frac{m}{1+\mu} \cdot \alpha_3$$

By (A 1)-(A 5), all terms apart from α_1 and h_1 can be signed unambiguously:

$$\alpha_2 < 0, \quad \alpha_3 > 0, \quad \alpha_4 > 0,$$
$$\beta_1 < 0, \quad \beta_2 > 0, \quad \beta_3 > 0, \quad \beta_4 < 0,$$
$$h_2 < 0.$$

However, appealing to the classification of effects established in the previous appendix, signs of the terms α_1 and h_1 follow the pattern:

$$\alpha_1 = \begin{cases} > 0 & \Leftrightarrow \tau(c^0) > 0 \Leftrightarrow \sigma(c^0) > 1 \\ = 0 & \Leftrightarrow \tau(c^0) = 0 \Leftrightarrow \sigma(c^0) = 1 \\ < 0 & \Leftrightarrow \tau(c^0) < 0 \Leftrightarrow \sigma(c^0) < 1 \end{cases}$$

$$sign(h_1) = -sign(\alpha_1)$$

Comparative statics: With all variables being constant in steady states, comparative statics results can be derived from the expression:

$$(B^* - A^*) \cdot \begin{bmatrix} d\,k \\ d\,m \\ d\,i \end{bmatrix} = h^* \cdot d\,\mu \tag{8.55}$$

The matrix $B^* - A^*$ is given by the expression:

$$B^* - A^* = \begin{bmatrix} w'(k) - 1 & -1 & 0 \\ \beta_1 & \beta_2 - \alpha_1 & -\alpha_2 \\ \beta_3 & \beta_4 - \alpha_3 & -\alpha_4 \end{bmatrix}$$

Applying Cramer's rule to (8.55) yields:

$$\frac{d\,k}{d\,\mu} = \frac{h_2 \cdot \alpha_2 - h_1 \cdot \alpha_4}{Det(B^* - A^*)} = \frac{m}{1+\mu} \cdot \frac{Det(A^*)}{Det(B^* - A^*)} \tag{8.56}$$

In (8.56), the sign of the numerator of $\frac{\partial k}{\partial \mu}$ is closely linked to the question of whether goods are substitutes or complements. In particular, the numerator is positive if the elasticity of substitution $\sigma(c^0)$ is greater than one, while for $\sigma(c^0) < 1$ the sign of the numerator is a priori ambiguous.

We turn now to a thorough analysis of the determinant $Det(B^* - A^*)$ showing up in the denominator of (8.56). Calculating $Det(B^* - A^*)$ yields:

$$Det(B^* - A^*) = [w'(k) - 1] \cdot [Det(A^*) + \alpha_2 \cdot \beta_4 - \alpha_4 \cdot \beta_2] - \alpha_4 \cdot \beta_1 + \alpha_2 \cdot \beta_3$$

Note that for β-type terms the following restrictions hold:

$$w'(k) \cdot \beta_4 + \beta_3 = 0 \tag{8.57}$$

$$w'(k) \cdot \beta_2 + \beta_1 = w'(k) \cdot \frac{1}{(1+\mu) \cdot m} \cdot u'(c^0) > 0 \tag{8.58}$$

Let θ_1^* and θ_2^* be defined as:

$$\theta_1^* = Det(A^*) + \alpha_2 \cdot \beta_4 - \alpha_4 \cdot \beta_2$$

$$\theta_2^* = Det(A^*) - \alpha_4 \cdot \frac{1}{(1+\mu) \cdot m} \cdot u'(c^0)$$

After some tidying up, the expression describing the determinant yields:

$$Det(B^* - A^*) = w'(k) \cdot \theta_2^* - \theta_1^* \tag{8.59}$$

To account for the intertemporal income effect we establish the lemma:

Lemma 1 *The terms θ_1^* and θ_2^* will always be negative: $\theta_1^* < 0, \theta_2^* < 0$.*

Proof: Let ϕ_1, ϕ_2, and ϕ_3 be defined as:

$$\phi_1 = (\alpha_1 - \beta_2) \cdot u'(c^1) \cdot \gamma'(i^*) -$$
$$f''(k) \cdot u'(c^1) \cdot \left[\frac{u''(c^0) \cdot c^0}{(1 - i^*)} \cdot c^0 + \frac{u''(c^1) \cdot (c^1 + \gamma(i^*))}{i^*} \cdot (c^1 + \gamma(i^*)) \right]$$

$$\phi_2 = \frac{1}{1+\mu} \cdot \frac{1}{m} \cdot u''(c^0) \cdot c^0 \cdot u'(c^1) \cdot \gamma'(i^*)$$

$$\phi_3 = f'(k) \cdot c^0 - (c^1 + \gamma(i^*)) \cdot \frac{1}{1+\mu}$$

Further simplifying the θ-type expressions, one obtains:

$$\theta_1^* = \phi_1 - \frac{u''(c^0) \cdot u''(c^1)}{i^* \cdot (1 - i^*)} \cdot \phi_3 \cdot [\phi_3 + f''(k) \cdot k \cdot c^0]$$

$$\theta_2^* = \phi_2 + \frac{u''(c^0) \cdot u''(c^1) \cdot (c^1 + \gamma(i^*)) \cdot c^0}{m \cdot i^*} \cdot \phi_3$$

It is easily verified that ϕ_1 and ϕ_2 will always be negative. Thus, $\theta_1^* < 0$ and $\theta_2^* < 0$ will be satisfied if $\phi_3 < 0$. However, $\phi_3 < 0$ follows from equations

(8.46) and (8.47) and the assumption that (8.44) is slack at the equilibrium: slackness of (8.44) implies $f'(k) > 1/(1 + \mu)$, and $c^1 > c^0$ follows then from (8.46). By (A 4), this implies: $u(c^1) > u(c^0)$. Consequently, according to (8.47), $u'(c^1) \cdot (c^1 + \gamma(i^*)) > u'(c^0) \cdot c^0$ needs to be satisfied. Combining this with (8.46), $\phi_3 < 0$ follows immediately. q.e.d.

Since $w'(k) = -k \cdot f''(k)$, (A 1) implies $w'(k) > 0$. Thus, $\theta_1^* < 0$, $\theta_2^* < 0$ ensures that the sign of $Det(B^* - A^*)$ in (8.59) is a priori ambiguous.

Proof of proposition 4: Using (8.59), let the threshold value θ^* for the intertemporal income effect be defined as:

$$\theta^* = \theta_1^*/\theta_2^*$$

Clearly, $\theta^* > 0$ needs to hold because of $\theta_1^* < 0$, $\theta_2^* < 0$, and $w'(k) < \theta^*$ implies in (8.59): $Det(B^* - A^*) > 0$. The classification of reaction effects given in proposition 4 follows then immediately from (8.56). q.e.d.

Dynamics: The analysis of the dynamics of the three-dimensional system (8.49)-(8.51) is substantially alleviated by the fact that the state variable k is entirely governed by the control variable m, while the choice of i has no repercussions over time, i.e. in the system (8.49)-(8.51) all realizations of i occur in period $t+1$. Thus, reflecting the static nature of the choice variable i, off-steady state dynamics of the linearized system (8.54) are to be analyzed by inspecting an appropriately manipulated, two-dimensional system in k_t and m_t. Note that the recursive structure of the matrix A^* makes it particularly easy to find the appropriate transformation. More specifically, by combining the second and third equation of the system (8.54), one easily eliminates the differential $d\,i_{t+1}$ and arrives at the two-dimensional system in k_t and m_t:[16]

$$\begin{bmatrix} k_{t+1} \\ m_{t+1} \end{bmatrix} = (I - J^*) \cdot \begin{bmatrix} k \\ m \end{bmatrix} + J^* \cdot \begin{bmatrix} k_t \\ m_t \end{bmatrix}, \quad \text{with:}$$

$$J^* = \begin{bmatrix} w'(k) & -1 \\ \frac{\beta_1 \cdot \alpha_4 - \beta_3 \cdot \alpha_2}{Det(A^*)} & \frac{\beta_2 \cdot \alpha_4 - \beta_4 \cdot \alpha_2}{Det(A^*)} \end{bmatrix}$$

As established in appendix II, off-steady state dynamics of the system (8.54) depend on the eigenvalues of the matrix J^*. In particular, the eigenvalues solve the characteristic equation:

$$p(\lambda) = \lambda^2 - Tr(J^*) \cdot \lambda + Det(J^*) = 0$$

Applying the standard solution formula yields:

$$\lambda_{1/2} = \frac{Tr(J^*)}{2} \pm \frac{1}{2} \cdot \sqrt{Tr(J^*)^2 - 4 \cdot Det(J^*)}$$

---

[16] Note that the analysis of dynamical properties of the system (8.54) requires $d\mu = 0$.

Expressions for the trace $Tr(J^*)$ and the determinant $Det(J^*)$ are given by:

$$Tr(J^*) = w'(k) + \frac{\beta_2 \cdot \alpha_4 - \beta_4 \cdot \alpha_2}{Det(A^*)}$$

$$Det(J^*) = w'(k) \cdot \frac{\beta_2 \cdot \alpha_4 - \beta_4 \cdot \alpha_2}{Det(A^*)} + \frac{\beta_1 \cdot \alpha_4 - \beta_3 \cdot \alpha_2}{Det(A^*)}$$

$$= \frac{\alpha_4 \cdot [w'(k) \cdot \beta_2 + \beta_1]}{Det(A^*)}$$

Finally, to assess whether λ_1 and λ_2 fall on the same side of unity, we factor the characteristic equation as $p(\lambda) = (\lambda - \lambda_1) \cdot (\lambda - \lambda_2)$ and evaluate the expression at $\lambda = 1$, using the restriction imposed by (8.57):

$$p(1) = 1 - Tr(J^*) + Det(J^*)$$

$$= \frac{-Det(B^* - A^*)}{Det(A^*)}$$

Proof of proposition 5:

By (8.58), the numerator of the term describing $Det(J^*)$ is always positive. Hence, $sign[Det(J^*)] = sign[Det(A^*)]$. As shown above, Tobin steady states with $w'(k) < \theta^*$ are characterized by the conditions: $Det(A^*) > 0$ and $Det(B^* - A^*) > 0$. This implies: $Det(J^*) > 0$, $p(1) < 0$. Thus, using the classification introduced in appendix II, steady states fall in region $1a$, i.e. steady states are a saddle (with associated eigenvalues $0 < \lambda_1 < 1$, $\lambda_2 > 1$), displaying monotone adjustment behaviour. q.e.d.

8.7 Appendix 3: The regime with an exogenous cash-in-advance constraint

As shown in the main section, for the regime with an exogenous cash-in-advance constraint equations (8.29) and (8.30) need to hold:[17]

$$k_{t+1} = w_t(k_t) - m_t \qquad (8.60)$$

$$\frac{1}{1+\mu} \cdot \frac{m_{t+1}}{m_t} \cdot u'(c_{t+1}^0) = f'(k_{t+1}) \cdot u'(c_{t+1}^1) \qquad (8.61)$$

Equilibrium levels of consumption are given by:

$$c_{t+1}^0 = \frac{m_{t+1}}{(1+\mu) \cdot (1 - \bar{\imath})} \qquad (8.62)$$

$$c_{t+1}^1 = \frac{f'(w_t(k_t) - m_t) \cdot (w_t(k_t) - m_t) - \Gamma(\bar{\imath})}{\bar{\imath}} \qquad (8.63)$$

---

[17]Remember that both (8.28) and (8.31) are assumed to hold as strict inequalities for small perturbations of the system around the steady state.

Totally differentiating (8.60)-(8.61) yields in matrix notation:

$$\overline{A} \cdot \begin{bmatrix} d\,k_{t+1} \\ d\,m_{t+1} \end{bmatrix} + \overline{h} \cdot d\,\mu = \overline{B} \cdot \begin{bmatrix} d\,k_t \\ d\,m_t \end{bmatrix} \tag{8.64}$$

Slightly abusing notation, we use for the elements of the matrices in equation (8.64) the same coefficients that we introduced in appendix 2 for the endogenous cash-in-advance regime:[18]

$$\overline{A} = \begin{bmatrix} 1 & 0 \\ 0 & \alpha_1 \end{bmatrix}, \quad \overline{B} = \begin{bmatrix} w'(k) & -1 \\ \beta_1 & \beta_2 \end{bmatrix}, \quad \overline{h} = \begin{bmatrix} 0 \\ h_1 \end{bmatrix}$$

Restating results derived above, signs of the coefficients are as following:

$$\alpha_1 = \begin{cases} > 0 & \Leftrightarrow \tau(c^0) > 0 \Leftrightarrow \sigma(c^0) > 1 \\ = 0 & \Leftrightarrow \tau(c^0) = 0 \Leftrightarrow \sigma(c^0) = 1 \\ < 0 & \Leftrightarrow \tau(c^0) < 0 \Leftrightarrow \sigma(c^0) < 1 \end{cases}$$

$$\text{sign}(h_1) = -\text{sign}(\alpha_1),$$
$$\beta_1 < 0, \; \beta_2 > 0.$$

Upon rearranging the linear approximation in (8.64), off-steady state dynamics are given by the two-dimensional system of first-order difference equations:

$$\begin{bmatrix} k_{t+1} \\ m_{t+1} \end{bmatrix} = (I - (\overline{A})^{-1} \cdot \overline{B}) \cdot \begin{bmatrix} k \\ m \end{bmatrix} + (\overline{A})^{-1} \cdot \overline{B} \cdot \begin{bmatrix} k_t \\ m_t \end{bmatrix} \tag{8.65}$$

Let $\overline{J}$ be defined as $\overline{J} = (\overline{A})^{-1} \cdot \overline{B}$. Note that the eigenvalues of the matrix $\overline{J}$ control the dynamics of the system. The matrix $(\overline{A})^{-1}$ is given by the expression:

$$(\overline{A})^{-1} = \begin{bmatrix} 1 & 0 \\ 0 & \frac{1}{\alpha_1} \end{bmatrix}$$

Calculating $\overline{J}$ yields:

$$\overline{J} = \begin{bmatrix} w'(k) & -1 \\ \frac{\beta_1}{\alpha_1} & \frac{\beta_2}{\alpha_1} \end{bmatrix}$$

Thus, one obtains for the trace $Tr(\overline{J})$ and the determinant $Det(\overline{J})$ the expressions:

$$Tr(\overline{J}) = w'(k) + \frac{\beta_2}{\alpha_1}$$

$$Det(\overline{J}) = w'(k) \cdot \frac{\beta_2}{\alpha_1} + \frac{\beta_1}{\alpha_1} = \frac{w'(k) \cdot \frac{1}{(1+\mu)\cdot m} \cdot u'(c^0)}{\alpha_1}$$

---

[18]Note that in appendix 2 all coefficients are evaluated at i^*, while now $\overline{i}$ is the relevant margin. However, this is the only difference.

The characteristic equation associated with $\bar{J}$ is given by:

$$p(\lambda) = \lambda^2 - Tr(\bar{J}) \cdot \lambda + Det(\bar{J}) = 0$$

Eigenvalues of the matrix $\bar{J}$ are determined by the formula:

$$\lambda_{1,2} = \frac{Tr(\bar{J})}{2} \pm \frac{1}{2} \cdot \sqrt{Tr(\bar{J})^2 - 4 \cdot D(\bar{J})}$$

In order to establish how λ_1 and λ_2 relate to plus and minus unity, we factor the characteristic equation as $p(\lambda) = (\lambda - \lambda_1) \cdot (\lambda - \lambda_2)$ and evaluate the expression at $\lambda = 1$ and $\lambda = -1$:

$$
\begin{aligned}
p(1) &= 1 - Tr(\bar{J}) + Det(\bar{J}) \\
&= \frac{[w'(k) - 1] \cdot [\beta_2 - \alpha_1] + \beta_1}{\alpha_1} \\
p(-1) &= 1 + Tr(\bar{J}) + Det(\bar{J}) \\
&= [1 + w'(k)] \cdot [1 + \frac{\frac{1}{(1+\mu)\cdot m} \cdot u'(c^0)}{\alpha_1}] - \frac{\beta_1}{w'(k) \cdot \alpha_1} \\
&= [1 + w'(k)] \cdot [1 + \underbrace{\frac{1}{1 - \frac{1}{\sigma(c^0)}}}_{\eta_1}] - \underbrace{\frac{\beta_1}{w'(k) \cdot \alpha_1}}_{\eta_2} \\
&= [1 + w'(k)] \cdot [1 + \eta_1] - \eta_2
\end{aligned}
$$

Finally, we calculate the critical expression $Tr(\bar{J})^2 - 4 \cdot D(\bar{J})]$:

$$Tr(\bar{J})^2 - 4 \cdot D(\bar{J}) = [w'(k) - \frac{\beta_2}{\alpha_1}]^2 - 4 \cdot \frac{\beta_1}{\alpha_1}$$

Proof of proposition 3:

Due to Samuelson's correspondence principle the distinction among steady state types as given in Proposition 2 carries over to the dynamical properties of steady states.

i) In a constellation with a unique steady state, the intertemporal income effect needs to be sufficiently small, i.e. the locus of the arbitrage relation needs to intersect the locus of the accumulation equation in m-k-plane from below. One easily shows that in such a constellation the numerator of $p(1)$ will always be negative, i.e. the condition $[w'(k) - 1] \cdot [\beta_2 - \alpha_1] + \beta_1 < 0$ will be satisfied.[19]

---

[19]Remember that the denominator of the reaction coefficient given in (8.37) measures the difference between the slopes of the arbitrage relation and the accumulation equation. Using this information, one easily verifies the claim upon explicit calculation of the numerator of $p(1)$.

Case 1: $\sigma(c^0) > 1$ *(Tobin steady state)*

$\sigma(c^0) > 1$ implies $\alpha_1 > 0$. Thus, we have: $Det(\overline{J}) > 0$, $p(1) < 0$. Using the classification introduced in appendix II at the end of the book, the steady state falls in region $1a$, i.e. the steady state is a *saddle* $(0 < \lambda_1 < 1 < \lambda_2)$, displaying monotone adjustment.

Case 2: $\sigma(c^0) = 1$ *(Superneutral steady state)*

$\sigma(c^0) = 1$ implies $\alpha_1 = 0$, and both $Det(\overline{J})$ and $Tr(\overline{J})$ tend to infinity as the unstable root passes from plus to minus infinity.

Case 3: $\sigma(c^0) < 1$ *(Anti-Tobin steady state)*

$\sigma(c^0) < 1$ implies $\alpha_1 < 0$, and one obtains: $Det(\overline{J}) < 0$, $p(1) > 0$. Thus, the eigenvalues are real, straddle zero, and fall on the same side of unity: $\lambda_1 < 0 < \lambda_2 < 1$. Furthermore, the sign of $p(-1)$ is a priori ambiguous. Note that $\eta_2 > 0$ will always be satisfied, while η_1 may fall on either side of -1, depending on the magnitude of $\sigma(c^0)$.

First, we show that Anti-Tobin steady states which arise from a sufficiently mild complementarity between cash and credit goods are saddlepath stable. To illustrate this, consider the interval $\frac{1}{2} < \sigma(c^0) < 1$, implying $\eta_1 < -1$. Thus, $p(-1) < 0$ will be satisfied, and the steady state falls in region $3b$ with associated eigenvalues: $\lambda_1 < -1$, $0 < \lambda_2 < 1$.

Second, we consider the interval: $0 < \sigma(c^0) < \frac{1}{2}$. This implies: $-1 < \eta_1 < 0$, and the sign of $p(-1)$ is now a priori ambiguous. In particular, we have:

$$w'(k) > -1 + \frac{\eta_2}{1+\eta_1} \quad \Leftrightarrow \quad p(-1) > 0$$

Note that $\frac{\eta_2}{1+\eta_1} = \frac{[f'(k)\cdot u''(c^1)\cdot \frac{d\,f'(k)\cdot k}{d\,k}\cdot\frac{1}{i^*}+f''(k)\cdot u'(c^1)]}{u'(c^0)} \cdot \frac{1}{2-1/\sigma(c^0)}$. Hence, for $(c^0, c^1) > 0$, $\sigma(c^0) \to 0$ implies $\frac{\eta_2}{1+\eta_1} \to 0$ and $p(-1) > 0$. Thus, below some critical value $\sigma^{cr} < 1/2$ the complementarity is sufficiently strong, and the steady state falls in region $7c$ or $7d$. Correspondingly, eigenvalues will satisfy the restriction: $-1 < \lambda_1 < 0 < \lambda_2 < 1$.

In summary, we can distinguish between the following subcases:

Case 3.1.: $\sigma^{cr} < \sigma(c^0) < 1$ *(case of a mild complementarity)*:

Eigenvalues are given by: $\lambda_1 < -1$, $0 < \lambda_2 < 1$. The steady state is a *saddle*, displaying monotone adjustment.

Case 3.2.: $0 < \sigma(c^0) < \sigma^{cr}$ *(case of a strong complementarity)*:

Eigenvalues are given by: $-1 < \lambda_1 < 0 < \lambda_2 < 1$. The steady state is a *sink*, and adjustment will ultimately be either monotone or oscillatory, depending on the sign of the dominant eigenvalue.

ii) To extend the classification to a situation with multiple equilibria is straightforward. In particular, assume that the locus of the arbitrage relation intersects the locus of the accumulation equation from above. Clearly, now the following condition will be satisfied: $[w'(k) - 1] \cdot [\beta_2 - \alpha_1] + \beta_1 > 0$.

Case 4: $\sigma(c^0) > 1$ (Anti-Tobin steady state)

The condition $\sigma(c^0) > 1$ implies $\alpha_1 > 0$, and we have: $Det(\overline{J}) > 0$, $p(1) > 0$, $[Tr(\overline{J})]^2 - 4 \cdot D(\overline{J}) > 0$. Thus, eigenvalues are real and fall on the same side of unity. One easily verifies that $\frac{\beta_2}{\alpha_1} > 1$ will be satisfied. Moreover, $w'(k) > 1$ follows from the restriction imposed on the relative slopes in m-k-plane. Thus, we have: $Tr(\overline{J}) > 2$. Therefore, both eigenvalues must exceed unity, and the steady state falls in region 8 $(1 < \lambda_1, \lambda_2)$, i.e. the steady state is a *source*.

Case 5: $\sigma(c^0) = 1$ (Superneutral steady state)

$\sigma(c^0) = 1$ implies $\alpha_1 = 0$, and both $Det(\overline{J})$ and $Tr(\overline{J})$ tend to infinity as one of the unstable roots passes from plus to minus infinity.

Case 6: $\sigma(c^0) < 1$ (Tobin steady state)

$\sigma(c^0) < 1$ implies $\alpha_1 < 0$, and we obtain: $Det(\overline{J}) < 0$, $p(1) < 0$. Thus, the eigenvalues are real and straddle both zero and unity: $\lambda_1 < 0, 1 < \lambda_2$. Similar to case 3, the sign of $p(-1)$ is a priori ambiguous. However, we have $p(-1) > 0$ if $0 < \sigma(c^0) < \sigma^{cr} < \frac{1}{2}$, i.e. the steady state falls in region $1b$ with associated eigenvalues: $-1 < \lambda_1 < 0, 1 < \lambda_2$. Conversely, $p(-1) < 0$ will be satisfied if $\sigma^{cr} < \sigma(c^0) < 1$, i.e. the steady state falls in region $2a$ or $2b$ with associated eigenvalues: $\lambda_1 < -1, 1 < \lambda_2$.

Again, we need to distinguish between two subcases:

6.1.: $\sigma^{cr} < \sigma(c^0) < 1$ (*Mild complementarity*):

Eigenvalues are given by: $\lambda_1 < -1, 1 < \lambda_2$. The steady state is a *source*.

6.2.: $0 < \sigma(c^0) < \sigma^{cr} < \frac{1}{2}$ (*Strong complementarity*):

Eigenvalues are given by: $-1 < \lambda_1 < 0, \lambda_2 > 1$. The steady state is a *saddle*, and since the stable eigenvalue is negative, adjustment will be oscillatory. q.e.d.

8.8   Appendix 4: Plots

Simulation 1:

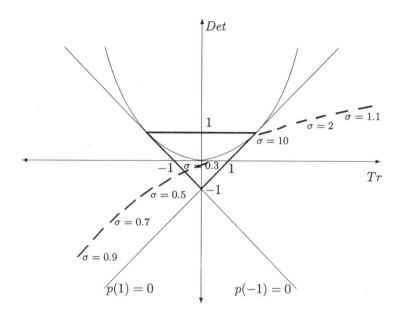

Plot 1: Stability behaviour

150

Simulation 2:

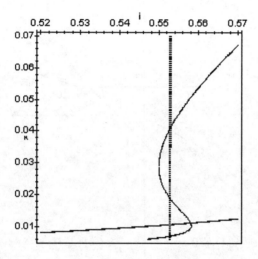

Plot 2: $\sigma = 0.99$

Simulation 3:

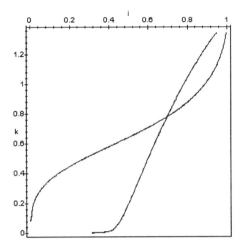

Plot 3a: $\sigma = 5$

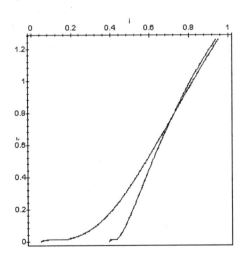

Plot 3b: $\sigma = 0.5$

152

Simulation 4:

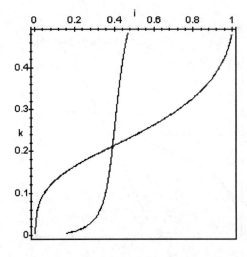

Plot 4a: $\sigma = 5$

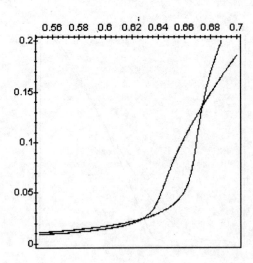

Plot 4b: $\sigma = 0.5$

Chapter 9

Variation 5: Differentiated goods, multiple means of payment, and alternative specifications of government activities

In the previous two chapters, our treatment of government activities in our discussion of economies subject to various cash-in-advance constraints has been rather crude. However, in this chapter we present more detailed specifications of some government activities, and it turns out that modifications both of the revenue and the expenditure side of the government's budget constraint can substantially change the interaction of inflation and capital formation. We use the framework introduced in chapter 8, and to keep the analysis as transparent as possible we concentrate on constellations with an 'exogenous cash-in-advance constraint'. Two specifications of this set-up are considered.

First, we modify the revenue side of the government's budget constraint and drop the assumption that money is the only outside asset of the economy. Instead, we present a specification, similar to chapter 6, in which both money and government bonds act as outside assets, and due to this modification any isolated discussion of purely monetary policy measures seems no longer appropriate. In contrast, as convincingly argued by Sargent/Wallace (1981), the impact of monetary policy now depends on the way one specifies the entire regime of monetary and fiscal policies. In particular, with the government participating in the capital market through the emission of bonds, the level of private capital formation will be critically affected by the mix of revenues resulting from seigniorage and additional bond financing. We present a framework in which the government is a net debtor towards the private sector. However, to isolate the additional effects resulting from the introduction of a second outside asset, it is assumed that the government runs a balanced primary budget. In fact, in our framework the government is exclusively concerned with a scheme of issuing bonds and money, thereby redistributing income between generations. To ensure that the results established in this section can be meaningfully compared with those derived previously, we concentrate on a regime in which fiscal policy measures are fully subordinated to the conduct of monetary policy, i.e. the path of bonds is taken to be endogenously determined. And it turns out that for such a regime a shift to a more inflationary policy can easily induce the crowding out of private investment projects, i.e. the Anti-Tobin effect may well prevail despite a seemingly 'monetarist' scenario.

Second, we abandon the ill-founded assumption that all government expenditures are unproductive. Instead, we present a framework in which both private and public capital are used as distinct inputs in the production of the output good of the economy. To isolate the additional effects caused by this modified specification of government expenditures, we assume again that money is the single outside asset of the economy. More specifically, we consider an economy in which the government spends all revenues resulting from seigniorage on public investment goods, thereby enhancing, for example, the quality of economywide used public infrastructure. Not surprisingly, with seigniorage revenues being directly linked to the creation of a productive input, the mechanics of the system work now strongly in favour of the Tobin effect. However, the dominance of the Tobin effect is not entirely uncontested. In fact, for the Tobin effect to prevail, we need to assume that there are decreasing returns to private and public capital. Only then it will be guaranteed that the expansionary impact effect of a shift to a more inflationary policy will be sufficiently dampened over time such that a new steady state equilibrium with a higher capital stock can be reached. Thus, under decreasing returns to private and public capital steady states will be stable, and we show that adjustment will be monotone, though indeterminate.

9.1 Differentiated goods, multiple means of payment, and multiple outside assets

Using the framework introduced in the previous chapter, we consider a version of an economy with an exogenous cash-in-advance constraint. Thus, as a convenient point of departure for our analysis, we reproduce the relevant equilibrium conditions (8.27)-(8.31) from chapter 8:

$$g_t = \frac{\mu}{1+\mu} \cdot m_t \tag{9.1}$$

$$f'(k_{t+1}) - \Gamma > \frac{1}{1+\mu} \cdot \frac{m_{t+1}}{m_t} \tag{9.2}$$

$$k_{t+1} = w_t(k_t) - m_t \tag{9.3}$$

$$\frac{1}{1+\mu} \cdot \frac{m_{t+1}}{m_t} \cdot u'(c_{t+1}^0) = f'(k_{t+1}) \cdot u'(c_{t+1}^1) \tag{9.4}$$

$$u(c_{t+1}^1) - u'(c_{t+1}^1) \cdot (c_{t+1}^1 + \gamma(\bar{i})) > u(c_{t+1}^0) - u'(c_{t+1}^0) \cdot c_{t+1}^0 \tag{9.5}$$

Equilibrium consumption levels of cash and credit goods are given by:

$$c_{t+1}^0 = \frac{m_{t+1}}{(1+\mu) \cdot (1-\bar{i})} \tag{9.6}$$

$$c_{t+1}^1 = \frac{f'(k_{t+1}) \cdot (k_{t+1}) - \Gamma(\bar{i})}{\bar{i}} \tag{9.7}$$

However, deviating from the analysis given in the previous chapter, the government is now assumed to issue two distinct outside assets, fiat money and interest-bearing bonds. To accommodate the coexistence of these assets, we impose exogenously that bonds do not qualify as hand-to-hand media of exchange. Thus, young agents can invest in government bonds (like physical capital) only with the assistance of intermediaries, and second period income resulting from bond holdings can never be used for payments to be made in cash. Moreover, we assume that government bonds and claims to physical capital are considered as perfect substitutes.

Let b_t denote the real amount of one-period bonds issued by the government per young agent in period t. Since bonds and capital are perfect substitutes, the equilibrium gross interest rate R_t^b on bonds, being paid in $t+1$, will be given by:

$$R_t^b = f'(k_{t+1}) \tag{9.8}$$

In order to isolate the effects caused by the introduction of a second outside asset, we assume that the government levies no taxes apart from the inflation tax. Moreover, government purchases g_t are zero. Thus, replacing (9.1), the modified budget constraint of the government is given by:

$$f'(k_t) \cdot b_{t-1} = b_t + \frac{\mu}{1+\mu} \cdot m_t \tag{9.9}$$

Equation (9.9) says that the principal and interest on government debt due in any period t has to be financed by funds, resulting either from seigniorage revenues or the sale of newly emitted bonds, maturing in $t+1$.

In the previous chapter, we argued that the strength of the intertemporal income effect and the question of whether goods are substitutes or complements are decisive for the interaction of inflation and capital formation. Now, this interaction will also be influenced by a crowding out effect resulting from the modified budget constraint (9.9). However, it seems desirable for the purposes of this chapter to isolate the crowding out effect as much as possible, and we assume therefore with respect to preferences:

(A 4*) The function u is given by:

$$u = ln(c)$$

Clearly, due to this assumption the cross-price effect between cash and credit goods will be zero, and substitution effects therefore no longer matter.

Moreover, we further simplify matters by introducing an extreme specification of processing costs $\Gamma(i)$ associated with non-cash payments:

(A 3*) Processing costs $\Gamma(i)$ are given by:

$$\Gamma(i) = \begin{array}{l} 0 \ \text{ for } 0 \leq i \leq \bar{i}, \\ \infty \ \text{ for } \bar{i} < i \leq 1 \end{array}$$

Evidently, assumption (A 3*) ensures that agents will never use cash at any location $i \leq \bar{i}$, as long as money is strictly return-dominated by credit. Thus, whenever the condition $f'(k_{t+1}) > \frac{1}{1+\mu} \cdot \frac{m_{t+1}}{m_t}$ is satisfied, we can safely concentrate on the analysis of a regime with an exogenous cash-in-advance constraint.

Upon these modifications, the binding arbitrage relation (9.4) can be rewritten as:

$$\frac{1}{1+\mu} \cdot \frac{m_{t+1}}{m_t} \cdot \frac{1}{c_{t+1}^0} = f'(k_{t+1}) \cdot \frac{1}{c_{t+1}^1} \tag{9.10}$$

Note that c_{t+1}^0 and c_{t+1}^1, as specified in (9.6) and (9.7), are now given by:

$$c_{t+1}^0 = \frac{m_{t+1}}{(1+\mu) \cdot (1-\bar{i})} \tag{9.11}$$

$$c_{t+1}^1 = \frac{f'(k_{t+1}) \cdot (k_{t+1} + b_t)}{\bar{i}} \tag{9.12}$$

Inserting (9.11) and (9.12) into (9.10), yields for the arbitrage relation:

$$m_t = \frac{1-\bar{i}}{\bar{i}} \cdot (k_{t+1} + b_t) \tag{9.13}$$

Thus, the steady state version of the modified system with multiple outside assets can be summarized as:

$$f'(k) \; > \; \frac{1}{1+\mu} \qquad (9.14)$$

$$[f'(k) - 1] \cdot b \; = \; \frac{\mu}{1+\mu} \cdot m \qquad (9.15)$$

$$k \; = \; w(k) - m - b \qquad (9.16)$$

$$m \; = \; \frac{1 - \bar{i}}{\bar{i}} \cdot (k + b) \qquad (9.17)$$

As far as the coordination problem between fiscal and monetary policies is concerned, we concentrate exclusively on a regime characterized by a 'passive' fiscal policy. Thus, we consider a regime in which the path of bonds adjusts endogenously and, as in the previous chapters, the rate of monetary expansion μ is exogenously given. Let $\Omega(k)$ be defined as: $\Omega(k) = k/w(k)$. Then, after substituting out for m and b in (9.15)-(9.17), one arrives at the two-equation system:

$$f'(k) \; > \; \frac{1}{1+\mu} \qquad (9.18)$$

$$\Omega(k) \; = \; \bar{i} - \frac{\mu}{1+\mu} \cdot (1 - \bar{i}) \cdot \frac{1}{f'(k) - 1} \qquad (9.19)$$

Existence of steady state equilibria: Similar to the analysis given in chapter 8, further assumptions need to be made with respect to technology in order to ensure the existence of a steady state solution of the system (9.18)-(9.19). Yet, appropriate sufficient conditions are easily specified, as the following slight modification of assumption (A 6) from chapter 8 shows:[1]

(A 6*) The function $f(k)$ satisfies the conditions:

(i) $w(0) > 0 \; \vee \; \lim_{k \to 0} \Omega(k) = \frac{k}{w(k)} < \bar{i}$,

(ii) $\lim_{k \to 0} f'(k) = \infty$,

(iii) $w'(k) > 0$, $w''(k) < 0$ for all $k > 0$.

Using assumption (A 6*), the existence of a steady state is easily established:[2]

---

[1]Assumption (A 6*) is satisfied, for example, by any Cobb-Douglas function and any CES function with elasticity of substitution no less than one. For details, see appendix I at the end of the book.

[2]In chapter 8, assumption (A 2) was introduced in order to account appropriately for the substitution effects on the side of consumers. In the context presented here, substitution effects no longer matter due to (A 4*). Thus, in establishing proposition 1 assumption (A 2) of chapter 8 can be dropped without loss of generality.

158

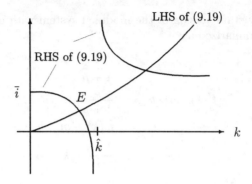

Figure 9.1: *Variation 5a - Steady state: existence*

Proposition 1 *Assume that assumption (A 1), as introduced in chapter 8, and assumptions (A 3*), (A 4*), and (A 6*) are satisfied. Then, there exists a unique steady state solution $(k, m, b) > 0$ of the system (9.14)-(9.17).*

Proof: Note that $\Omega(k)$ will always be positive. Concavity of $w(k)$ as given by part (iii) of (A 6*) implies that $\Omega(k)$ is strictly increasing in k. Thus, the LHS of (9.19) rises in k as illustrated in figure 9.1. By (A 1), the RHS of (9.19) declines monotonically in k for $k \in (0, \widehat{k})$, with $\widehat{k}$ being defined by $f'(\widehat{k}) = 1$. By part (ii) of (A 6*), the RHS of (9.19) approaches $\overline{i}$ for $k \downarrow 0$ and $-\infty$ for $k \uparrow \widehat{k}$, respectively. Thus, considering the interval $(0, \widehat{k})$, there must exist a unique intersection k by part (i) of (A 6*) and continuity of the curves. Clearly, for $\mu > 0$, $f'(k) > f'(\widehat{k}) > 1/(1+\mu)$ will be satisfied by (A 1). Finally, one easily confirms that $(m, k) > 0$ is implied by $\Omega(k) < \overline{i} < 1$.[3] q.e.d.

Comparative statics: Taking for granted the passive nature of fiscal policy, it is straightforward to establish how a permanent switch to a more inflationary policy impacts on the level of the capital stock:

Proposition 2 *Assume that the rate of monetary expansion μ is permanently raised. Then, in the new steady state the capital stock will be lower than before, i.e. the Anti-Tobin effect will prevail.*

---

[3] As indicated in figure 9.1, equation (9.19) may well have a second solution with $k > 0$. Clearly, $f'(k) < 1$ needs to hold for such a solution, and according to (9.15) this is not consistent with $(m, b) > 0$.

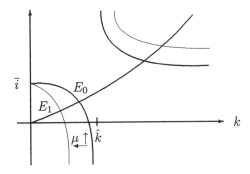

Figure 9.2: *Variation 5a - Steady state: comparative statics*

Proof: Differentiating (9.19) yields:

$$\frac{\partial k}{\partial \mu} = \frac{\frac{1}{(1-f'(k))} \cdot \frac{1-\bar{i}}{(1+\mu)^2}}{\Omega'(k) - \frac{\mu}{1+\mu} \cdot (1-\bar{i}) \cdot \frac{f''(k)}{(f'(k)-1)^2}}$$

Since $f'(k) > 1$ needs to be satisfied at any steady state with $(m, b) > 0$, the numerator of the reaction coefficient will be negative. Concavity of $w(k)$ implies $\Omega'(k) > 0$. Thus, by part (iii) of (A 6*) and (A 1), the denominator will be positive, thereby ensuring that the overall effect will be negative. q.e.d.

To see why the Anti-Tobin effect prevails, note that a change in μ leaves both the accumulation equation (9.16) and the arbitrage relation (9.17) unaffected. Thus, reflecting our extreme specification of preferences, a change in μ impacts on the capital stock exclusively through the crowding out effect captured by (9.15), i.e. through the change in the stance of the government in the capital market. Equation (9.15) says that for a given level of real balances a higher inflation rate increases revenues of the government resulting from seigniorage. However, this in turn enables the government to pursue a more expansionary fiscal policy, and the associated rise in the interest rate needs to be brought about by a fall in the capital stock. As illustrated in figure 9.2, the mechanics of this crowding out effect have a simple graphical representation: while the change in μ leaves the term $\Omega(k)$ unaffected, it induces a downward shift of the relevant branch of the RHS of (9.19). As a result, in the new steady state the capital stock needs to be lower than before.

Not surprisingly, for specifications using less restrictive utility functions, the crowding out effect remains no longer uncontested, and less clear-cut results obtain. In particular, it is not difficult to show that the crowding out effect and the substitution effect will work in opposite directions if cash and credit goods act at the margin as substitutes. The results established in this section should therefore be interpreted with some caution. However, the results do strongly indicate that any proper specification of the coordination problem between fiscal and monetary policies leads to a considerable complication of the debate about the Tobin effect.

9.2 Differentiated goods, multiple means of payment, and productive government expenditures

As in the previous section, we consider a version of an economy with an exogenous cash-in-advance constraint along the lines of chapter 8. Again, we simplify matters by assuming:[4]

(A 3*) Processing costs $\Gamma(i)$ are given by:

$$\Gamma(i) = \begin{array}{l} 0 \text{ for } 0 \leq i \leq \bar{i}, \\ \infty \text{ for } \bar{i} < i \leq 1 \end{array}$$

(A 4*) The function u is given by:

$$u = ln(c)$$

However, deviating from the framework presented in chapter 8, we assume that private and public capital act as distinct, complementary inputs in the production of the single output good of the economy. Let $\bar{k}_t$ denote the stock of public capital per young agent provided by the government in period t. For the sake of simplicity, we assume that production occurs according to a Cobb-Douglas function $F(\bar{k}_t, K_t, L_t,) = \bar{k}_t^{\beta} \cdot K_t^{\alpha} \cdot L_t^{1-\alpha}$, where α and β denote the output elasticities with respect to private and public capital, respectively. As in previous chapters, we normalize the labour endowment per young agent: $L_t = 1$. Thus, rewriting the production function in intensive form, our assumptions with respect to technology can be summarized as:

(A 6*) The production function is of Cobb-Douglas type:

$$f(k_t, \bar{k}_t) = \bar{k}_t^{\beta} \cdot k_t^{\alpha} \qquad \text{with: } 0 < \alpha, \beta < 1$$

---

[4]Thus, due to (A 4*) we concentrate again on a constellation with a zero cross-price effect between cash and credit goods, i.e. changes in the inflation rate do not lead to substitution effects on the side of consumers.

Similar to the investment technology of the private sector, there is a lag of one period for public capital to be produced and installed. Like private capital, public capital provided by the government is assumed to depreciate entirely within the production process. Moreover, money is again the only outside asset of the economy, and the government levies no taxes apart from the inflation tax. Thus, assuming that all government revenues are spent on public investment goods, the government's budget constraint is given by:

$$\overline{k}_{t+1} = \frac{\mu}{1+\mu} \cdot m_t \tag{9.20}$$

Under these specifications, the steady state conditions for an economy with productive government expenditures and an exogenous cash-in-advance constraint can be summarized as:

$$\frac{\partial f(k,\overline{k})}{\partial k} = \alpha \cdot k^{\alpha-1} \cdot \overline{k}^{\beta} > \frac{1}{1+\mu} \tag{9.21}$$

$$\overline{k} = \frac{\mu}{1+\mu} \cdot m \tag{9.22}$$

$$w(k,\overline{k}) = (1-\alpha) \cdot k^{\alpha} \cdot \overline{k}^{\beta} = k + m \tag{9.23}$$

$$m = \frac{1-\overline{i}}{\overline{i}} \cdot k \tag{9.24}$$

Rearranging (9.21) and inserting (9.24) into (9.23) and (9.22), yields the system in k and $\overline{k}$:

$$\overline{k} > [\frac{1}{(1+\mu) \cdot \alpha}]^{\frac{1}{\beta}} \cdot k^{\frac{1-\alpha}{\beta}} \tag{9.25}$$

$$\overline{k} = \frac{\mu}{1+\mu} \cdot \frac{1-\overline{i}}{\overline{i}} \cdot k \tag{9.26}$$

$$\overline{k} = (\frac{1}{(1-\alpha) \cdot \overline{i}})^{\frac{1}{\beta}} \cdot k^{\frac{1-\alpha}{\beta}} \tag{9.27}$$

Existence of steady state equilibria: By virtue of the specific functional forms describing preferences and technology, one easily calculates a condition under which there exists a unique steady state equilibrium. As shown in figure 9.3, the system (9.25)-(9.27) has generically two distinct graphical representations, depending on the magnitude of the term $\alpha + \beta$. Disregarding the borderline case of $\alpha + \beta = 1$, equations (9.26) and (9.27) have a unique intersection $(k, \overline{k}) > 0$. Moreover, strict return-dominance of money as required by (9.25) will be satisfied whenever the locus of (9.25) at equality remains below the locus of (9.27). By comparison of (9.25) at equality and (9.27), it is straightforward to derive a critical restriction on parameters, ensuring the existence of a unique steady state equilibrium:

162

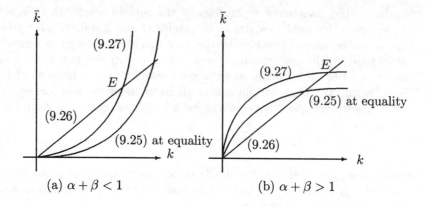

Figure 9.3: *Variation 5b - Steady state: existence*

Proposition 3 *The economy with productive government expenditures as described by (9.25)-(9.27) has a unique steady state $(m, k, \overline{k}) > 0$ if the following restriction on parameters is satisfied: $\frac{\alpha}{1-\alpha} > \frac{\overline{i}}{1+\mu}$.*

Proof: The restriction on parameters follows directly from comparing the coefficients in (9.25) and (9.27). q.e.d.

Plausible parameter constellations satisfying the restriction are easily found. For example, let α and $\overline{i}$ be given by: $\alpha = 0.4$ and $\overline{i} = 2/3$. Then, for any $\mu > 0$ the restriction will be satisfied. Finally, combining (9.26) and (9.27), one obtains for the steady state value of the private capital stock k:

$$k = [1 - \alpha]^{\frac{1}{1-\alpha-\beta}} \cdot [1 - \overline{i}]^{\frac{\beta}{1-\alpha-\beta}} \cdot \overline{i}^{\frac{1-\beta}{1-\alpha-\beta}} \cdot \left[\frac{\mu}{1+\mu}\right]^{\frac{\beta}{1-\alpha-\beta}} \qquad (9.28)$$

Comparative statics: The effects of a switch to a permanently more inflationary policy are readily established by referring to figure 9.4. In particular, a change in μ leaves (9.27) unaffected, but it induces an upward rotation of (9.26) and a downward rotation of (9.25) at equality, respectively. Evidently, the effect on the capital stock depends on the magnitude of the term $\alpha + \beta$:

Proposition 4 *Consider an economy with productive government expenditures that has a unique steady state. Assume that the rate of monetary expansion μ is permanently raised. Then, the Tobin effect (Anti-Tobin effect) prevails with respect to both the private capital stock k and the overall capital stock $k + \overline{k}$ if the restriction $\alpha + \beta < 1$ ($\alpha + \beta > 1$) is satisfied.*

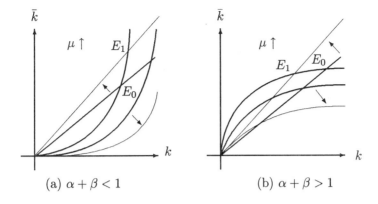

Figure 9.4: *Variation 5b - Steady state: comparative statics*

Proof: The result follows immediately from differentiating equations (9.26) and (9.28). q.e.d.

Given the strong link between seigniorage revenues and the creation of public capital, the ambiguity of this result is at first sight rather surprising. However, the ambiguity reflects that a new steady state with a higher capital stock can only be attained if the two types of capital inputs are jointly not overly productive. In particular, for the Tobin effect to prevail, the technology must be subject to decreasing returns to private and public capital, i.e. the empirically plausible restriction $\alpha + \beta < 1$ needs to be satisfied. In contrast, under increasing returns to private and public capital the expansionary impact effect resulting from productive government expenditures turns into a self-enforcing process of rapid capital accumulation which does not converge to a more capital-intensive steady state. In fact, as the following proposition confirms, steady states characterized by the condition $\alpha + \beta > 1$ will never be stable:

Proposition 5 *Consider an economy with productive government expenditures that has a unique steady state. If the economy exhibits decreasing returns to private and public capital ($\alpha + \beta < 1$) the steady state will be locally stable, and adjustment behaviour will be monotone, though indeterminate. Conversely, under increasing returns to private and public capital ($\alpha + \beta > 1$) the steady state will be unstable.*

Proof: see appendix.

Complementing the aspects addressed in previous sections, the results established in this section support the view that long run effects of inflation should also depend on the structure of government expenditures. In fact, the results derived in this section challenge our sceptical attitude towards the Tobin effect and give us, therefore, the chance to conclude in a conciliatory manner. Clearly, for the debate on long run effects of inflation it must be of some importance whether revenues resulting from seigniorage are used in a productive manner. And if this is the case, this should make it more likely for the Tobin effect to prevail.

9.3 Appendix

Proof of proposition 5:

Using equations (9.3), (9.4), and (9.20), one easily verifies that off-steady state dynamics of the system (9.22)-(9.24) are governed by the following three-equation system in $k_t, \overline{k}_t$, and m_t:

$$\overline{k}_{t+1} = \frac{\mu}{1+\mu} \cdot m_t \tag{9.29}$$

$$k_{t+1} = (1-\alpha) \cdot k_t^\alpha \cdot \overline{k}_t^\beta - m_t \tag{9.30}$$

$$m_t = \frac{1-\overline{i}}{\overline{i}} \cdot k_{t+1} \tag{9.31}$$

As in previous chapters, real balances m_t are a control variable with a free initial condition, but now the system is characterized by two state variables, the private capital stock k_t and the public capital stock $\overline{k}_t$. Reflecting the recursive structure of the equations, the Jacobian matrix of the system (9.29)-(9.31) is not invertible, i.e. equilibrium dynamics cannot be classified along the lines of the procedure outlined in appendix II. Alternatively, similar to the dynamical analysis given in chapter 7, we employ a procedure which exploits directly the recursive structure. In particular, substituting out for $m_t, \overline{k}_t$, and $\overline{k}_{t+1}$ yields the following first-order, non-linear difference equation in k_t:

$$k_{t+1} = \overline{i} \cdot (1-\alpha) \cdot [\frac{\mu}{1+\mu} \cdot \frac{1-\overline{i}}{\overline{i}}]^\beta \cdot k_t^{\alpha+\beta} \tag{9.32}$$

To establish the dynamical behaviour of (9.32), we investigate its linear expansion around the steady state. Accordingly, differentiating (9.32) yields:

$$d\,k_{t+1} = \overline{i} \cdot (1-\alpha) \cdot [\frac{\mu}{1+\mu} \cdot \frac{1-\overline{i}}{\overline{i}}]^\beta \cdot (\alpha+\beta) \cdot k^{\alpha+\beta-1} \cdot d\,k_t \tag{9.33}$$

However, one easily verifies that (9.33) simplifies considerably if one inserts the steady state value k given by (9.28). In fact, (9.33) reduces to:

$$d\,k_{t+1} = (\alpha+\beta) \cdot d\,k_t \tag{9.34}$$

Thus, the dynamics of the system will be locally governed by the scale parameter $\alpha + \beta$. In particular, stability of the steady state will be ensured if the economy is characterized by decreasing returns to private and public capital $(\alpha + \beta < 1)$. Note that the stability coefficient is not influenced by the initial choice of m_t. Thus, adjustment will be indeterminate. Moreover, since $\alpha + \beta > 0$ by assumption, adjustment towards the steady state will be monotone. In contrast, the steady state will be unstable if the economy exhibits increasing returns to private and public capital $(\alpha + \beta > 1)$. q.e.d.

Summary

This study investigates the long run interaction of inflation and real economic activity as traditionally addressed in the literature on money and growth. In a prominent contribution to this literature, Tobin (1965) arrives at the well-known result that one should expect inflation and economic activity to be positively correlated. Importantly, this so-called Tobin effect hinges critically on the assumption that money and capital enter the portfolios of agents as substitutes: with inflation acting like a tax on real balances, this assumption ensures that a more inflationary policy induces a portfolio shift from money to capital, thereby leading to a higher level of overall activity. More recently, however, empirical and theoretical studies have challenged this view.

Essentially, we argue in this book that critical aspects of the debate about the Tobin effect can be reexamined within a version of the overlapping generations model with production as developed by Diamond (1965). Generally speaking, we show that the unequivocal predominance of the Tobin effect in the standard version of the Diamond model vanishes if mechanisms are incorporated that support the 'complementarity hypothesis' with respect to money and credit. More specifically, we demonstrate that such mechanisms can easily be established if informational imperfections in the credit market, liquidity aspects of money, and the notion of multiple means of payment are adequately included.

In more detail, our argument proceeds as following. In chapter 4, we present a monetary version of the standard Diamond model with production. The proposed version assumes that money acts as the single outside asset of the economy. Moreover, the capital market works entirely frictionless, and details of how transactions are settled remain unaddressed. In short, in this economy money acts purely as a store of value. Restating a well-known result of the literature, we show that the Tobin effect prevails under conditions which ensure the existence of a unique monetary steady state. Also, we show that local dynamics around the monetary steady state are uniquely determined along a stable saddlepath, displaying monotone adjustment.

Chapters 5-9 propose variations on the base model discussed in chapter 4, and in all cases we introduce modifications which give money a more interesting role to play. In chapter 5, we discuss a version of the base model due to Azariadis/Smith (1996) in which credit markets are subject to an informational friction. This leads to a situation in which high inflation rates tend to be associated with a regime of credit rationing on the side of intermediaries, and money and capital cease to be substitutes. As a result, inflation has a detrimental impact on capital formation and the Anti-Tobin effect prevails. Moreover, equilibrium dynamics may well become indeterminate and exhibit endogenous fluctuations in the neighbourhood of the monetary steady state.

In chapter 6, we outline a version of the base model by Schreft/Smith (1997) in which outside money competes as outside asset with interest-bearing government bonds. However, a modified timing of events guarantees that money overcomes the return differential due to its unique liquidity features. As a result, money and all interest-bearing assets are no longer substitutes, and this leads again to a situation in which the mechanics of the base model are critically affected. In particular, a constellation with two monetary steady states may well arise. In such a constellation, the steady state characterized by a low level of economic activity is shown to be of Anti-Tobin nature and local dynamics are saddlepath stable, with adjustment behaviour being monotone. In contrast, at the high level equilibrium the Tobin effect is shown to prevail. Moreover, local dynamics are indeterminate and adjustment behaviour towards the steady state may well be subject to endogenous volatility.

In chapters 7-9, we present our own research and develop versions of the base model which can be used to deal with aspects related to the transactions role of money. In chapter 7, we account for the transactions role of money by adapting a standard cash-in-advance constraint to the base model. Our analysis concentrates on the intertemporal dimension of this constraint, and we show that the mechanics of the model work strongly in favour of the Anti-Tobin effect. Moreover, we establish that monetary steady states cease to be saddlepath stable. We demonstrate that further restrictions need to be imposed to rule out that steady states are entirely unstable. Yet, further investigating this issue in a set-up with Cobb-Douglas-type preferences and a Cobb-Douglas production function, we show that now the unique monetary steady state will always be entirely stable, with adjustment behaviour towards the steady state being monotone, though indeterminate.

In chapter 8, we specify a version of the base model with a rich spatial arrangement and multiple means of payment, facilitating an endogenous treatment of the cash-in-advance constraint. However, our arrangement is such that a standard version of an exogenously imposed cash-in-advance constraint can be discussed as a special case arising from a corner solution. Concentrating on intratemporal aspects of the portfolio decision of agents, we show for the regime with an 'endogenous constraint' that the Tobin effect is strongly supported. Corresponding equilibria are shown to be saddlepath stable, and adjustment behaviour towards the steady state is monotone. Whenever the corner solution of an 'exogenous constraint' applies, the range of available goods can be rigidly divided into so-called 'cash goods' (which require payment in cash) and credit goods (which can be paid for by check). Under standard specifications comparative statics results and dynamical properties depend now simply on whether consumers regard cash and credit goods at the margin as substitutes or complements. If goods are substitutes the Tobin effect obtains and steady states are saddlepath stable, displaying monotone adjustment behaviour. If goods are complements the Anti-Tobin effect obtains and steady states can be either a saddle or a sink, with adjustment behaviour being not necessarily monotone. Moreover, for both regimes we construct constellations with multiple steady states.

Finally, chapter 9 extends the analysis given in chapter 8 and presents more detailed specifications of government activities. Two specifications are considered. First, modifying the revenue side of the government's budget constraint, we assume that outside money is no longer the only outside asset, but rather coexists with interest-bearing bonds. In general, effects of inflation will now depend on the way fiscal and monetary policies are coordinated. However, we present a regime that closely resembles a 'monetarist' scenario and show that a shift to a more inflationary policy may easily induce the crowding out of private investment projects, thereby giving rise to the Anti-Tobin effect. Second, modifying the expenditure side of the government's budget constraint, we demonstrate that long run effects of inflation also depend on the mix of productive and unproductive uses of government expenditures. More specifically, we show for a regime with productive government activities that the Tobin effect is likely to dominate, with adjustment behaviour being monotone, though indeterminate.

As a common theme, all of the variations described in chapters 5-9 give rise to the possibility that the Anti-Tobin effect prevails. Moreover, local dynamics may well be indeterminate, and adjustment behaviour towards the steady state is not always monotone. Also, multiple monetary steady states may well occur. In short, the variations presented in chapters 5-9 show that the standard mechanics of the Tobin effect are seriously at risk if one accounts for aspects of money that go beyond the narrow store of value function implied by the pure overlapping generations friction.

Appendix I: Technology

Throughout our analysis in part II we have alluded to various properties of two prominent production functions, the Cobb-Douglas and the CES function. This appendix summarizes compactly these properties. Following the notation introduced in chapter 4, let K, L, and k denote capital, labour, and the capital-labour ratio, respectively. The parameter A stands for some exogenously specified measure of overall productivity, and the parameter α governs the shares of factor incomes in total output.

1) Cobb-Douglas production function

Consider the production function:

$$F(K, L) = A \cdot K^\alpha \cdot L^{1-\alpha} \quad \text{with: } A > 0, \alpha \in (0, 1) \tag{1}$$

Let the production function in intensive form $f(k)$ be defined as: $f(k) \equiv F(K/L, 1)$. Thus, one obtains:

$$f(k) = A \cdot k^\alpha \tag{2}$$

Note that the Cobb-Douglas function is homogenous of degree one, i.e. it satisfies: $F(K, L) = L \cdot F(K/L, 1) = L \cdot f(k)$.

i) *Concavity of $f(k)$*:

Calculating the first and second derivative of $f(k)$ yields:

$$
\begin{aligned}
f'(k) &= A \cdot \alpha \cdot k^{\alpha-1} & (3) \\
f''(k) &= A \cdot \alpha \cdot (\alpha - 1) \cdot k^{\alpha-2} & (4)
\end{aligned}
$$

Thus, $f'(k) > 0, f''(k) < 0$ will be satisfied for all $k > 0$, i.e. the function $f(k)$ is strictly concave. Moreover, one easily verifies:

$$f(0) = 0, \quad \lim_{k \to 0} f'(k) = \infty, \quad \lim_{k \to \infty} f'(k) = 0 \tag{5}$$

170

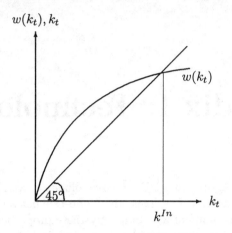

Figure A.1: *Wage function w(k): Cobb-Douglas function*

ii) *Properties of w(k):*

Since the Cobb-Douglas function is homogenous of degree one, factor payments will exhaust output: $w(k) = f(k) - k \cdot f'(k)$. Accordingly, one obtains from (2) and (3) for the wage function:

$$w(k) = (1 - \alpha) \cdot A \cdot f(k) \qquad (6)$$

In chapter 4, we claimed that the Cobb-Douglas function satisfies (A 2**). For simplicity, we restate assumption (A 2**) as given in chapter 4:

(A 2**) The function $f(k)$ admits the following behaviour of $w(k)$:

(1) $w(0) > 0 \;\; \vee \;\; w'(0) > 1$,

(2) $\lim\limits_{k\to\infty} \frac{w(k)}{k} < 1$,

(3) $w'(k) > 0$, $w''(k) < 0$ for all $k > 0$.

The claim is quickly verified: combining (5) and (6) yields: $\lim_{k\to 0} w'(k) > 1$. Thus, part (1) of (A 2**) is satisfied. By (5), we have: $\lim_{k\to\infty} f'(k) = 0$. Clearly, this implies: $\lim_{k\to\infty} \frac{w(k)}{k} = 0 < 1$. Thus, part (2) of (A 2**) is also satisfied. Finally, according to (6), concavity of $f(k)$ translates into concavity of $f(k)$, as required by part (3) of (A 2**). Note that $w(0) = f(0) = 0$. Thus, the function $w(k)$ can be graphed as illustrated in figure A.1.[1]

---

[1]Chapters 5, 6, and 9 rely on assumptions which are slightly more restrictive than

iii) *Properties of $f'(k) \cdot k$:*

In chapters 7 and 8, the production function $f(k)$ is assumed to satisfy the condition:

(A 2) (i) $\lim\limits_{k \to 0} f'(k) \cdot k = 0$, (ii) $\frac{d\,f'(k)\cdot k}{d\,k} > 0$ for all $k > 0$

For the Cobb-Douglas function the relevant terms are given by:

$$f'(k) \cdot k = \alpha \cdot f(k), \quad \frac{d\,f'(k) \cdot k}{dk} = \alpha \cdot f'(k) \tag{7}$$

Clearly, $\lim_{k \to 0} f'(k) \cdot k = 0$ and $\frac{d\,f'(k)\cdot k}{d\,k} > 0$ for $k > 0$ follow from (3) and (5), respectively, i.e. (A 2) is satisfied.

2) Constant elasticity of substitution (CES) production function

Consider now the production function:[2]

$$F(K, L) = A \cdot [\alpha \cdot K^{-\rho} + (1-\alpha) \cdot L^{-\rho}]^{-\frac{1}{\rho}} \quad \text{with: } A > 0, \alpha \in (0,1), \rho > -1 \tag{8}$$

Let η denote the elasticity of substitution between the factors in the production process. One easily verifies that this elasticity is given by the constant value $\eta = \frac{1}{1+\rho}$, with: $\eta \in (0, \infty)$.[3] The production function in intensive form is given by:

$$f(k) = A \cdot [\alpha \cdot k^{-\rho} + (1 - \alpha)]^{-\frac{1}{\rho}} \tag{9}$$

Again, one easily confirms that the function $F(K, L)$ is linear homogenous.

i) *Concavity of $f(k)$:*

Calculating the first and second derivative of $f(k)$ yields:

$$f'(k) = \alpha \cdot A^{-\rho} \cdot [\frac{f(k)}{k}]^{1+\rho} \tag{10}$$

$$f''(k) = -\alpha \cdot A^{-\rho} \cdot (1+\rho) \cdot [\frac{f(k)}{k}]^{\rho} \cdot [\frac{w(k)}{k^2}] \tag{11}$$

(A 2**). In particular, in chapter 5 the additional assumption $\lim_{k \to \infty} \frac{w(k)}{k} = 0$ needs to be satisfied, chapter 6 requires $\lim_{k \to 0} f'(k) = \infty$ and $\lim_{k \to \infty} f'(k) < 1$, and chapter 9 uses the assumptions $\lim_{k \to 0} \frac{k}{w(k)} < \bar{i} < 1$ and $\lim_{k \to 0} f'(k) = \infty$. However, our calculations confirm that the Cobb-Douglas function satisfies these conditions as well.

[2]For a similar, though less detailed discussion of properties of the CES production function, see Azariadis (1993, ch. 13). The CES production function was introduced into the literature by Arrow/Chenery/Minhas/Solow (1961).

[3]The technical rate of substitution (i.e. the ratio of the marginal products) is given by the expression: $\frac{F_K}{F_L} = \frac{\alpha}{1-\alpha} \cdot (\frac{K}{L})^{-(1+\rho)}$. Thus, the elasticity of substitution is given by the constant value: $\eta = \frac{1}{1+\rho}$.

Thus, $f'(k) > 0, f''(k) < 0$ will be satisfied for all $k > 0$, i.e. the function $f(k)$ is strictly concave, irrespective of the magnitude of the elasticity of substitution η.

ii) *Properties of $w(k)$:*

Again, since $F(K, L)$ is linear homogenous, the wage function is given by the term: $w(k) = f(k) - k \cdot f'(k)$. Combining (9) and (10), one obtains:

$$w(k) = (1 - \alpha) \cdot A^{-\rho} \cdot f(k)^{1+\rho} \tag{12}$$

Define the constant $c > 0$ as following:

$$c = \alpha \cdot (1 - \alpha) \cdot (1 + \rho) \cdot A^{-2 \cdot \rho}$$

Differentiating with respect to k yields, after some tidying up:

$$w'(k) = c \cdot f(k)^\rho \cdot [\frac{f(k)}{k}]^{1+\rho} \tag{13}$$

$$w''(k) = c \cdot f(k)^{1+2\cdot\rho} \cdot k^{-(2+\rho)} \cdot [\frac{(1 + 2 \cdot \rho) \cdot \alpha \cdot k^{-\rho}}{\alpha \cdot k^{-\rho} + 1 - \alpha} - (1 + \rho)] \tag{14}$$

In chapter 4, we claimed that the CES function satisfies assumption (A 2**) only if the elasticity of substitution is no less than one ($\eta > 1$). In particular, we claimed that for $0 < \eta < 1$ the function $w(k)$ is not globally concave and that the equation $w(k) = k$ may well be solved by two distinct, positive values of k. We address now these claims in turn.

ii a) $\eta > 1 \Leftrightarrow \rho \in (-1, 0)$

Consider again all three parts of assumption (A 2**) as stated above:

ad 1): From (9), one obtains: $\lim_{k \to 0} f(k) = A \cdot (1 - \alpha)^{-\frac{1}{\rho}} > 0$. Inserting this expression into (12) yields: $\lim_{k \to 0} w(k) > 0$. Thus, part (1) of (A 2**) is satisfied.

ad 2): Combining (9) and (12), one obtains: $\frac{w(k)}{k} = \frac{1-\alpha}{\alpha \cdot k^{-\rho} + 1 - \alpha} \cdot \frac{f(k)}{k}$. Note that $\frac{f(k)}{k}$ simplifies to: $\frac{f(k)}{k} = A \cdot [\alpha + (1 - \alpha) \cdot k^\rho]^{-\frac{1}{\rho}}$. Moreover, it is straightforward to verify the limits: $0 < \lim_{k \to \infty} \frac{f(k)}{k} = A \cdot \alpha^{-\frac{1}{\rho}} < \infty$, $\lim_{k \to \infty} \frac{1-\alpha}{\alpha \cdot k^{-\rho} + 1 - \alpha} = 0$. Thus, $\lim_{k \to \infty} \frac{w(k)}{k} = 0$, i.e. part (2) of (A 2**) is satisfied.[4]

---

[4] At the end of chapter 4 we claimed that part (2) of assumption (A 2**) is less restrictive than the condition $\lim_{k \to \infty} f'(k) = 0$. Note that the CES production function confirms this claim, since $\lim_{k \to \infty} f'(k) = \alpha \cdot A^{-\rho} \cdot \lim_{k \to \infty} [\frac{f(k)}{k}]^{1+\rho} = A \cdot \alpha^{-\frac{1}{\rho}} > 0$, while part (2) of (A 2**) is satisfied.

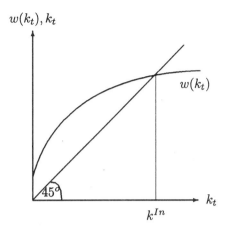

Figure A.2: *Wage function $w(k)$: CES function ($\eta > 1$)*

ad 3): According to (13), $w'(k) > 0$ will be satisfied for all $k > 0$. Let z be defined as: $z = \frac{(1+2\cdot\rho)\cdot\alpha\cdot k^{-\rho}}{\alpha\cdot k^{-\rho}+1-\alpha} - (1+\rho)$. By (14), $sign[w''(k)] = sign[z]$. Rearranging yields:

$$z < 0 \quad \Leftrightarrow \quad \rho < \frac{(1+\rho)\cdot(1-\alpha)}{\alpha} \cdot k^{\rho} \tag{15}$$

Thus, $w''(k) < 0$ will be satisfied for all $k > 0$, i.e. the function $w(k)$ is strictly concave, as required by part (3) of (A 2**). In summary, the function $w(k)$ can be graphed as shown in figure A.2.[5]

ii b) $0 < \eta < 1 \Leftrightarrow \rho > 0$

To demonstrate that for $0 < \eta < 1$ assumption (A 2**) is not satisfied, it suffices to show that $w(k)$ is no longer globally concave. Since $\rho > 0$, the sign of z in (15) is a priori ambiguous. However, rearranging (15) yields the condition:

$$w''(k) > 0 \quad \Leftrightarrow \quad k < \bar{k}, \text{ with: } \bar{k} = (\frac{\rho}{1+\rho} \cdot \frac{\alpha}{1-a})^{\frac{1}{\rho}} > 0$$

---

[5]Again, we discuss briefly for $\eta > 1$ the additional assumptions imposed in chapters 5, 6, and 9. As shown above, the condition $\lim_{k\to\infty} \frac{w(k)}{k} = 0$ introduced in chapter 5 will always be satisfied. Chapter 6 requires: $\lim_{k\to 0} f'(k) = \infty$ and $\lim_{k\to\infty} f'(k) < 1$. One easily verifies that the first condition will always be met. Using the result established in the previous footnote, we have: $\lim_{k\to\infty} f'(k) = A\cdot\alpha^{-\frac{1}{\rho}} > 0$. However, $\lim_{k\to\infty} f'(k) < 1$ will be satisfied if, for example, the productivity parameter A is sufficiently small. Finally, the assumptions used in chapter 9 will be satisfied, since we have: $\lim_{k\to 0} w(k) > 0$ and $\lim_{k\to 0} f'(k) = \infty$.

174

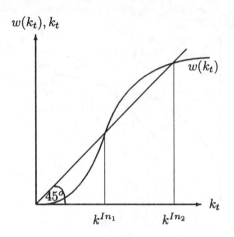

Figure A.3: *Wage function $w(k)$: CES function $(\eta < 1)$*

Thus, $w(k)$ is no longer globally concave. However, to establish the shape of the function $w(k)$ in more detail, we calculate the limits: $\lim_{k\to 0} w(k)$, $\lim_{k\to 0} w'(k)$, and $\lim_{k\to\infty} \frac{w(k)}{k}$. First, evaluating (9) at $k = 0$, yields: $\lim_{k\to 0} f(k) = 0$. Thus, by (12): $\lim_{k\to 0} w(k) = 0$. Second, according to (13), we establish the limits: $\lim_{k\to 0}[\frac{f(k)}{k}]^{1+\rho} = 0$ and $\lim_{k\to 0} f(k)^{\rho} = 0$. Thus, by (13), one obtains: $\lim_{k\to 0} w'(k) = 0$. Finally, using again the decomposition $\frac{w(k)}{k} = \frac{1-\alpha}{\alpha \cdot k^{-\rho}+1-\alpha} \cdot \frac{f(k)}{k}$, one obtains: $\lim_{k\to\infty} \frac{1-\alpha}{\alpha \cdot k^{-\rho}+1-\alpha} = 1$, $\lim_{k\to\infty} \frac{f(k)}{k} = 0$. Hence, $\lim_{k\to\infty} \frac{w(k)}{k} = 0$. Moreover, one easily verifies in (12) that the productivity parameter A acts like a shift parameter of the wage function $w(k)$. Thus, for A being sufficiently large, the equation $w(k) = k$ will be solved by two distinct, positive values, as illustrated in figure A.3.

iii) *Properties of $f'(k) \cdot k$:*

Using (10), one obtains:

$$f'(k) \cdot k = \alpha \cdot A^{-\rho} \cdot [\frac{f(k)}{k}]^{1+\rho} \cdot k = \alpha \cdot A^{-\rho} \cdot f(k)^{1+\rho} \cdot k^{-\rho} \qquad (16)$$

Differentiating with respect to k and manipulating the resulting expression, yields:

$$\frac{d\,f'(k) \cdot k}{d\,k} = \alpha \cdot A^{-\rho} \cdot [\frac{f(k)}{k}]^{1+\rho} \cdot [(1+\rho) \cdot \alpha \cdot A^{-\rho} \cdot [\frac{f(k)}{k}]^{\rho} - \rho] \qquad (17)$$

We show now that assumption (A 2) as stated above holds globally for $\eta > 1$, while it is only locally satisfied for $0 < \eta < 1$.

iii a) $\eta > 1 \Leftrightarrow \rho \in (-1, 0)$

Evaluating the relevant expressions in (16) at $k = 0$, yields: $\lim_{k \to 0} k^{-\rho} = 0$, $\lim_{k \to 0} f(k)^{1+\rho} = [A \cdot (1 - \alpha)^{-\frac{1}{\rho}}]^{1+\rho} > 0$. Thus, $\lim_{k \to 0} f'(k) \cdot k = 0$, i.e. the first part of (A 2) is satisfied. Moreover, for $\rho \in (-1, 0)$ the sign of the derivative in (17) is unambiguously positive for all $k > 0$, i.e. the second part of (A 2) is satisfied as well.

iii b) $0 < \eta < 1 \Leftrightarrow \rho > 0$

We establish the limit: $\lim_{k \to 0} [\frac{f(k)}{k}]^{1+\rho} = A^{1+\rho} \cdot \alpha^{-\frac{1+\rho}{\rho}} > 0$. Thus, by (16), we have: $\lim_{k \to 0} f'(k) \cdot k = 0$, i.e. the first part of (A 2) is satisfied. For $\rho > 0$, the sign of the derivative in (17) is a priori ambiguous. However, by rearranging terms one can establish:

$$\frac{d\, f'(k) \cdot k}{d\, k} > 0 \iff k < \widetilde{k}, \text{ with: } \widetilde{k} = [\frac{\alpha}{(1 - \alpha) \cdot \rho}]^{\frac{1}{\rho}} > 0$$

Thus, the second part of (A 2) holds no longer globally. Yet, for $k \in (0, \widetilde{k})$ the condition is locally satisfied.

Appendix II: Dynamics

This appendix outlines briefly the procedure which we use throughout the second part of the book to study dynamical properties of two-dimensional systems of nonlinear, first-order difference equations. Clearly, a comprehensive treatment of all the technical details involved is beyond the scope of the book. Instead, we draw in this appendix heavily on the presentation of the material given in Azariadis (1993, chapter 6) and reproduce key results which deal with dynamical properties of 'planar systems'.[1] However, in classifying the figurations of possible solutions we deviate slightly from Azariadis (1993) and follow instead the more detailed treatment presented in Baumol (1958, 1970).

Consider the autonomous first-order system of nonlinear difference equations where both functions f and g are continuously differentiable:

$$x_{t+1} = f(x_t, y_t) \tag{1}$$
$$y_{t+1} = g(x_t, y_t) \tag{2}$$

Assume that there exists a steady state solution (x, y) for the system (1)-(2) such that $x = f(x, y)$ and $y = g(x, y)$. To characterize the behaviour of the system (1)-(2) around the steady state by means of a linear system, we use the first-order Taylor approximation:

$$\begin{bmatrix} x_{t+1} \\ y_{t+1} \end{bmatrix} = \begin{bmatrix} x \\ y \end{bmatrix} + J(x, y) \cdot \begin{bmatrix} x_t - x \\ y_t - y \end{bmatrix}, \quad \text{with:} \tag{3}$$

$$J(x, y) = \begin{bmatrix} \frac{\partial f(x,y)}{\partial x} & \frac{\partial f(x,y)}{\partial y} \\ \frac{\partial g(x,y)}{\partial x} & \frac{\partial g(x,y)}{\partial y} \end{bmatrix}$$

More specifically, we assume that (x, y) is a hyperbolic equilibrium, i.e. we assume that no eigenvalue of the Jacobian matrix $J(x, y)$ has modulus exactly 1. Hence, the linear approximation (3) can be used to assess the stability behaviour of the original system (1)-(2):

---

[1]For more detailed presentations of techniques relevant for the analysis of discrete dynamical systems, see, for example, Gandolfo (1996) and Tu (1994).

Theorem 1 *(Hartman-Grobman) Let (x, y) be a hyperbolic steady state equilibrium of the system (1)-(2). If the Jacobian matrix $J(x, y)$ is invertible, there is a neighbourhood U of (x, y) in which the nonlinear system (1)-(2) is topologically equivalent to the linear system (3). In particular, this implies that the stability of the equilibrium (x, y) of the system (1)-(2) can be determined by examining the eigenvalues of the Jacobian matrix $J(x, y)$.*

For two-dimensional systems the stability of equilibria can be classified as:

Theorem 2 *(Nonlinear stability) Let (x, y) be a hyperbolic steady state equilibrium of the system (1)-(2).*
(a) If both eigenvalues of $J(x, y)$ have moduli strictly less than one the steady state (x, y) is asymptotically stable (i.e. a sink).
(b) If both eigenvalues of $J(x, y)$ have moduli greater than one the steady state (x, y) is asymptotically unstable (i.e. a source).
(c) If one eigenvalue of $J(x, y)$ has modulus less than one and the other greater than one the steady state (x, y) is a saddle.

Let $Tr(J)$ and $Det(J)$ stand for the trace and the determinant of the matrix $J(x, y)$, respectively. The eigenvalues of the matrix $J(x, y)$ are roots of the characteristic polynomial:

$$p(\lambda) = \begin{vmatrix} \frac{\partial f(x,y)}{\partial x} - \lambda & \frac{\partial f(x,y)}{\partial y} \\ \frac{\partial g(x,y)}{\partial x} & \frac{\partial g(x,y)}{\partial y} - \lambda \end{vmatrix} = \lambda^2 - Tr(J) \cdot \lambda + Det(J) = 0 \quad (4)$$

Using the solution formula for quadratic equations, one obtains:

$$\lambda_{1,2} = \frac{Tr(J)}{2} \pm \frac{1}{2} \cdot \sqrt{Tr(J)^2 - 4 \cdot Det(J)} \quad (5)$$

According to (5), the eigenvalues of $J(x, y)$ are determined by the values of the trace $Tr(J)$ and the determinant $Det(J)$. However, these values decide not only whether the steady state is locally stable, but they provide also detailed information with respect to the exact configuration of solution orbits. Thus, we derive now a comprehensive graphical classification of stability-types of steady state equilibria in $Det(J)$-$Tr(J)$-plane. To this end, we derive four auxiliary lines:

(i) Assume that the discriminant in (5) equals zero:

$$Tr(J)^2 - 4 \cdot Det(J) = 0 \quad (6)$$

As shown in figure A.4, equation (6) defines in $Det(J)$-$Tr(J)$-plane a parabola through the origin. For combinations of $Det(J)$ and $Tr(J)$ above the parabola the discriminant is negative and eigenvalues of $J(x,y)$ are complex. In contrast, for combinations of $Det(J)$ and $Tr(J)$ below the parabola eigenvalues are real.

(ii) The polynomial in (4) can be factored as: $p(\lambda) = (\lambda - \lambda_1) \cdot (\lambda - \lambda_2)$. Assuming that eigenvalues are real, we want to establish whether the eigenvalues fall on the same side of some constant a. Evaluating p at a yields:

$$p(a) = (a - \lambda_1) \cdot (a - \lambda_2) \tag{7}$$

Obviously, λ_1 and λ_2 fall on the same side of a if and only if $p(a) > 0$. In the light of theorem 2, we want to know how λ_1 and λ_2 relate to the critical values 1 and -1. Thus, using (4), our second auxiliary line is given by:

$$p(1) = 0 \quad \Leftrightarrow \quad Det(J) = -1 + Tr(J) \tag{8}$$

For points above this line, the two eigenvalues fall on the same side of 1, while in the region below this line they fall on different sides of 1.

(iii) Similarly, the third auxiliary line is given by:

$$p(-1) = 0 \quad \Leftrightarrow \quad Det(J) = -1 - Tr(J) \tag{9}$$

Accordingly, in the region above this line both eigenvalues fall on the same side of -1, and the opposite is true for the region below this line.

(iv) One easily verifies from (5) that eigenvalues satisfy the relation:

$$\lambda_1 \cdot \lambda_2 = Det(J) \tag{10}$$

Consider now the case of complex eigenvalues which come in conjugate pairs:

$$\lambda_{1/2} = a \pm i \cdot b \tag{11}$$

Then, according to (10) we have:

$$a^2 + b^2 = Det(J) \tag{12}$$

Note that the LHS of (12) equals the square of the modulus of the eigenvalues. To assess the stability behaviour of the system, we want to know how the modulus relates to 1. Clearly, for $Det(J) > 1$ (< 1) the modulus of the eigenvalues will be greater (less) than one. Thus, the forth auxiliary line is given by:

$$Det(J) = 1 \tag{13}$$

Finally, note that the parabola as given by (6) is tangential to the two lines $p(1) = 0$ at $(2, 1)$ and $p(-1) = 0$ at $(-2, 1)$. Therefore, as shown in figure A.4, the four auxiliary lines divide the $Det(J)$-$Tr(J)$-plane in 8 regions, and we establish now the stability behaviour of equilibria and the shape of solution orbits corresponding to these regions.

As a general feature, solutions of difference equations can not be represented by continuous curves, but rather by sequences of points that induce a stepped profile of solution orbits. Moreover, the shape of these orbits will depend on whether eigenvalues are real or complex and various configurations are conceivable. More specifically, if eigenvalues are conjugate complex orbits will be *fluctuating* around the steady state solution. In contrast, if eigenvalues are real the component of the solution path associated with a positive eigenvalue displays *monotone* behaviour (decreasing or increasing), while a negative eigenvalue influences the solution in an *oscillatory* manner.[2] Yet, as shown in detail by Baumol (1958, 1970), the contributions of the two eigenvalues to the solution path can interact in a complicated manner. To illustrate this point, remember that in a situation with two distinct, real eigenvalues λ_1 and λ_2 with associated eigenvectors e_1 and e_2 the general solution of the linear system (3) will be given by:

$$\begin{bmatrix} x_t \\ y_t \end{bmatrix} = \begin{bmatrix} x \\ y \end{bmatrix} + A_1 \cdot \begin{bmatrix} e_{11} \\ e_{12} \end{bmatrix} \cdot \lambda_1^t + A_2 \cdot \begin{bmatrix} e_{21} \\ e_{22} \end{bmatrix} \cdot \lambda_2^t \qquad (14)$$

Moreover, for the sake of a simple illustration let us assume that both eigenvalues have the same sign. As a result, the two time-dependent components of the solution are subject to similar forces, both of them being either monotone or oscillatory. Yet, in such a situation the signs of the constant coefficients A_1 and A_2 to be obtained from the initial conditions of the system will decide whether the time-dependent components tend to reinforce or counteract each other. In fact, two negative (positive) eigenvalues may well be compatible with a solution path that exhibits initially monotone (oscillatory) behaviour if the counteracting moment happens to be sufficiently strong.[3] However, in any case the eigenvalue that is smaller in absolute value exerts a non-negligible influence only in the initial phase of the adjustment process. Correspondingly, in the long run the profile of the time path will ultimately reflect the influence exerted by the dominant eigenvalue (i.e. the eigenvalue that is larger in absolute value). Thus, whenever appropriate, we establish in the following the sign of the dominant eigenvalue, thereby indicating whether the adjustment path will ultimately be monotone or oscillatory.

---

[2] However, the literature does not always distinguish explicitly between oscillatory and fluctuating behaviour since both cases can be interpreted as a form of endogenously arising volatility. For an example in this spirit, see Azariadis (1993), p. 67.

[3] For an appropriate example, see Baumol (1958), p. 274.

I) Case of real and distinct eigenvalues: $Tr(J)^2 - 4 \cdot Det(J) > 0$

Region 1: $p(1) < 0$, $p(-1) > 0$, i.e. the eigenvalues fall on different sides of 1 and on the same side of -1. Thus, we have $\lambda_1 > 1$, $\lambda_2 \in (-1,1)$, and the steady state is a *saddle*.

'Saddlepath stability': Assume that we have one state (or predetermined) variable and one control variable with a free initial condition. Then, there is a unique path approaching the steady state. In particular, the saddlepath solution requires in terms of equation (14) that the control variable jumps exactly to the level that eliminates the unstable eigenvalue. Thus, the sign of the remaining stable eigenvalue decides whether convergence along the saddlepath is monotone or oscillatory.

1a: $Det(J) > 0$: The eigenvalues have the same sign, i.e. $\lambda_1 > 1$, $\lambda_2 \in (0,1)$, and adjustment towards the steady state is monotone.

1b: $Det(J) < 0$: The eigenvalues are of opposite sign, i.e. $\lambda_1 > 1$, $\lambda_2 \in (-1,0)$, and adjustment towards the steady state is oscillatory.

Region 2: $p(1) < 0$, $p(-1) < 0$, i.e. the eigenvalues straddle both 1 and -1. Thus, we have: $\lambda_1 > 1$, $\lambda_2 < -1$, and the steady state is a *source*.

2a: Since $Tr(J) < 0$ and $Det(J) < 0$, it follows from (5) that the dominant eigenvalue is negative.

2b: Since $Tr(J) > 0$ and $Det(J) < 0$, it follows from (5) that the dominant eigenvalue is positive.

Region 3: $p(1) > 0$, $p(-1) < 0$, i.e. the eigenvalues fall on the same side of 1 and on different sides of -1. Thus, we have: $\lambda_1 < -1$, $\lambda_2 \in (-1,1)$, and the steady state is a *saddle*. Again, assume the system is saddlepath stable as discussed for region 1.

3a: $Det(J) > 0$: The eigenvalues have the same sign, i.e. $\lambda_1 < -1$, $\lambda_2 \in (-1,0)$, and adjustment towards the steady state is oscillatory.

3b: $Det(J) < 0$: The eigenvalues are of opposite sign, i.e. $\lambda_1 < -1$, $\lambda_2 \in (0,1)$, and adjustment towards the steady state is monotone.

Region 4: $p(1) > 0$, $p(-1) < 0$, i.e. the eigenvalues fall on the same side of both 1 and -1. $Det(J) > 0$, i.e. the eigenvalues have the same sign. Moreover, since $Tr(J) < -2$ we have $\lambda_1, \lambda_2 < -1$, and the steady state is a *source*.

Region 7: $p(1) > 0$, $p(-1) < 0$, i.e. the eigenvalues fall on the same side of both 1 and -1. Since $\lambda_1 \cdot \lambda_2 = Det(J)$ needs to hold, $Det(J) \in (-1,1)$ implies $\lambda_1, \lambda_2 \in (-1,1)$, i.e. the steady state is a *sink*.

7a: $Det(J) > 0$, $Tr(J) < 0$, i.e. λ_1, $\lambda_2 \in (-1,0)$.

7b: $Det(J) > 0$, $Tr(J) > 0$, i.e. λ_1, $\lambda_2 \in (0,1)$.

7c: $Det(J) < 0$, i.e. the eigenvalues are of opposite sign: $-1 < \lambda_1 < 0 < \lambda_2 < 1$. Since $Tr(J) > 0$ and $Det(J) < 0$, it follows from (5) that the dominant eigenvalue is positive.

7d: $Det(J) < 0$, i.e. the eigenvalues are of opposite sign: $-1 < \lambda_1 < 0 < \lambda_2 < 1$. Since $Tr(J) < 0$ and $Det(J) < 0$, it follows from (5) that the dominant eigenvalue is negative.

In short, regions *7a* and *7d* have dominant eigenvalues that are associated with oscillatory adjustment, while regions *7b* and *7c* are ultimately subject to monotone adjustment.

Region 8: $p(1) > 0$, $p(-1) < 0$, i.e. the eigenvalues fall on the same side of both 1 and -1. $Det(J) > 0$, i.e. the eigenvalues have the same sign. Moreover, since $Tr(J) > 2$, we have λ_1, $\lambda_2 > 1$, and the steady state is a *source*.

II) Case of complex eigenvalues: $Tr(J)^2 - 4 \cdot Det(J) < 0$

Region 5: $Det(J) > 1$, i.e. the eigenvalues have modulus greater than 1, and the steady state is a *source*. Moreover, orbits are fluctuating, i.e. the steady state is an unstable focus.

Region 6: $Det(J) < 1$, i.e. the eigenvalues have modulus less than 1, and the steady state is a *sink*. Again, orbits are fluctuating, i.e. the steady state is a stable focus.

In summary, one easily verifies from figure A.4 that combinations of the trace and the determinant inside the stability triangle drawn in bold face are asymptotically stable. Points outside the triangle are for arbitrary initial conditions asymptotically unstable. However, for systems with one predetermined variable and one control variable with a free initial condition, there exists in regions 1 and 3 a uniquely defined saddlepath that converges asymptotically towards the steady state. Similarly, for such systems adjustment behaviour in all regions inside the stability triangle is locally indeterminate, since there exists an infinite amount of values for the free initial condition of the control variable with associated converging adjustment paths.

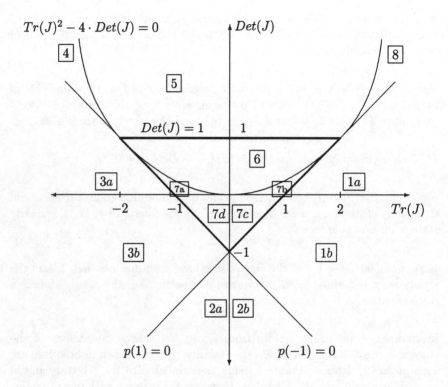

Figure A.4: *Classification of steady state dynamics*

References

1. Aiyagari, R./Wallace, N./Wright, R., Coexistence of money and interest-bearing securities, *Journal of Monetary Economics*, 37, 397-419, 1996.

2. Akerlof, G./Dickens, W./Perry, G., The macroeconomics of low inflation, *Brookings Papers on Economic Activity*, 1, 1-76, 1996.

3. Andrés, J./Hernando, I., Does inflation harm economic growth ? Evidence for the OECD, *NBER Working Paper*, No. 6062, 1997.

4. Arrow, K./Chenery, H./Minhas, B./Solow, R., Capital-labour substitution and economic efficiency, *Review of Economics and Statistics*, 63, 225-50, 1961.

5. Azariadis, C., *Intertemporal macroeconomics*, Basil Blackwell, Oxford, 1993.

6. Azariadis, C./Smith, B., Private information, money, and growth, *Journal of economic growth*, 1, 309-32, 1996.

7. Azariadis, C./Smith, B., Financial intermediation and regime switching in business cycles, *American Economic Review*, 88/3, 516-36, 1998.

8. Backus, D./Kehoe, P., International evidence on the historical properties of business cycles, *American Economic Review*, 82/4, 864-88, 1992.

9. Barro, R., Inflation and growth, chapter 3, in: Barro, R., *Determinants of economic growth*, A cross-country empirical study, MIT Press, 1997.

10. Baumol, W., Topology of second order linear difference equations with constant coefficients, *Econometrica*, 26, 258-85, 1958.

11. Baumol, W., *Economic dynamics: an introduction*, 3rd edition, Macmillan, London, 1970.

12. Bencivenga, V./Smith, B., Financial intermediation and endogenous growth, *Review of Economic Studies*, 58, 195-209, 1991.

13. Bencivenga, V./Smith, B., Deficits, inflation, and the banking system in developing countries: the optimal degree of financial repression, *Oxford Economic Papers*, 44, 767-790, 1992.

14. Benhabib, J./Farmer, R., Indeterminacy and increasing returns, *Journal of Economic Theory*, 63/1, 19-41, 1994.

15. Bernanke, B./Gertler, M., Agency costs, net worth, and business fluctuations, *American Economic Review*, 79/1, 14-31, 1989.

16. Bhattacharya, J./Guzman, M./Huybens, E./Smith, B., Monetary, fiscal, and reserve requirement policy in a simple monetary growth model, *International Economic Review*, 38/2, 321-50, 1997.

17. Blanchard, O., Debt, deficits, and finite horizons, *Journal of Political Economy*, 93/2, 223-47, 1985.

18. Blanchard, O., Why does money affect output ? A survey, in: Friedman, M./Hahn, F. (ed.), *Handbook of monetary economics*, Volume II, Chapter 15, North-Holland, Amsterdam, 1990.

19. Blanchard, O./Fischer, S., *Lectures on macroeconomics*, MIT Press, Cambridge/Mass., 1989.

20. Blanchard, O./Kahn, C., The solution of linear difference models under rational expectations, *Econometrica*, 48/5, 1305-11, 1980.

21. Boyd, J./Smith, B., Capital market imperfections in a monetary growth model, *Economic Theory*, 11/2, 241-73, 1998.

22. Brock, W., Money and growth: the case of long run perfect foresight, *International Economic Review*, 15, 750-77, 1974.

23. Bruno, M./Easterly, W., Inflation crises and long-run growth, *Journal of Monetary Economics*, 41, 3-26, 1998.

24. Bryant, J./Wallace, N., Open-market operations in a model of regulated, insured intermediaries, *Journal of Political Economy*, 88/1, 146-73, 1980.

25. Bryant, J./Wallace, N., A price discrimination analysis of monetary policy, *Review of Economic Studies*, 51, 279-88, 1984.

26. Bullard, J./Keating, J., The long-run relationship between inflation and output in postwar economies, *Journal of Monetary Economics*, 36, 477-96, 1995.

27. Burmeister, E./Dobell, A., Money and economic growth, in: *Mathematical theories of economic growth*, Chapter 6, MacMillan, 1970.

28. Calvo, G., On models of money and perfect forseight, *International Economic Review*, 20/1, 83-103, 1979.

29. Chari, V./Jones, L./Manuelli, R., The growth effects of monetary policy, *Federal Reserve Bank of Minneapolis, Quarterly Review*, 19/4, 18-32, 1995.

30. Clower, R., A reconsideration of the microfoundations of monetary theory, *Western Economic Journal*, 6, 1-8, 1967.

31. Coleman, W., Money and output: a test of reverse causation, *American Economic Review*, 86/1, 90-111, 1996.

32. Cukierman, A./Kalaitzidakis, P./Summers, L./Webb, S., Central bank independence, growth, investment, and real rates, *Carnegie-Rochester Conference Series on Public Policy*, 39, 95-140, 1993.

33. Danthine, J.-P./ Donaldson, J./ Smith, L., On the superneutrality of money in a stochastic dynamic macroeconomic model, *Journal of Monetary Economics*, 20, 475-99, 1987.

34. De Gregorio, J., The effects of inflation on economic growth, *European Economic Review*, 36, 417-25, 1992.

35. De Gregorio, J., Inflation, taxation, and long-run growth, *Journal of Monetary Economics*, 31, 271-98, 1993.

36. Diamond, P., National debt in a neoclassical growth model, *American Economic Review*, 55/5, 1126-50, 1965.

37. Diamond, P., Aggregate demand management in search equilibrium, *Journal of Political Economy*, 90, 881-94, 1982.

38. Diamond, D./Dybvig, P., Bank runs, deposit insurance, and liquidity, *Journal of Political Economy*, 91/3, 401-19, 1983.

39. Dixit, A./Pindyck, R., *Investment under uncertainty*, Princeton University Press, Princeton, 1994.

40. Dornbusch, R./Frenkel, J., Inflation and growth, *Journal of Money, Credit, and Banking*, 5, 141-56, 1973.

41. Fama, E., Banking in the theory of finance, *Journal of Monetary Economics*, 6, 39-57, 1980.

42. Fama, E., Financial intermediation and price level control, *Journal of Monetary Economics*, 12, 7-28, 1983.

43. Farmer, R., *The macroeconomics of self-fulfilling prophecies*, MIT Press, Cambridge/Mass., 1993.

186

44. Farmer, R./Guo, J., Real business cycles and the animal spirits hypothesis, *Journal of Economic Theory*, 63/1, 42-72, 1994.

45. Feldstein, M., The costs and benefits of going from low inflation to price stability, *NBER Working Paper*, No. 5469, 1996.

46. Fischer, S., A framework for monetary and banking analysis, *Economic Journal* (supplement), Conference Papers, 1-16, 1982.

47. Fischer, S., Growth, macroeconomics, and development, *NBER Macroeconomics Annual*, 6, 329-79, 1991.

48. Fischer, S., The role of macroeconomic factors in growth, *Journal of Monetary Economics*, 32, 485-512, 1993.

49. Gale, D., Money and growth, in: *Money and disequilibrium*, Chapter 2, Cambridge University Press, Cambridge, 1983.

50. Galor, O./Ryder, H., Existence, uniqueness, and stability of equilibrium in an overlapping generations model with productive capital, *Journal of Economic Theory*, 49, 360-75, 1989.

51. Gandolfo, G., *Economic dynamics*, 3rd edition, Springer Verlag, Berlin, 1996.

52. Ghosh, A./Phillips, S., Warning: inflation may be harmful to your growth, *IMF Staff Papers*, 45/4, 1998.

53. Gomme, P., Money and growth revisited, Measuring the costs of inflation in an endogenous growth model, *Journal of Monetary Economics*, 32, 51-77, 1993.

54. Grier, K./Tullock, G., An empirical analysis of cross-national economic growth, 1951-80, *Journal of Monetary Economics*, 24, 259-76, 1989.

55. Groshen, E./Schweitzer, M., The effects of inflation on wage adjustments in firm-level data: grease or sand ?, *Federal Reseve Bank of New York, Staff Reports*, 9, 1996.

56. Hahn, F., On some problems of proving the existence of an equilibrium in a monetary economy, in: F.Hahn/F.Brechling, *The theory of interest rates*, London, 1965.

57. Hahn, F., On money and growth, *Journal of Money, Credit, and Banking*, 1, 175-84, 1969.

58. Hahn, F., Discussion, in: Kareken, J./Wallace, N. (ed.), *Models of monetary economics*, Federal Reserve Bank of Minneapolis, 161-65, 1980.

59. Hahn, F., *Money and inflation*, Basil Blackwell, Oxford, 1982.

60. Hahn, F., Liquidity, in: Friedman, M./Hahn, F. (ed.), *Handbook of monetary economics*, Volume I, Chapter 2, North-Holland, Amsterdam, 1990.

61. Hahn, F./Solow, R., Perfectly flexible wages, in: *A critical essay on modern macroeconomic theory*, Chapter 2, Blackwell Publishers, Oxford, 1995.

62. Hellwig, M., The challenge of monetary theory, *European Economic Review*, 37, 215-42, 1993.

63. Herbertsson, T./Gylfason, T., Does inflation matter for growth ?, *CEPR Discussion Paper*, No. 1503, 1996.

64. Howitt, P., Money and growth revisited, in: H.Barkai (ed.), *Monetary theory and thought*, Basingstoke, 1993.

65. Huo, T., Inflation and capital accumulation in a two-sector cash-in-advance economy, *Journal of Macroeconomics*, 19/1, 103-15, 1997.

66. Ireland, P., Money and growth: an alternative approach, *American Economic Review*, 84/1, 47-65, 1994.

67. Jones, L./Manuelli, R., Growth and the effects of inflation, *Journal of Economic Dynamics and Control*, 19, 1405-28, 1995.

68. Keynes, J.M., *A tract on monetary reform* (1923), in: The collected writings of John Maynard Keynes, Volume 4, Cambridge University Press, Cambridge, 1972.

69. King, R./Levine, R., Finance, entrepreneurship, and growth, *Journal of Monetary Economics*, 32, 513-42, 1993.

70. King, R./Plosser, C., Money, credit, and prices in a real business cycle, *American Economic Review*, 74/3, 363-80, 1984.

71. Kiyotaki, N./Wright, R., On money as a medium of exchange, *Journal of Political Economy*, 97/4, 927-54, 1989.

72. Kiyotaki, N./Wright, R., A search theoretic approach to monetary economics, *American Economic Review*, 83/1, 63-77, 1993.

73. Kormendi, R./Meguire, P., Macroeconomic determinants of growth, Cross country evidence, *Journal of Monetary Economics*, 16, 141-63, 1985.

74. Krugman, P., Stable prices and fast growth: just say no, in: *The Economist*, August 31, 1996.

75. Levine, R./Renelt, D., A sensitivity analysis of cross-country growth regressions, *American Economic Review*, 82/4, 942-63, 1992.

76. Lucas, R., Some international evidence on output-inflation tradeoffs, *American Economic Review*, 63/3, 326-34, 1973.

77. Lucas, R., Econometric policy evaluation: a critique, in: Brunner, K./Meltzer, A. (ed.), *The Phillips curve and labor markets*, Vol. 1 of Carnegie-Rochester Conference Series on Public Policy, North-Holland, Amsterdam, 19-46, 1976.

78. Lucas, R., Interest rates and currency prices in a two-country world, *Journal of Monetary Economics*, 10, 335-59, 1982.

79. Lucas, R., On the mechanics of economic development, *Journal of Monetary Economics*, 22, 3-42, 1988.

80. Lucas, R./Stokey, N., Optimal fiscal and monetary policy in an economy without capital, *Journal of Monetary Economics*, 12/1, 55-93, 1983.

81. Lucas, R./Stokey, N., Money and interest in a cash-in-advance economy, *Econometrica*, 55/3, 491-513, 1987.

82. Mankiw, G., Real business cycles: A new keynesian perspective, *Journal of Economic Perspectives*, 3/3, 79-90, 1989.

83. Marquis, M./Reffett, K., Equilibrium growth in a monetary economy with transactions costs, *Bulletin of Economic Research*, 47/3, 233-51, 1995.

84. McCandless, G./Weber, W., Some monetary facts, *Federal Reserve Bank of Minneapolis, Quarterly Review*, 19/3, 2-11, 1995.

85. McKinnon, R., *Money and capital in economic development*, Brookings, Washington D.C., 1973.

86. Mino, K./Shibata, A., Monetary policy, overlapping generations, and patterns of growth, *Economica*, 62, 179-94, 1995.

87. Mitsui, T./Watanabe, S., Monetary growth in a turnpike environment, *Journal of Monetary Economics*, 24, 123-37, 1989.

88. Mundell, R., Growth, stability, and inflationary finance, *Journal of Political Economy*, 73, 97-109, 1965.

89. Nagatani, K., A note on Professor Tobin's money and economic growth, *Econometrica*, 38, 171-75, 1970.

90. Olivera, H., A note on passive money, inflation, and economic growth, *Journal of Money, Credit, and Banking*, 3, 137-44, 1971.

91. Orphanides, A./Solow, R., Money, inflation and growth, in: Friedman, M./Hahn, F. (ed.), *Handbook of monetary economics*, Volume I, Chapter 6, North-Holland, Amsterdam, 1990.

92. Patinkin, D., Financial intermediation and the logical structure of monetary theory, *American Economic Review*, 51/1, 95-116, 1961.

93. Patinkin, D., *Money, interest, and prices: an integration of monetary and value theory*, 2nd edition, Harper and Row, New York, 1965.

94. Prescott, E., A multiple means-of-payment model, in: Barnett, W./Singleton, K., *New approaches to monetary economics*, Cambridge University Press, Cambridge, 1987.

95. Rebelo, S., Long-run policy analysis and long-run growth, *Journal of Political Economy*, 99/3, 500-21, 1991.

96. Romer, P., Increasing returns and long-run growth, *Journal of Political Economy*, 94/5, 1002-37, 1986.

97. Rothschild, M./Stiglitz, J., Equilibrium in competitive insurance markets: the economics of incomplete information, *Quarterly Journal of Economics*, 91, 629-50, 1976.

98. Roubini, N./Sala-i-Martin, X., Financial repression and economic growth, *Journal of Development Economics*, 39, 5-30, 1992.

99. Samuelson, P., An exact consumption-loan model of interest with or without the social contrivance of money, *Journal of Political Economy*, 66, 467-82, 1958.

100. Sarel, M., Nonlinear effects of inflation on economic growth, *IMF Staff Papers*, 43/1, 1996.

101. Sargent, T./Wallace, N., Some unpleasant monetarist arithmetic, *Federal Reserve Bank of Minneapolis, Quarterly Review*, 1-17, Fall 1981.

102. Schreft, S., Transaction costs and the use of cash and credit, *Economic Theory*, 2, 283-96, 1992.

103. Schreft, S./Smith, B., The effects of open market operations in a model of intermediation and growth, *Review of Economic Studies*, 65, 519-50, 1998.

104. Schreft, S./Smith, B., Money, banking, and capital formation, *Journal of Economic Theory*, 73, 157-82, 1997.

105. Shaw, E., *Financial deepening in economic development*, Oxford University Press, Oxford, 1973.

190

106. Sidrauski, M., Rational choice and patterns of growth in a monetary economy, *American Economic Review*, 57/2, 534-44, 1967.

107. Sidrauski, M., Inflation and economic growth, *Journal of Political Economy*, 75, 796-810, 1967a.

108. Stiglitz, J./Weiss, A., Credit rationing in markets with imperfect information, *American Economic Review*, 71/3, 393-409, 1981.

109. Stockman, A., Anticipated inflation, and the capital stock in a cash-in-advance economy, *Journal of Monetary Economics*, 8, 387-93, 1981.

110. Svensson, L., Money and asset prices in a cash-in-advance economy, *Journal of Political Economy*, 93/5, 919-44, 1985.

111. Tirole, J., Asset bubbles and overlapping generations, *Econometrica*, 53/6, 1499-1528, 1985.

112. Tobin, J., Money and economic growth, *Econometrica*, 33/4, 671-84, 1965.

113. Tobin, J., A general equilibrium approach to monetary theory, *Journal of Money, Credit, and Banking*, 1, 15-29, 1969.

114. Tobin, J., Money and finance in the macroeconomic process, *Journal of Money, Credit, and Banking*, 14/2, 171-204, 1982.

115. Tobin, J./Brainard, W., Financial intermediaries and the effectiveness of monetary controls, *American Economic Review*, 53/2, 383-400, 1963.

116. Townsend, R., Optimal contracts and competitive markets with costly state verification, *Journal of Economic Theory*, 21, 265-93, 1979.

117. Townsend, R., Models of money with spatially separated agents, in: Kareken, J./Wallace, N. (ed.), *Models of monetary economics*, Federal Reserve Bank of Minneapolis, 265-303, 1980.

118. Tu, P., *Dynamical systems*, 2nd edition, Springer Verlag, Berlin, 1994.

119. Turnovsky, S., *Methods of macroeconomic dynamics*, MIT Press, Cambridge/Mass., 1995.

120. Van der Ploeg, F./Alogoskoufis, G., Money and endogenous growth, *Journal of Money, Credit, and Banking*, 26, 771-91, 1994.

121. Wallace, N., The overlapping generations model of fiat money, in: Kareken, J./Wallace, N. (ed.), *Models of monetary economics*, Federal Reserve Bank of Minneapolis, 49-96, 1980.

122. Wallace, N., A legal restrictions theory of the demand for money and the role of monetary policy, *Federal Reserve Bank of Minneapolis, Quarterly Review*, Winter 1983.

123. Wang, P./Yip, C., Alternative approaches to money and growth, *Journal of Money, Credit, and Banking*, 24/4, 553-62, 1992.

124. Weil, P., Is money net wealth ?, *International Economic Review*, 32/1, 37-53, 1991.

125. Woodford, M., Monetary policy and price level determinacy in a cash-in-advance economy, *Economic Theory*, 4, 345-80, 1994.

126. Wu, Y./Zhang, J., Endogenous growth and the welfare costs of inflation: a reconsideration, *Journal of Economic Dynamics and Control*, 22, 465-82, 1998.

127. Yaari, M., Uncertain lifetime, life insurance, and the theory of the consumer, *Review of Economic Studies*, 32, 137-50, 1965.

List of Figures

Lecture Notes in Economics and Mathematical Systems

For information about Vols. 1–290
please contact your bookseller or Springer-Verlag

Vol. 329: G. Tillmann, Equity, Incentives, and Taxation. VI, 132 pages. 1989.

Vol. 330: P.M. Kort, Optimal Dynamic Investment Policies of a Value Maximizing Firm. VII, 185 pages. 1989.

Vol. 331: A. Lewandowski, A.P. Wierzbicki (Eds.), Aspiration Based Decision Support Systems. X, 400 pages. 1989.

Vol. 332: T.R. Gulledge, Jr., L.A. Litteral (Eds.), Cost Analysis Applications of Economics and Operations Research. Proceedings. VII, 422 pages. 1989.

Vol. 333: N. Dellaert, Production to Order. VII, 158 pages. 1989.

Vol. 334: H.-W. Lorenz, Nonlinear Dynamical Economics and Chaotic Motion. XI, 248 pages. 1989.

Vol. 335: A.G. Lockett, G. Islei (Eds.), Improving Decision Making in Organisations. Proceedings. IX, 606 pages. 1989.

Vol. 336: T. Puu, Nonlinear Economic Dynamics. VII, 119 pages. 1989.

Vol. 337: A. Lewandowski, I. Stanchev (Eds.), Methodology and Software for Interactive Decision Support. VIII, 309 pages. 1989.

Vol. 338: J.K. Ho, R.P. Sundarraj, DECOMP: An Implementation of Dantzig-Wolfe Decomposition for Linear Programming. VI, 206 pages.

Vol. 339: J. Terceiro Lomba, Estimation of Dynamic Econometric Models with Errors in Variables. VIII, 116 pages. 1990.

Vol. 340: T. Vasko, R. Ayres, L. Fontvieille (Eds.), Life Cycles and Long Waves. XIV, 293 pages. 1990.

Vol. 341: G.R. Uhlich, Descriptive Theories of Bargaining. IX, 165 pages. 1990.

Vol. 342: K. Okuguchi, F. Szidarovszky, The Theory of Oligopoly with Multi-Product Firms. V, 167 pages. 1990.

Vol. 343: C. Chiarella, The Elements of a Nonlinear Theory of Economic Dynamics. IX, 149 pages. 1990.

Vol. 344: K. Neumann, Stochastic Project Networks. XI, 237 pages. 1990.

Vol. 345: A. Cambini, E. Castagnoli, L. Martein, P Mazzoleni, S. Schaible (Eds.), Generalized Convexity and Fractional Programming with Economic Applications. Proceedings, 1988. VII, 361 pages. 1990.

Vol. 346: R. von Randow (Ed.), Integer Programming and Related Areas. A Classified Bibliography 1984–1987. XIII, 514 pages. 1990.

Vol. 347: D. Ríos Insua, Sensitivity Analysis in Multiobjective Decision Making. XI, 193 pages. 1990.

Vol. 348: H. Störmer, Binary Functions and their Applications. VIII, 151 pages. 1990.

Vol. 349: G.A. Pfann, Dynamic Modelling of Stochastic Demand for Manufacturing Employment. VI, 158 pages. 1990.

Vol. 350: W.-B. Zhang, Economic Dynamics. X, 232 pages. 1990.

Vol. 351: A. Lewandowski, V. Volkovich (Eds.), Multiobjective Problems of Mathematical Programming. Proceedings, 1988. VII, 315 pages. 1991.

Vol. 352: O. van Hilten, Optimal Firm Behaviour in the Context of Technological Progress and a Business Cycle. XII, 229 pages. 1991.

Vol. 353: G. Ricci (Ed.), Decision Processes in Economics. Proceedings, 1989. III, 209 pages 1991.

Vol. 354: M. Ivaldi, A Structural Analysis of Expectation Formation. XII, 230 pages. 1991.

Vol. 355: M. Salomon. Deterministic Lotsizing Models for Production Planning. VII, 158 pages. 1991.

Vol. 356: P. Korhonen, A. Lewandowski, J . Wallenius (Eds.), Multiple Criteria Decision Support. Proceedings, 1989. XII, 393 pages. 1991.

Vol. 357: P. Zörnig, Degeneracy Graphs and Simplex Cycling. XV, 194 pages. 1991.

Vol. 358: P. Knottnerus, Linear Models with Correlated Disturbances. VIII, 196 pages. 1991.

Vol. 359: E. de Jong, Exchange Rate Determination and Optimal Economic Policy Under Various Exchange Rate Regimes. VII, 270 pages. 1991.

Vol. 360: P. Stalder, Regime Translations, Spillovers and Buffer Stocks. VI, 193 pages . 1991.

Vol. 361: C. F. Daganzo, Logistics Systems Analysis. X, 321 pages. 1991.

Vol. 362: F. Gehrels, Essays in Macroeconomics of an Open Economy. VII, 183 pages. 1991.

Vol. 363: C. Puppe, Distorted Probabilities and Choice under Risk. VIII, 100 pages . 1991

Vol. 364: B. Horvath, Are Policy Variables Exogenous? XII, 162 pages. 1991.

Vol. 365: G. A. Heuer, U. Leopold-Wildburger. Balanced Silverman Games on General Discrete Sets. V, 140 pages. 1991.

Vol. 366: J. Gruber (Ed.), Econometric Decision Models. Proceedings, 1989. VIII, 636 pages. 1991.

Vol. 367: M. Grauer, D. B. Pressmar (Eds.), Parallel Computing and Mathematical Optimization. Proceedings. V, 208 pages. 1991.

Vol. 368: M. Fedrizzi, J. Kacprzyk, M. Roubens (Eds.), Interactive Fuzzy Optimization. VII, 216 pages. 1991.

Vol. 369: R. Koblo, The Visible Hand. VIII, 131 pages.1991.

Vol. 370: M. J. Beckmann, M. N. Gopalan, R. Subramanian (Eds.), Stochastic Processes and their Applications. Proceedings, 1990. XLI, 292 pages. 1991.

Vol. 371: A. Schmutzler, Flexibility and Adjustment to Information in Sequential Decision Problems. VIII, 198 pages. 1991.

Vol. 372: J. Esteban, The Social Viability of Money. X, 202 pages. 1991.

Vol. 373: A. Billot, Economic Theory of Fuzzy Equilibria. XIII, 164 pages. 1992.

Vol. 374: G. Pflug, U. Dieter (Eds.), Simulation and Optimization. Proceedings, 1990. X, 162 pages. 1992.

Vol. 375: S.-J. Chen, Ch.-L. Hwang, Fuzzy Multiple Attribute Decision Making. XII, 536 pages. 1992.

Vol. 376: K.-H. Jöckel, G. Rothe, W. Sendler (Eds.), Bootstrapping and Related Techniques. Proceedings, 1990. VIII, 247 pages. 1992.

Vol. 427: F. W. van Tongeren, Microsimulation Modelling of the Corporate Firm. XVII, 275 pages. 1995.

Vol. 428: A. A. Powell, Ch. W. Murphy, Inside a Modern Macroeconometric Model. XVIII, 424 pages. 1995.

Vol. 429: R. Durier, C. Michelot, Recent Developments in Optimization. VIII, 356 pages. 1995.

Vol. 430: J. R. Daduna, I. Branco, J. M. Pinto Paixão (Eds.), Computer-Aided Transit Scheduling. XIV, 374 pages. 1995.

Vol. 431: A. Aulin, Causal and Stochastic Elements in Business Cycles. XI, 116 pages. 1996.

Vol. 432: M. Tamiz (Ed.), Multi-Objective Programming and Goal Programming. VI, 359 pages. 1996.

Vol. 433: J. Menon, Exchange Rates and Prices. XIV, 313 pages. 1996.

Vol. 434: M. W. J. Blok, Dynamic Models of the Firm. VII, 193 pages. 1996.

Vol. 435: L. Chen, Interest Rate Dynamics, Derivatives Pricing, and Risk Management. XII, 149 pages. 1996.

Vol. 436: M. Klemisch-Ahlert, Bargaining in Economic and Ethical Environments. IX, 155 pages. 1996.

Vol. 437: C. Jordan, Batching and Scheduling. IX, 178 pages. 1996.

Vol. 438: A. Villar, General Equilibrium with Increasing Returns. XIII, 164 pages. 1996.

Vol. 439: M. Zenner, Learning to Become Rational. VII, 201 pages. 1996.

Vol. 440: W. Ryll, Litigation and Settlement in a Game with Incomplete Information. VIII, 174 pages. 1996.

Vol. 441: H. Dawid, Adaptive Learning by Genetic Algorithms. IX, 166 pages.1996.

Vol. 442: L. Corchón, Theories of Imperfectly Competitive Markets. XIII, 163 pages. 1996.

Vol. 443: G. Lang, On Overlapping Generations Models with Productive Capital. X, 98 pages. 1996.

Vol. 444: S. Jørgensen, G. Zaccour (Eds.), Dynamic Competitive Analysis in Marketing. X, 285 pages. 1996.

Vol. 445: A. H. Christer, S. Osaki, L. C. Thomas (Eds.), Stochastic Modelling in Innovative Manufacturing. X, 361 pages. 1997.

Vol. 446: G. Dhaene, Encompassing. X, 160 pages. 1997.

Vol. 447: A. Artale, Rings in Auctions. X, 172 pages. 1997.

Vol. 448: G. Fandel, T. Gal (Eds.), Multiple Criteria Decision Making. XII, 678 pages. 1997.

Vol. 449: F. Fang, M. Sanglier (Eds.), Complexity and Self-Organization in Social and Economic Systems. IX, 317 pages, 1997.

Vol. 450: P. M. Pardalos, D. W. Hearn, W. W. Hager, (Eds.), Network Optimization. VIII, 485 pages, 1997.

Vol. 451: M. Salge, Rational Bubbles. Theoretical Basis, Economic Relevance, and Empirical Evidence with a Special Emphasis on the German Stock Market.IX, 265 pages. 1997.

Vol. 452: P. Gritzmann, R. Horst, E. Sachs, R. Tichatschke (Eds.), Recent Advances in Optimization. VIII, 379 pages. 1997.

Vol. 453: A. S. Tangian, J. Gruber (Eds.), Constructing Scalar-Valued Objective Functions. VIII, 298 pages. 1997.

Vol. 454: H.-M. Krolzig, Markov-Switching Vector Autoregressions. XIV, 358 pages. 1997.

Vol. 455: R. Caballero, F. Ruiz, R. E. Steuer (Eds.), Advances in Multiple Objective and Goal Programming. VIII, 391 pages. 1997.

Vol. 456: R. Conte, R. Hegselmann, P. Terna (Eds.), Simulating Social Phenomena. VIII, 536 pages. 1997.

Vol. 457: C. Hsu, Volume and the Nonlinear Dynamics of Stock Returns. VIII, 133 pages. 1998.

Vol. 458: K. Marti, P. Kall (Eds.), Stochastic Programming Methods and Technical Applications. X, 437 pages. 1998.

Vol. 459: H. K. Ryu, D. J. Slottje, Measuring Trends in U.S. Income Inequality. XI, 195 pages. 1998.

Vol. 460: B. Fleischmann, J. A. E. E. van Nunen, M. G. Speranza, P. Stähly, Advances in Distribution Logistic. XI, 535 pages. 1998.

Vol. 461: U. Schmidt, Axiomatic Utility Theory under Risk. XV, 201 pages. 1998.

Vol. 462: L. von Auer, Dynamic Preferences, Choice Mechanisms, and Welfare. XII, 226 pages. 1998.

Vol. 463: G. Abraham-Frois (Ed.), Non-Linear Dynamics and Endogenous Cycles. VI, 204 pages. 1998.

Vol. 464: A. Aulin, The Impact of Science on Economic Growth and its Cycles. IX, 204 pages. 1998.

Vol. 465: T. J. Stewart, R. C. van den Honert (Eds.), Trends in Multicriteria Decision Making. X, 448 pages. 1998.

Vol. 466: A. Sadrieh, The Alternating Double Auction Market. VII, 350 pages. 1998.

Vol. 467: H. Hennig-Schmidt, Bargaining in a Video Experiment. Determinants of Boundedly Rational Behavior. XII, 221 pages. 1999.

Vol. 468: A. Ziegler, A Game Theory Analysis of Options. XIV, 145 pages. 1999.

Vol. 469: M. P. Vogel, Environmental Kuznets Curves. XIII, 197 pages. 1999.

Vol. 470: M. Ammann, Pricing Derivative Credit Risk. XII, 228 pages. 1999.

Vol. 471: N. H. M. Wilson (Ed.), Computer-Aided Transit Scheduling. XI, 444 pages. 1999.

Vol. 472: J.-R. Tyran, Money Illusion and Strategic Complementarity as Causes of Monetary Non-Neutrality. X, 228 pages. 1999.

Vol. 473: S. Helber, Performance Analysis of Flow Lines with Non-Linear Flow of Material. IX, 280 pages. 1999.

Vol. 474: U. Schwalbe, The Core of Economies with Asymmetric Information. IX, 141 pages. 1999.

Vol. 475: L. Kaas, Dynamic Macroelectronics with Imperfect Competition. XI, 155 pages. 1999.

Vol. 476: R. Demel, Fiscal Policy, Public Debt and the Term Structure of Interest Rates. X, 279 pages. 1999.

Vol. 477: M. Théra, R. Tichatschke (Eds.), Ill-posed Variational Problems and Regularization Techniques. VIII, 274 pages. 1999.

Vol. 478: S. Hartmann, Project Scheduling under Limited Resources. XII, 221 pages. 1999.

Vol. 479: L. v. Thadden, Money, Inflation, and Capital Formation. IX, 192 pages. 1999.